# Find that Special Someone

Jeraldine Saunders. Her name is synonymous with bringing romance to the high seas. Now she can help bring love and romance into your life, too! With Jeraldine's practical advice, you'll learn to use your horoscope, numerology, and other mystic arts to uncover insightful hints that will give your love life a serious boost.

You'll discover how to banish the two enemies of love: fear and low self-esteem. Stop putting up that protective wall out of fear of being rejected or hurt! Instead, realize that there are people out there who are trying to get through to you—they want to love you and want your love in return. And, discover there is no way to truly express love except through self-love.

Plus, learn easy and fun ways to help you find Mr. or Ms. Right. Discover how compatible you and a potential partner are based on your astrological signs . . . learn to read your lover's facial expressions . . . decipher your friend's innermost nature with numerology . . . determine your lover's capacity for faithfulness with palm reading . . . and much more.

You deserve love . . . let *Love Signs* help you attract that special someone into your life—today!

# About the Author

Jeraldine Saunders is a powerful, multifaceted best-selling author whose years of astrological practice, books, and lectures have made her a worldwide success. She is in the World *Who's Who of Women*. She has appeared on *Good Morning America, Merv Griffin,* and more than 850 other TV and radio talk shows in the U.S.A., Canada, Europe, and the lands of the Pacific.

Jeraldine's book *The Love Boats* was the forerunner of her hit television series, *The Love Boat,* now syndicated in 112 countries.

# To Write to the Author

If you wish to contact the author or would like more information about this book, please write to the author in care of Llewellyn Worldwide and we will forward your request. Both the author and publisher appreciate hearing from you and learning of your enjoyment of this book and how it has helped you. Llewellyn Worldwide cannot guarantee that every letter written to the author can be answered, but all will be forwarded. Please write to:

Jeraldine Saunders
c/o Llewellyn Worldwide
P.O. Box 64383, Dept. K618-1
St. Paul, MN 55164-0383, U.S.A.

Please enclose a self-addressed, stamped envelope for reply, or $1.00 to cover costs. If outside U.S.A., enclose international postal reply coupon.

## FIND YOUR TRUE

*astrology*
*numbers*
*handwriting*
*palm reading*
*face reading*
*and aura reading*

## LOVE USING

# Love
# Signs

## Jeraldine Saunders

*Third Edition*

1998
Llewellyn Publications
St. Paul, Minnesota, U.S.A.

THIRD EDITION
Second Printing, 1998
(formerly titled *Signs of Love)*

Second Llewellyn edition, first printing, 1995
First Llewellyn edition, two printings, 1990
Originally published by Pinnacle Books, 1977

Cover design by Anne Marie Garrison
Third edition editing and design by Christine Snow

**Library of Congress Cataloging-in-Publication Data**
Saunders, Jeraldine.
    Love signs: find your true love using astrology, numbers, handwriting,
palm reading, face reading, and aura reading / by Jeraldine Saunders: with
foreword by Sydney Omarr. — 3rd ed.
      p. cm.
    Originally published under title: Signs of love
    Includes index.
    ISBN 1-56718-618-1 (pbk.)
    1. Astrology. 2. Love–Miscellanea. 3. Mate selection–Miscellanea.
4. Sex–Miscellanea. 5. Astrology and sex. 6. Occultism. I. Saunders, Jeraldine. Signs of love. II. Title.
    BF1729.L6S27     1998
    133.5'864677—dc21                    98-20404
                                                              CIP

Llewellyn Worldwide does not participate in, endorse, or have any authority or responsibility concerning private business transactions between our authors and the public.
    All mail addressed to the author is forwarded but the publisher cannot, unless specifically instructed by the author, give out an address or phone number.

Llewellyn Publications
A Division of Llewellyn Worldwide, Ltd.
P.O. Box 64383, Dept. K618-1
St. Paul, MN 55164-0383

Printed in the United States of America

*To Gail*

# Other Books by the Author

The Love Boats (Pinnacle Books)

Cruise Diary (Houghton-Mifflin)

Complete Guide to a Successful Cruise (Contemporary Books)

Frisco Lady (Pinnacle Books)

Frisco Fortune (Pinnacle Books)

Legacy of Love (Medallion Books)

Spanish Serenade (Harper & Row)

Hypoglycemia: The Disease Your Doctor Won't Treat (Kensington)

Love Boats: Above and Below Decks with Jeraldine Saunders
(Llewellyn)

# contents

# $\mathcal{L}$OVE IS THE SIGN

## *foreword*

$\mathcal{M}$any so-called scientists insist that astrology is a fossil science. Well, if that's so, astrology is the liveliest corpse I know. If the truth be known, astrology is very much alive and kicking in the world today. More and more people, young and old, are turning to astrology. Astrology shows that persons are more concerned with love, money, and health, in that order. Some individuals may dispute whether money should come before health, but there is no dispute about love! Love leads the way, always! Astrologers from time immemorial—from the beginning of recorded history—have been bombarded with questions and exhortations about love.

Today, loneliness is one of the greatest—if not the greatest—malady facing most people, young and old. We have arrived at a time of modern technology, yet, increasingly, young people lead the way around the world in alcoholism and suicide. Astrology can be used to avoid pitfalls because astrology teaches us our place in time—the right time—the time to reap and the time to sow.

To be ignorant of astrology is to ignore the poetry of our personal universe. Astrology equates love with self-esteem, and to have self-esteem is to take the first major step toward love.

Astrology is that scientific art which deals with the synchronicity between planetary positions and mundane affairs, including human character and potential, and which deals with the Jungian concept that "everything born or done at this moment of time has the qualities of this moment of time."

Once you become familiar with astrology, you are at home in your own universe. You realize that the very time you were born connects with universal intelligence, that nothing happens by chance.

When you begin to wonder about the planets and how they revolve around the Sun, you realize that we have just touched the tip of the iceberg of the universal intelligence, permitting us to gain some insights. For example, we know in astrology that the Sun is the giver of life. In a horoscope we all have a Fifth House. Leo is the natural fifth sign of the Zodiac, representing love and children; and the Sun, the giver of life, is the ruler of Leo, the Fifth House. It would not take Sherlock Holmes to deduce that love is life—that without the Sun there is no life—ergo, without love there is no life.

When we say that a person is lifeless, what we're really saying is that a person is without love. When we say a person is lively and so full of life, we mean that the person exudes—or radiates—the warmth that is the Sun; so there will come a day in the not-too-distant future when our maladies—emotional, financial, and spiritual—all the way up and down the scale, will be eradicated once love is understood. The power and impact of love, when love is fully understood and utilized, is the best medicine in the world. (The very word when numericized equals nine, and in adding the numbers together to reduce to one digit, as in numerology, we find that 360 degrees is also equal to nine, a completion of the circle.) No medicine can or will compare to love.

When love is understood, when we recognize the signs of love, if you will, then we will be recognizing how to attain—to reach—our fullest potential. We can live life to the hilt here and now. The first step is to understand the rudiments of astrology, beginning with our own horoscopes, which include our month, day, year, hour, and place of birth, and to realize that the very moment our birth indicates not only our professional and our financial potential, but most important of all, our love potential.

The signs of love? They are all about…they are all of the signs, and to distinguish one from the other is the stuff of life.

Indeed, Jeraldine Saunders sheds a brilliant light into the true signs of love, and I am sure her illuminating and intelligible work will serve a purpose greater than the pedantic, posing, thick-bound, horn-rimmed-glasses kind of volume that might lay claim to everything from balancing the budget to winning the latest war.

To the signs of love! Let us perceive them whenever and wherever encountered. Amen!

—Sydney Omarr
Santa Monica, California

# Simply Love

What is this thing called LOVE?
It is a blessing sent from Heaven above.
It is wonderful, delightful—that very special rapture
That you must pursue until you, or it, has made the capture.

LOVE is here, there, and everywhere.
It fills the Universe and pervades the air.
Whoever you are and whatever you do,
LOVE is present, and completely surrounds you.

You dispute this fact of Natural Law?
Do you say LOVE is not, because you never saw
Or felt your very soul respond to its urge?
What a useless, meaningless, fearful dirge!

Only you can control LOVE's destiny in your day.
To awaken it, you must give it, that is the way
To get LOVE to return to you,
Release it, let it escape into yonder blue.

Out it will rush, then it will come back
Tenfold or more; the tide will never slack.
You will wonder at all this good,
And it's proper that you should.

Learn to LOVE in the largest sense.
Cease being narrow, self-indulgent and tense.
Read here of LOVE, its true definition,
You'll find life Paradise and not Perdition.

—Arthur Andrews

# $\mathscr{D}$O YOU WONDER WHY?

## *preface to the second edition*

$\mathscr{D}$o you wonder why people in the same family with the same environment, the same upbringing, etc. can be so different?

Do you wonder if you will be lucky in love? Is there a soul mate for you? Do you wonder where your talents lie? Will you find your true purpose in life? These and many other questions are answered in this book.

It's no wonder *Love Signs* has maintained its popularity for so long. It gives you understanding about fate and free will. It will ignite your soul's power and help make your dreams come true.

Word of mouth has made *Love Signs* a popular, dual-purpose volume. It is fun-filled information that gives quick insight about the reader and their loved ones. Readers have taken this book to a gathering and through utilizing birth dates, Sun signs, palm reading, face reading, and handwriting analysis, it's become the life of the party! Meanwhile, subliminally, all involved learned ancient truths for individual betterment.

*I thank all my readers of the previous edition.*

The mail I have received from readers show bright, intellectually motivated seekers of the truth. The only persons who put down these subjects discussed in this book are those who have not studied them. Each section is chockfull of truth hidden behind levity. In the astrology section, I have gone around the zodiac informing how each sign relates to the other signs. In this expanded new edition, I have added how we relate to another person who has our own Sun sign.

After lecturing at sea on these topics while I was a cruise director, I took my own advice. I used these truths and attribute my successful autobiography, *The Love Boats*, and my creation of the TV series to following the information found in this book. Think of *Love Signs* as the blueprint leading to the wealth of your unique talent and creative energy, hidden beneath the surface, just waiting to be discovered through the application of the knowledge herein.

In the near future, with our now ever-expanding technology, these underlying principles will be utilized in enhancing not only our physical comforts but our mind and spirit as well.

Happy sailing through these pages.

—Jeraldine Saunders
June 1998

# Acknowledgments

I would like to thank my editor, a great Leo, Andrew Ettinger, for his patience and encouragement. And Taurean Gaye Tardy, for her faith and dedication. A special thanks to a brilliant Virgo, Dr. Leo Fishbeck, for his inspiration. A huge thanks to the talented Aquarian, Bob Skeetz, for creating the haikus. But most of all, thank you to my dearly loved Libra husband, Arthur R. Andrews.

And in this new edition, a big thank you to editor Christine Snow and artist Anne Marie Garrison and all the loving people at Llewellyn Publications.

# $\mathcal{S}$igns of Love

*SIGNS OF LOVE help you discover*
*The ways to catch and hold your lover,*
*How to please, and how to know*
*That your love is special and will surely grow.*

*Ignorance is not bliss nor a delight,*
*Knowledge you must have—knowledge must be right.*
*So read these words and read them well!*
*For true love demands wisdom—not a spell.*

—Arthur Andrews

# ℒOVE SIGNS

## FOR ALL

## *introduction*

> *Sure Man was born to meditate on things,*
> *And to contemplate the eternal springs*
> *Of God and Nature, glory, bliss and pleasure;*
> *That Life and love might be his heavenly treasure.*
> —Traherne

Confucius said, "If you would slay the dragon, you must first learn his habits."

Let's assume, if you are a man, that you bought this book because you would like to be a little more of a "ladykiller," or that you would like to capture the right one alive and drag her, not kicking too hard, to a minister, a judge, or to your own native habitat.

For better or for worse....

Or for fun and games.

Or, if you are a woman, let us assume that you are looking for a not-too-domesticated, partially housebroken, live, virile, intelligent, moderately hairy, success-oriented male of the species.

Let's assume that your past track record has been hit and miss, win a few and lose a bunch!

Could be there's a better way to go!

Flying blind with a highly volatile cargo of vulnerable, uninsurable emotions is like playing Russian roulette with a fully loaded gun.

What you need are guidelines.

Learn something about the beauty of the beast before you venture into the cave with an unknown quantity that may be too inert to be interesting or too dangerous to be alone with in the dark.

Even before recorded history, man has scanned the night skies and noted the correlation between mundane and personal happenings and planetary (especially Lunar) positions in the heavens.

Old-time preachers often warned parents to lock up their daughters at the time of the full Moon, to preserve their virtue.

Not so weirdly there is a tremendous amount of useful and interesting data available to all who would like a little more love in their lives.

Let's say that Computer Miss-Match broke down the day they promised you Ms./Mr. Right and paired you instead with someone who was psychologically and physiologically wrong for you.

Let's say you couldn't get off the ground with that alleged airline stewardess from Unbelievable Dates, Inc., or was it Dial-a-Dog Dating Unlimited?

Not only were you unwilling to fly her, she was equally reluctant to take you aboard.

Now, are you ready to look at some more reliable and fun ways of choosing the person or persons who can join with you to find a most meaningful joy of life?

We will start out with the signs of love in the twelve astrological signs of the zodiac. Then we will move on to face reading, graphology, palm reading, aura reading, and numerology.

These have been the tools in my personal "problem solving kit"—these, plus some good old-fashioned Irish extrasensory perception.

Men and women of all ages seem to home in on me when their problems reach a critical mass. It is no surprise that people bring their problems and their confidences regarding *l'amour* to me.

Through the years, more by accident than design, I have acquired considerable expertise in what genius Sydney Omarr has dubbed "borderline" areas.

These areas encompass the Mantic Arts we shall explore in this book. Obviously, personal experience also enters the picture. I am in love with love.

I feel, like many of you, that I blossom when I am in love.

When we reach for love, we are reaching for life.

In my past professions I was both in the midst and at the sidelines of the unending effort to find warmth, appreciation, romance, and even seduction.

You might say it was a unique profession for a woman, since I was the only female cruise director of a cruise ship in the world. My responsibility was to see to the needs of passengers on the cruise because they wanted fun and games and entertainment. I had this job seven days a week, eleven months a year, for seven years.

My duties included giving lectures and private personal readings. My tools were the borderline skills, powerful tools in learning and understanding the love needs and gifts of my passengers.

I am a people watcher, people studier, and people helper.

With you, Dear Readers, I will share my findings and my secrets—some of them, anyway.

Being a Cupid at heart, I get a vicarious thrill just thinking about how much happier you will feel after you have learned and practiced what you will read about in this book.

Nature gave us the need to love and be loved.

Many people have said, "You can't fight nature, it's bigger than both of us!" Not a very original approach.

More like an aboriginal prelude to something very much desired by young and old.

Surface as well as deeper feelings are invited, challenged, pursued, resisted, sometimes surrendered, sometimes hurt, sometimes exalted. We may be brought to the brink of true love or swept over the edge in temporary passion and infatuation.

"Love is never lost," said Washington Irving. "Even if not recip- rocated, it will flow back and soften and purify the heart."

Maybe it is more important to love than be loved. Actually, you are more apt to find love by giving it than by looking for it.

Your work, art, music, athletics, money, responsibilities, duties, crossword puzzles—all can be satisfying parts of life, but there is a missing ingredient. Love and dreams together are part of the spice ingredient that turns existence into living!

Cynics and purveyors of sour grapes deny this scornfully. They fool themselves and rob themselves. Their dreams don't deal with wish fulfillment but with frustration.

They are afraid to be fully alive. Shakespeare said, "Ah! There's the rub!"

To dream.

And to dream of love.

LOVE—the answer to the human condition. Its motivation is to fulfill deepest desires and highest aspirations. It brings the greatness of meaning and dignity to life. We cannot fear and love at the same time. Now we will release love! This imprisoned splendor has been waiting for the ecstasy of giving.

We can extend our journey of fulfillment past the three dimen- sions of body, emotion, and intellect to a fourth dimension—that of the spiritual—when we learn our own unique purpose in life. This fourth dimension can keep us in harmony with ourselves and allow us to rejoice in the fullness that you have just added to your life.

Every person born into this world has a definite place to fill, where he or she is to live, love, and serve, paying a price to justify a particular existence. We are given inner needs and desires, satisfied only in love and its spiritual commitment.

Love disciplines and controls us so that our actions fit our destiny. Everyone is here to learn how to love, and it is in loving that we learn our true fulfillment and our lessons in life. Remember, this life is not a dress rehearsal for something else.

We are all here to learn, all "diamonds in the rough." Surely during our lives, abrasive persons and situations come to us which help us to rise above them and become more polished, more radiant and beautiful on the inside, where it counts.

Love is not to be found. It consists not in finding the right person, but in *becoming* the right person. There is no other way to truly express love except through self-love.

I would like to impress upon you the importance in helping each other to feel:

> Significant
> Secure
> Appreciated
> Beloved
> Understood

Move out into life and become lovable, but don't run amok boasting of conquests while you are seeking in quantity that which can be found only in quality, or while you are seeking in sex that which can be found only in true love. Allow a strong feeling of love to flow out to all persons and to all living things.

How much touching did you do last week? Yesterday? Did you shake some hands? Did you pat any backs? How many people did you hug?

Did you blow any kisses? Did you merge auras with your lover? If you did, are you any the poorer for the touches and kisses you gave and received?

If you withheld touches, kisses, pats on the back, or physical love, are you any richer? Has this frugality of emotional support for others (deserved or otherwise) piled up any reserve that contributes to your or anyone's enjoyment of life?

Nonverbal communication—touching and being touched in or out of the nude—beats arguments and bickering. When spiritual friendship and love are joined with sensual love, as we lower the protective walls and shed protective clothing, we find we are filled with overflowing love.

The more we nourish the negative and repressive voice within us, the more apt we are to feel that the affirmative, more tolerant one must be leading us astray.

Essentially, love is not an emotion, not sentimentality, not a sensual or sexual experience; but it may use any or all of these as a conduit into which it flows. Zen masters have told us that:

> *When we walk we should walk;*
> *When we sit we should sit;*
> *When we talk we should really say things.*

Should we not love when we love?

If we are self-consciously analyzing "shoulds" and "shouldn'ts" instead of actively loving when we feel love, we are short-circuiting and short-changing ourselves.

Feelings! Joy! Glee! Abandonment! Laughter! Touching! Surely they are vital parts of the machinery that makes the world go round—at least the ingredients of the lubricant, or the brighter colors in the paint job.

Our attitudes control our lives. It is of paramount importance that we know how to harness and control this great force.

Since the universe is the greatest university, it is here that we are to learn how to love, that we may be healthy and happy. We, not nature, are the culprits when we misuse or abuse our creativity in a way that is against nature. We create our own sadness or happiness.

One beautiful outcome that you will derive from the study of this book is the confirming evidence that nature does not do things haphazardly, that there is an order to the universe. Perhaps I should share with you one of my favorite quotations from the late, great scientist, Dr. Albert Einstein. This giant among intellects declared, "God does not play dice with the universe." So, why should we play dice with our lives?

Life is for loving and the common goal of spirituality sustains this axiom.

*Love Signs* deals with finding and holding someone worth loving through the use of the Mantic Arts. Through the right application of the knowledge and power herein lies wisdom—wisdom that life is not just for existing, life is for loving.

So, let's LEARN TO LOVE BY LOVING!

# $\mathscr{A}$N INVITATION

*chapter one*

TO LOVE

*If music be the food of love, play on.*
—William Shakespeare,
from *Twelfth Night*

$\mathscr{L}$ove, the magic ingredient that is the very essence of life, is sought after by everyone everywhere on the face of this Earth. The need to love and be loved in return lies deep within our souls, silently awaiting a seductive summons, an invitation to life's dance.

Come, join the dance, and be assured that no matter what awaits you—success or failure—you will always be welcome. The music plays for you, too.

Let the signs of love be instrumental in showing you how to achieve perfect harmony between yourself and your loved ones through the power of love—a power that will enable you to express life according to how you feel about yourself, a power that can help you attain lasting, mutual love and happiness.

# Eliminating the Enemies of Love

We will strive for a mood of mystic thoughtfulness, using the Mantic Arts not merely for intellectual analysis, but for a kind of quickened appreciation that causes us to be attentive to the significance of living and loving. Rightmindedness is the directing of attention to those matters that are first in importance. We must not allow isolation and a feeling of separateness to keep us from being able to realize the true significance of love.

The enemies of love are low self-worth (low self-esteem) and fear. They are very prominent in our society. The good news is that we can make them disappear—if we will face them. The past must be released, and we must let go of everything that doesn't help promote a beautiful future.

## Low Self-Worth

Childlike qualities can add much to life by helping us to be playful and joyful. When we were young and unable to use our reason to understand the cause of our feelings, we may have developed wrongly conceived ideas into, not childlike, but childish attitudes. These are the feelings at which we must take a completely new and mature look. With this new look, we must take the responsibility of changing those wrong impressions that we acquired in childhood.

We know that people are interested in love, money, and health— in that very order. If love is of paramount importance to us, then we must learn how to make ourselves lovable—and you can make yourself lovable. You do have this power over yourself. You have the ability to think beyond the past. You have the ability to make that child within you realize that everyone is lovable! In other words, to eliminate the number-one enemy of love (low self-worth), we must retrain our feelings about ourselves first before we can love others, or be loved by them.

As you can understand, the early years in a child's life are very important, for that is when the child develops deep-seated impressions about oneself, according to the manner in which he or she is cared for, loved, or rejected. For the first five years, at least, the ego is in a delicate balance. As we grow older, anything that reinforces our wrongful conception that we are not lovable only adds to our low self-esteem.

People tend to treat us in the way that we think about ourselves. A dead giveaway of low self-esteem is rigidity about many matters and intolerance of oneself or others. As you learn to love yourself more, you will automatically become compassionate, not only toward yourself, but toward others, too. If you have high self-esteem, you won't allow others to use you badly. Being withdrawn is another symptom of low self-esteem—it is not allowing yourself to open up to others because you are unsure of yourself.

The study of your horoscope, numerology, or any of the other Mantic Arts contained in this book are all aids in helping you to know that you are okay, that you are unique, that no one else is exactly like you. Realize that there are many others out there who are trying to get through to you—wanting to love you and wanting your love in return. Don't put up that protective wall for fear of the possibility of rejection or of being hurt.

As you learn about your unique self, you can be your real, very own self. Always remember, someone out there is looking for someone just like you! Cherish your uniqueness.

## Fear

Now for the number two enemy of love, fear. It manifests itself as jealousy, possessiveness, unusually high expectations, manipulation, and attention-getting.

Fear is only an illusion. It is the illusion that creates the feeling of separateness—the false sense of isolation—that exists only in your imagination. As you face up to who you really are honestly, and realize that you are okay, you must not apply any blame to yourself in the process.

When you are no longer occupied with your low self-esteem and are free of fear, an automatic alertness flows toward other people, whether they are your family, friends, or lovers. You are now free to experience loving relationships. With this new awareness, you will find yourself becoming involved with others so that the inner sense of isolation is eliminated and you are then eager for commitment.

Commitment is getting out and getting involved. It is spontaneous. Commitment can't be created out of guilt. Commitment is the natural result of your discovery of love within you.

Your newfound awareness of the love within you brings with it an inner illumination and the ability to become a magnet for love. Now life takes on a new dimension, for out of the imagination of the heart come the real issues of life.

Once free of the enemies of love, you are free to love, even to plan life wisely. It is not the peace and leisure at the end of life that you are seeing; it is the leisure to live and love along the way; and the mental capacity to live leisurely in a world of haste reveals the true scholar. Those hasten most who are unsure of their destination. By studying the Mantic Arts herein, we can enjoy the adventures along the way, for then we each are following our own unique path. Then every upset, every incident, becomes alive with purpose and rich with meaning.

Your own inner peace is the motionless center of your moving world. (This mathematical concept that the center of a rotating mass is motionless is a truth that the student can only realize slowly.) The calm serenity that encompasses all the phenomena of your living is your Nirvana. It is only our lack of understanding who we are that makes the road of life difficult and obstructs nature with a thousand artificial hazards and predicaments. Be patient and kind, and in time love will be kind through you. For love is a verb, just as God is a verb; each expression is interchangeable.

Love keeps everything together; it is the cohesive force of the universe. It keeps the planets moving and the Moon, stars, and all nature in place. By just looking out our window and observing nature, we can see love in action, and, indeed, it is beautiful to behold.

By living in harmony with your world, and by not isolating yourself, you will see that love is a creative force. Learn to love that which you are, and then you will be capable not only of receiving and feeling love, but also of expressing it.

Eliminate the fear. Eliminate the low self-image. Be kinder to yourself; consider all that you've been through. Instead of reproach, give yourself a pat on the back. Build your commitment to loving the Source that is within you, with all your mind, your heart, and your soul.

When you commit yourself to eliminating the enemies of love, then you are ready to accept the invitation to love, and your inner Divine Intelligence will joyously create within you the *art of loving!*

# $\mathcal{T}$HE ASTROLOGY OF LOVE

## *chapter two*

*Astrology is Astronomy brought down to
earth and applied to the affairs of man.*
—Ralph Waldo Emerson

$\mathcal{T}$ell me, thou star," wrote Percy Bysshe Shelley
in one of his romantic poems; they are words that
remain an invitation to look beyond our Earth for
the true meaning of love. How often, when we are
with a loved one, we do just that—lie together on
the grass and gaze at the stars, dreaming dreams
together, wishing wishes together. Heavenly bodies
and human love have been tied together in romantic metaphor after romantic metaphor throughout
the history of literature. And for good reason.

We are all beings of Earth, but at the same time, we are all beings of the universe; its stars and planets all have influences on us and on our emotions.

Astrology has become one of the most popular occult sciences in recent years. Perhaps this is a natural evolution of things, because the different influences of the planets and stars on each of us are almost as obvious as the different influences of our various cultures. It is just as obvious that a person who grew up in the Midwest has grown up with different influences from one who grew up in the East. Someone who was born at a time and place that put Taurus in the astrological position of his or her Sun sign has grown with an influence different from one who was born with a Libra Sun.

The position of the planets and stars in relationship to the place on Earth where you were born determines the major influences on your inner personality. Each fraction of a second that the Earth moves on its axis and within its orbit, it alters its gravitational relationship with the planets and stars of the galaxy; and each spot on the Earth's surface is also affected differently by these gravitational changes. For us, this means that no two people can possibly be astrologically identical, unless they are born at the identical spot in the same instant—a physical impossibility!

Though astrology is a complex scientific art, much can be determined about a person by merely knowing his or her Sun sign (zodiac sign). This is the sign we say we are when someone asks, "What's your sign?" It indicates the position of the Sun at the time of your birth in relation to one of twelve zodiacal signs. Knowing your Sun sign and your lover's Sun sign can tell you much about each other's natural tendencies and about your compatibility as a romantic duo.

Let's look at the twelve signs (listed on the next page), one by one, to see what each means in the realm of love. Remember, this is your major sign, and these are your major characteristics. But remember, too, should you want to delve into the more intricate details of the astrology of love, that a complete astrological chart can tell you much more about you and your loved one.

# The Twelve Love Signs

| ARIES | ♈ | Fire | Ruled by Mars, a planet of action. Rules the head. |
| TAURUS | ♉ | Earth | Ruled by Venus, the goddess of Love. Rules the throat. |
| GEMINI | ♊ | Air | Ruled by Mercury, the messenger. Rules the lungs, both arms. |
| CANCER | ♋ | Water | Ruled by the Moon, the imaginative planet. Rules the breasts. |
| LEO | ♌ | Fire | Ruled by the Sun, the planet of vitality. Rules the heart. |
| VIRGO | ♍ | Earth | Ruled by Mercury (and Vulcan). Rules the intestines. |
| LIBRA | ♎ | Air | Ruled by Venus (like Taurus). Rules the kidneys. |
| SCORPIO | ♏ | Water | Ruled by Mars (action) and Pluto, the planet of reconstruction. Rules the genitals. |
| SAGITTARIUS | ♐ | Fire | Ruled by Jupiter, the planet of expansion. Rules the thighs. |
| CAPRICORN | ♑ | Earth | Ruled by Saturn, the teacher and the task master. Rules the knees. |
| AQUARIUS | ♒ | Air | Ruled by Uranus, the planet of genius and progress. Rules the calves. |
| PISCES | ♓ | Water | Ruled by Neptune, the planet of illusion. Rules the feet. |

# *Meanings of the Signs*

## Aries (March 21–April 20)

♈ Aries individuals are the sexual scalp hunters of the zodiac. Frequently "first nighters," Aries men and women often have more than one iron in the fire, in both business and love.

There is an exciting impatience about them. Quick on the draw, they shoot now and ask questions later. In any romantic encounter with an Aries, be prepared for the rush act: "I want you now or never" would be a typical Aries approach. An Aries convinces you that you seem to have known each other all your lives, notwithstanding the fact you haven't even finished your first drink. And don't expect your refusals to be heard; Aries people have a strong dislike for the word "No," and a reluctance to hear it.

If your Aries companion has ever had a complete astrological chart cast, try to find out in which of the twelve signs the planet Venus is located. Two Venus positions to watch for especially are Venus in Aries and Venus in Pisces. Aries natives who, on the first date, say you're the most wonderful person in the world, probably have their Venus, as well as their Sun, in Aries. When you hear your Aries companions speculate that your meeting might have been fated, they most likely have their Venus in Pisces.

Though quite spontaneous in starting relationships, Aries are not known for their follow-up. Oh, you may hear from them from time to time, often at ridiculous hours of the night. They might be calling from a pay phone around the corner and want to come right over.

***The Aries Man.*** It has been said of the Aries male, "He is the anyplace, anytime, anybody's sign when it comes to love." Probably not entirely true, unless you read "anytime" to mean "soonest."

Definitely in the predator class, the Aries male is an enthusiastic, impulsive tracker and a relentless pursuer, once he selects his target.

He is in a rush, and because Aries is a Mars-ruled Sun sign, he is highly competitive. He wants the prize, whether his game of the day is business or love.

Being a pursuer, however, he also enjoys the chase itself, including the initial efforts of his prey to elude or escape him. Of course, if he had his way, he'd skip the courtship and the amenities and get down to brass snaps and zippers. He's the guy who, before the main course of your first dinner together is served, begins an internal psychodrama in which he is piloting you toward his sleeping quarters and overcoming your protests with charm.

Prepare yourself for this energetic variety of the male species; often, he's so sex hungry he could wear some women out!

Single, the Aries man is apt to fluctuate in his choice of outlets for this excessive energy between his business and his love life. So, if it's a long-term relationship you desire with your Aries companion, you'll have to give a lot of praise, love, sex, and understanding to housebreak him. But be careful! He often deludes himself that his most recent conquest is the best of all, the one he's searched for all his life. (Watch those Venus positions!) His impatience and impulsiveness, his rashness and capacity for self-delusion, could all combine to propel him into that most dreaded condition of all— the hasty marriage.

If you keep a level head, and understand the great deal of giving you'll have to do, a permanent relationship with an Aries man can be a rewarding experience, and certainly not wanting for emotion and sexual activity. Often, Aries men want to father a large brood of children. (Almost as often, they are simply too impatient to take proper precautions.) So, this is at least one subject to talk very seriously about before beginning a long-term relationship.

The right marriage would have a beneficial effect on the health, wealth, and public reputation of the Aries man.

***The Aries Woman.*** She is all woman, and too much so for some men to handle. Aries women can be one of two basic types: the submissive, repressed Aries lamb, or the hyper Aries ram. I feel that the lamb type is an early phase of the true Aries woman; most Aries women who seem to be this type are merely going through a stage while they wait for their horns to grow.

They're in a hurry to get on with life's experiences, and sexual initiation may come early in life—earlier, anyway, than for the more cautious signs. And once they have experienced sexual delight, they develop an unequivocal taste and need for more.

Men often think of them as "good sports" or "one of the guys," because Aries women often are genuinely interested in career and material success, those realms that until recently were the exclusive domain of men. But when they start mixing business with pleasure, you can bank on the appearance of the purely female Aries. They project it exceedingly well.

Aries women, like Aries men, are pursuers. Sometimes their male friends may wonder what is happening, especially if the men think they're doing the pursuing. There's another side to the aggressive Aries woman that cannot be overlooked: she loves, and is extremely vulnerable to, flattery. And she likes to be where the action is (it's usually where she is).

You'll probably find that your Aries lover likes to go out to a chic restaurant before getting down to the real business of the evening. Her path of pursuit favors a route with a high tab. But more often than not it's worth it.

One astounded male, speaking of an encounter with an Aries woman, remarked, "Beautiful! But I felt raped." Apparently, however, he was not upset by the events of the evening, for he went on, "I never met a woman like her before. I was afraid I'd never find another." (Do you like stories with happy endings? They were married within three weeks.)

Although the typical Aries woman will seem to have more than her fair share of affairs, including some quickies of little consequence, she does have domestic and maternal potential. Once she decides that a permanent relationship is the next challenge, she works at it with imagination, energy, and love. But brace yourself here for stormy moments of violent temper, and don't get too hung up on them, because generally she forgets them quickly.

She will expect her husband and her children to be go-getters and winners, and she will provide much of the inspiration for this, as well as great rewards for their successful efforts.

## Taurus (April 21–May 21)

People born under the Sun sign Taurus are the temperamental reverse of the hasty Aries type. They won't be rushed from the table, the bar, or the bed. They seem to think time really is on their side. If you are to enjoy life to the very hilt, a Taurean might say, "Then take it slow and easy."

Because they are of a fixed, earthy sign ruled by the planet Venus, they have the capacity to develop an obsessive nature in the areas of sex and material luxury. They often have a first-cabin complex. A possessive zodiacal type anyway, they are unhappy if they don't have the very best, and this includes the best in love and sex.

On first meeting, Taureans seem quiet and contemplative. It is up to you to break the ice, most often, but that is not at all difficult. Their simple dignity and quietness shouldn't be taken for extreme sensitivity or self-centeredness. They want to be wanted. Once that first conversation gets flowing, you'll probably hear the archetypal Taurean voice: a rich, sensual tone.

Staying power is the most noticeable attribute of the Taurus. Don't plan to get home early on your first date.

**The Taurus Man.** Does the new man in your life have doe eyes and the wide-open apprehensive look of a young deer surprised by a predator? Is he muscular with a strong jaw shaded by a heavy beard? Chances are, he's a Taurus.

The Taurus man likes to sample the merchandise before he makes a long-term commitment, but once the idea of making a commitment begins to form in his head, he's the jealous type and expects complete loyalty. On the other hand, he will return your loyalty with stubborn steadfastness.

These are sensual men who find immense enjoyment in things of the body—good sex, good food, and a comfortable bed. He considers himself an expert in these areas, and is apt to invite you to his place for one of his gourmet dinners and some fine wine. He'll be more relaxed in his own home, and if he is particularly attracted to you, he'll become quite a tosser of the bull in an atmosphere which he finds comfortable.

He's not going to rush you into bed, but if that's his goal, you may end the evening there. His sexual drive borders on the satyric sometimes, and he'll demand a woman with equal desires and without sexual inhibitions. Conservative as he may seem on the surface, he is not, by any means, wed to the missionary position. Taurus men are often fond of oral sex, and they expect reciprocation from their partners.

They're often concerned with what others think of them, and this includes what others think of their love mate, and what their love mate thinks of them. So you'll have to offer praise for their sexual prowess—don't take it for granted.

If you've been seeing one Taurean man for a while, he's probably already thinking in terms of forever with you. Once he becomes a permanent partner, your restauranting will suffer a severe cutback, and your kitchen will become a focal point in your home—that, and the bedroom. Don't be too surprised if, on your first anniversary, he buys you a second refrigerator. Food and gourmet cookery are important to the household of the Taurus male, and he'll be wanting to spend much of his time at home. If you aren't a gourmet cook, he'll teach you, and you'd better learn, for he'll be inviting friends and business associates over for dinner all the time. It's best you understand this before any long-term plans are made.

Of course, his desire for financial success will assure you of material security, and he'll always buy you the best—even though the best will have a heavy concentration on fine cookware. But you will be regarded with respect and love, and if he can at all afford it, the Taurus husband will make no complaints about hiring you a housekeeper to assist with the upkeep of his castle.

So, if it's loyalty and a solid home life you desire, as well as lasting, potent sex, Taurus could be your match. One caveat: they are slow to anger, but when they reach the limit of their patience—which is there in abundance—the bellow of the enraged bull will be heard for miles.

*The Taurus Woman.* The Taurus woman is the mistress of the grand entrance. She steps slowly and surely, displaying her well-chosen clothes and jewelry with aplomb. You'll notice her when she speaks, and, like the Taurus man, her voice is rich and resonant.

If she's interested in you, her eyes will telegraph her sultry message and draw out the slightest interest you may have toward her. You will probably sense her feelings of love for her own body. She spends much time and money to keep it in the best possible condition. Fine clothes, cosmetics, perfumes, and jewelry enhance her well-toned physique. She probably takes yoga and exercise classes, and many Taurean women study dance, because they love music and body movement.

If the idea of a Taurean woman appeals to you, check out a Kundalini yoga class, where she may very well be learning to develop her already potent sexual energies.

Body contact is important to the sensual Taurus woman. She loves the kind of date that includes dinner in a fine restaurant and late-night dancing. And then…well, the best is yet to come. Once is not enough for her, but few Taurus women fail to inspire the best in bed from their men, due in part at least to their unabashed delight in restoring still another erection in their men for sexual encores. She'll probably make you feel like the Man of the Year in bed.

But don't take her bedroom process for granted. She, too, demands to be pleasured with the best. And she won't be rushed initially. Like the Taurus male, she'll take her time getting there, and once she's there, she'll take her time being there.

As a permanent partner, the Taurus woman is loyal and steadfast, patient and home oriented. She will expect the best from her husband—a comfortable house, material security, and a good kitchen. Like her Taurus brother, she may be a gourmet cook, and will like to entertain at home. Be prepared to play the host to her hostess at numerous dinner parties. And her dinner parties will be the best presented with the finest food served on the finest serving ware, the best crystal, the richest silver.

Taurean women are luxury items and desire men who are capable of high sexual proficiency as well as high potential for satisfying their expensive material tastes. If you can afford her, she can be the ideal lifetime partner.

But if she becomes jealous of or angry with her mate, her warning will be barely visible. Like the namesake of her sign, she'll stamp the ground once, just to let you know her divine patience is about to go out the window. If you don't mend your ways on the spot, watch out, unless you're the world's greatest toreador.

# Gemini (May 22–June 21)

Ⅱ With their more-the-merrier flirtatious attitude toward the opposite sex, and their desire to talk about it stronger than their desire to get on with it, Geminis can be a problem.

The natives of this sign, though they are not sinister types, have something of a Dr. Jekyl-Mr. Hyde personality. They can talk the leg off an iron pot, and they love to play the devil's advocate. This can play havoc with the nerves of those who need a little more action and a little less verbiage.

You can't get into a fight or a bed with any Gemini without considerable palaver first, unless they are the ones trying to promote something interesting. They rarely bore you, but unless you are a pretty special live wire yourself, you may bore a Gemini, especially after the initial excitement of the conquest loses its glow. And don't count on being the only attraction for your newly met Gemini; they like to engage more than one person at a time in conversation—whenever that conversation takes place.

But if you're truly interested in a Gemini person, don't worry too much about their faults; they need something to work off all that nervous energy, and love can be just the therapy for them.

***The Gemini Man.*** Flirtatious, witty, charming, your new potential love is also a talker. He loves to argue, discuss, and debate. He knows all the verbal tricks, and his part of the conversation may lead you to believe he's quite the Casanova. If this is true of the man in your life, chances are he's a Gemini.

To some Gemini men, women are like a deck of cards—they give them all quite a shuffle. Then, they'll play some of them and discard others. If a woman is not immediately of personal interest to him, he'll let her know right away. In the beginning, he'll be looking for a personal female sounding board, an idea person, someone with whom to talk and establish a meaningful communication. He won't be thinking of disrobing a woman physically until he's sure it'll be interesting first to disrobe her mentally.

Novelty is attractive to the Gemini man; he's open to experimentation, both mentally and sexually. As a matter of fact, it wouldn't be all that unusual for a Gemini man to combine the two; many times, he'll love to talk about sex first before getting down to it, and then review the act afterward. You won't really have to participate in the discussion that much—just listen, as such discussions take on the character of a monologue, anyway. Sometimes, he won't say a word about sex, before or after. Not aloud, at any rate. But you can be sure his mind is previewing and reviewing.

Some Gemini men may be kiss-and-tell types. In that case, your romantic interlude could become the subject of gossip, or maybe the center of one of his interesting anecdotes for his next lady—post-mortem judgment included.

The Gemini man in his Dr. Jekyll self is a dream to be with; but when that Mr. Hyde surfaces, watch out; grab your purse and your patience and head for the exit, at least temporarily. With luck, his devilish side will have gone into hiding by the time you return.

When a Gemini man marries, it doesn't necessarily mean his woman-shuffling days are over; he may marry more than once. A permanent relationship with a Gemini man is guaranteed to be free from boredom. He'll always be as interesting as he is fastidious and changeable.

***The Gemini Woman.*** For the man who claims he is looking for a woman who possesses both a body and a brain, the Gemini woman can be a challenging and often frustrating temptation. Whoever coined the phrase about women being fickle must have based his evidence on Gemini women.

There are two extremes of the Gemini woman. One can be summed up by the question this extreme may pose: "Why can't you love me for myself?" Retranslated, that means: "What does sex have to do with love?"

The other extreme is the sensual, wandering Gemini woman, who is always puzzled about why her men can't understand that she can love two people (or more) at once.

The typical Gemini woman tends to be slender, with a smaller bosom than the other signs. Her aliveness is reflected in her large eyes, which seem full of mischief and worldliness. Her long fingers may go into play during one of her bubbly, chatty conversations. She is a beauty, and she is not dumb.

Like her Gemini brother, she may intellectualize about sex and the concept of love more than she puts it into practice, and she tends to compartmentalize life's complexities. She has such a compartment for sensuality, but none for sexual perversions, which she views with fear or disgust.

Gemini is not wildly enthusiastic about a lot of sexual activity or about childbearing; however, she has quite a flair for acting, and can convince her playmate that she enjoys only what she has the choice to take or leave. But make no mistake, she loves the companionship, sympathy, and conversation that goes with a relationship, even though her interest in the erotic is largely verbal and a pose intended to please.

She is quite adaptable to any situation except one—a boring situation or a boring person. Most of the time, she would rather curl up with a good book than with a tiresome, overly aggressive sexual male.

Gemini women need very special men, ones who are willing to listen and are able to put some of her words into action, gently.

## Cancer (June 22–July 23)

♋ Cancerians are extremely complex individuals. I call them the twelve-for-the-price-of-one sign, and not without good reason. They are ruled by the fastest piece of astrological equipment—as well as the nearest to Earth—the magnetic and mysterious Moon. The Moon changes position in the sky, moving through each astrological sign once every two and a half days. This gives Cancers fast-changing moods (sometimes so dramatic as to be personality changes), a new mood every two and a half days, twelve a month!

If you like the kind of person who loves to fondle, touch, and snuggle, you'll find Cancer to be your dream, because loving and touching are what they're all about. Because Cancer is ruled by the Moon, these individuals can become quite stimulated when it is full. If they're feeling sexy, a sweet madness comes over them. If they're feeling sentimental, tears gush and sobbing shakes the building. If they're feeling angry, they can become quite tyrannical and unreasonable.

Both men and women born under the sign of Cancer are delightful packages of sexuality, with a strong tendency toward the emotional, whether they're sad or glad about the people and events around them.

***The Cancer Man.*** The male Moonchild is overly sensitive and takes offhand comments about himself too personally. How he loves to fondle and be fondled! Yet how important it is for him to have the right atmosphere and a sensitive love partner. He is the person in the zodiac who most fears rejection; he needs a great deal more reassurance and emotional support than any other sign.

If he says, "I love you," and you come back with, "Big deal" or "I bet you say that to all the girls," you just don't know how to handle a Cancer man. Tell him that you love him, need him, and appreciate him, and elaborate on your devotion to him with your body.

He is one part sentimentalist, one part sensualist, and one part little boy. Usually, he'd rather take you to his place than go to yours the first time you're alone together. There is a certain cozy security that he feels about his place, and you're bound to feel it too—unless, of course, he still lives with his parents. In that case, his fear of awakening or disturbing them will put a wet blanket on your evening.

Cancers tend to have reserve stockpiles of food and drink at hand, and would feel extremely insecure if their cupboards were bare. They also tend to have reserve stockpiles of women at hand. Many Cancer men are inclined to play around, because their hunger for sex is a matter of moods. They feel more secure when, if you are not in the mood, they know someone else who may be.

Women bring out the Cancer man's sensual and sentimental sides. If you can satisfy those two sides of their nature, you'll probably meet the little boy side, too. But remember, watch for those Full Moon nights, when the Cancer man's sensuality, emotionalism, and desire will peak.

***The Cancer Woman.*** Like her Cancer brother, she is a sensitive one, and tends to easily bruise emotionally. She, like her male counterpart, may have strong ties to the family, especially her mother, and looks forward to being a mother someday—nay, *expects* to be a mother someday.

Sensual as well as changeable, Cancer women tend to be buxom, with a certain delightful timidity or shyness which makes them attractive to many kinds of men.

She may seem magnetic and mysterious, like her ruling Moon, especially on the first date, but her sensuality will show through before the evening is out. However, it's not wise to view the Cancer woman as a one night stand. She needs security and sensitivity in her men.

Because of her changeability, her mate may think he's living with twelve different women. Be prepared for emotional outbursts and confessions of love, for these she has in plenty. Don't be too shocked at her mercurialness, for her temper may flare, and she may hold a grudge if a spat isn't resolved right away.

Her many-sidedness makes her a complex woman, one who needs a good protector, much reassurance, and sensitivity; she is a woman who has a certain sentimental liking for old-fashioned etiquette, and she wants her permanent mate to be a good provider.

Cancer women tend to seek lasting relationships, and would probably feel unfulfilled if they are denied children. Because of their ties to their parents, especially to their mothers, Cancer women will expect their lovers and husbands to extend themselves for their parents in times of need.

If it is a loving wife and mother you seek, Cancer may be the sign to follow.

## Leo (July 24–August 23)

♌ The words "audience" and "audition" come to mind in any exploration of the inner workings of this rather straightforward sign, the king or queen of two-legged beasts. To gain applause, they'll sing, dance, and tell jokes; they'll take up sports, outdoor and indoor. Many people, on a crucial date with a Leo, have the uneasy feeling that what does or does not follow is the consequence of their success or failure in a tryout.

There is, of course, another side to Leo: warm, generous, humorous, and loyal. Remember that Leos are proud, fixed in their opinions, and in need of compliments and approval. One way or another, they will acquire an audience, whether on a large or small-scale basis.

Leos love to be the boss. Actually, they make quite able administrators, and, because of their creative nature, they keep life from descending into boredom, even when they're at the wheel of yours.

*The Leo Man.* If you were to compare the male Leo to a bird, you'd have to imagine the peacock; think of his dramatic, colorful feathers, which he likes to preen and show off to his best advantage. He expects applause and appreciation, both of which will cause him to make pleasant sounds.

But if you criticize or oppose him, beware, for you'll soon find he has sharp claws, and the sounds you'll hear will be more like lion's growls. Here, the analogy with the peacock ends. He is, ultimately, the king of beasts, a predator seeking women to conquer and dominate. His ideal woman is most likely a worshipping mistress, submissive, attractive, and showy.

He considers himself a lover-boy and a king—the lion at the office, in the living room, and in the bedroom. Sex, to him, is a demonstration of prowess, as well as an expression of personal warmth, playfulness, sport, and love. The Leo man needs to shine, and sometimes a relationship with him may seem to take on master-slave overtones.

Because he has childlike or little-boy moods, you'll have to tolerate his addiction to the use of first-person singular in his monologues, which often will be composed of anecdotes about himself, his family, or his business achievements. Further, you'll have to pamper and humor him. For instance, he wants to be proud of his women; he'll dress them in satins and silk—figuratively, at least—and will pay for their time at the hairdresser. It's a good idea to play it safe and tell him early on in the relationship that he's a great provider and a spectacular lover.

Notwithstanding his egocentricities, he knows how to get around women. He can make you feel like an empress (his) at the same time that he's trying to get you to become his permanent mistress or wife, and general serving maid.

So, if you take up with a Leo on a permanent basis, be prepared for the singular life with the domestic lion. First of all, you'll probably have to hit upon a strategy for getting him on a diet. Although princely in appearance early in life, he'll tend toward a widening waistline as his hair thins.

Leo men usually want some children to carry on the family name, or at least the family business if there is one; then, too, children are proof of his strength, virility, and potency. Like his wife, his children are also his people. He'll be proud of them and talk endlessly of their accomplishments.

The proud man, the generous man, the active man, the center-stage man—that is Leo.

***The Leo Woman.*** Sleek, sensual, regal, and magnetic, the predatory pussycat known as the Leo woman has many faces. She can be matriarchal and tyrannical, and she can be warm and generous.

Many Leo women are professional beauties, models, or show-business people. Others are into the arts, women's organizations, or are heads of their departments at work. Because she considers herself pretty important, she prefers the company of important men; her ideal man probably would be a well-built, handsome, rich man whose name gets around in the right circles.

Young or old, the Leo woman seems quite impressive and somewhat of a prize package to the man who is looking. There is an exciting and often daring quality to the way she dresses; it's reflected again in the way her eyes seem to be looking for something or someone special.

She chooses her clothes to enhance her self-image, and she dresses for dramatic effect.

Now, Leo women do not always choose their lovers wisely, and this is due to the Leo blind side. Yes, she has one. Remember, she loves to be complimented and stroked; she thrives on being the center of attention. Further, she is hot-blooded and spontaneous, wanting what she wants when she wants it (and plenty of it). Many have a strong exhibitionist streak. Sometimes it's verbal; often, it's physical. Any man with a faculty for the analytical will be able to spot these needs and use them to his benefit.

To maintain good public relations with the female Leo, you'll have to bring gifts. Discussions of your previous wives or lovers are a no-no.

Because Leo women are strong in their spontaneity, they tend to marry in haste and may attract spouses who are weaker than they are. Sometimes, the wedding of complimentary types works out well and comfortably. When it doesn't, the unhappy Leo wife can—like the Aries in similar circumstances—become a shrew of formidable proportions.

So play it safe with the queen of the jungle; be prepared to make your Leo woman happy and purring or you can keep the parson out of the act.

## Virgo (August 24–September 23)

♍ Virgos have taken something of a beating from most writers of astrology books, and it's way past time to set the record straight. They are cruelly written off as overly fastidious or insulting; they are pictured as people who conduct their lives by straightening the paintings on other people's walls, adjusting drapery, and emptying ashtrays. It's been said that they're too critical and analytical to be lovable, and that they're slaves to fashion and fad diets.

No one wants to admit to being a Virgo. They've had too much bad press.

Being a Virgo myself, as well as having observed others of the sign, I find that they are quite loving. They can be very earthy. It's true, they are a little more discriminating in their choices of lovers than some of the more spontaneous signs. They do have an eye for detail, and they tend to be neat and tidy people—but whoever said that these have to be negative traits? To a Virgo, someone with a loud mouth or something making loud noises are things to be avoided.

In the words of a Virgo playboy (who had no expertise in astrology, incidentally), "No woman is perfect, so I must settle for that little piece of perfection in all women."

***The Virgo Man.*** Virgo men are as many-faceted as an intricately cut diamond. There's the fussbudget type, supercritical and analytical, with a bookkeeper's mind; no woman is good enough for this type of Virgo. They make great bachelors.

Then there are the service- or healer-oriented ones, who may set up dental or medical offices, trade agencies, or a business revolving around the maintenance of buildings, automobiles, and clothing sales; don't be surprised to find a Virgo running your local dry-cleaning service. They have a great facility for bringing people together for business purposes. Quality control in any sort of industry, as well as literary or clerical work, comes quite naturally to them.

Though there are exceptions, most Virgo men will be well dressed and well groomed. They may bathe more frequently than non-Virgo men—often before and after making love.

What would a Virgo man be looking for in a woman? A better, refined type of person. What would he settle for? A woman with the potential for perfection, someone he feels he can improve upon. And what is his first step with a new potential lover? Getting rid of all her clothing he doesn't like. He'll help you select the right thing to wear, starting you off, perhaps, by buying a few items which he thinks will look better on you than your present hopeless wardrobe. From then on, he picks and you pay. Next, he may try to change your eating habits, introducing you to his latest health diet. But it's all in your interest; he wants you to look and feel better.

The Virgo man may find fault with his mate's cooking, unless she is extraordinarily proficient in the kitchen. He himself is likely to be a pretty good chef, with a meticulously filed list of recipes. The Virgo man's attitude toward sex is that it is a normal body function—like eating, breathing, sleeping, and exercising. He probably thinks of it more as a treatment than a treat, and feels that too much pleasure is bad for one's self-control. However, because he needs to be proficient at what he does, he'll probably make special efforts to become proficient in bed. Some Virgo men may even do a mental review on your responsiveness, as well as their own performance, after you've made love. Bathing—sometimes together—may become a pre- or post-lovemaking ritual.

Most men of this sign like a woman who is trim and attractive, and who will not get sick. It is not unusual to find a Virgo man who considers pregnancy repulsive. Yet they make good fathers, even though their children, at times, find them hard to please. To both wife and children, the Virgo may say, "I don't like to be critical, but…" and proceed to analyze or criticize.

Some Virgos tend to play the withholding game where allowances and alimony are concerned; they'll make you wait for the money. One thing few Virgos are, however, is tight-fisted; they are notorious for their gifts to special people and on special occasions. And the gifts will be chosen to a tee, with the recipient's wants and needs in mind.

***The Virgo Woman.*** Like the Leo woman, Ms. Virgo enjoys being fussed over by her hairdresser or a sales person, but she is harder to please than Leo and always on the lookout for someone who can do a better job. She can be lured by the very best in apparel, perfumes, and jewelry.

Virgo women may tend to think about sex more often than they put it into practice. Some prefer that men keep their wandering hands to themselves, at least until the preliminary groundwork has been laid. Because they have a certain feeling of specialness about themselves, they may be the kind of women who save their bodies for special people, not just any Tom, Dick, or Harry.

The gifted astrologer and comic, Bob Skeetz, recently gave Virgos a backhanded compliment when he cracked, "It isn't true that Virgos have an obsession with virginity. They're just as sexy as Scorpios. The only problem is that they don't want to do it when you want to do it." He added that they always make their lovers take a bath first.

Well, there are some men who may allege that Virgo women consider sex an unsanitary form of recreation that leads to perspiration, messy hairdos, and pregnancy. They fail to understand that with Virgo women, there are certain amenities which must be observed.

A little intelligent, informed conversation is a good starter. But even before that, be sure that the flowers you bring her are really fresh—you might even include an unusual or delicate vase with it. She may not remember who gave it to her in years to come, but she'll treasure it and use it again and again.

If you offer a Virgo woman a drink, be sure to offer the best, chosen for its style and taste—not just something to consume unheedingly. And be sure to ask her opinion of the wines and liquors.

Before you can touch the Virgo woman, you must have established her respect and trust. The canard that Ms. Virgo will end an old, persnickety maiden is not true; she is discriminating, however, and will hold out for a better deal, so long sometimes that she'll begin wondering if there are any decent men around at all. She is not the type to go through the ordeal of housebreaking a "potential" into a husband.

But once a man insinuates himself into a Virgo's bedroom, he'll find the woman of this sign to be warm, supportive, eager to please—but also anxious to improve him in every way. And she'll make a terrific mother, even though she may expect too much of her children in their early years.

## Libra (September 24–October 23)

These are beautiful people, people with style, and the ability to attract others of better classes. They like to work and socialize in pairs, and they maneuver easily.

Librans, like Virgos, are turned off by loudmouths and people who curse too much. But they're extremely diplomatic. They can say unpleasant things in clever double-talk and seem to sound innocuous. A Libran can tell you to go to hell in such a nice way, you might seriously consider going there.

They are romantic beings, but they have to be fed first, and their food is the entire social trip, complete with dressing up, grooming, and all the amenities and pleasantries.

To the Libran, the word "dalliance" means to caress and fondle as well as to delay. Translated: don't rush them!

Cool rationality, social adeptness, the power to attract others, the expectation of loyalty, and the ability to see both sides of any argument are some of the main traits of the typical Libra.

***The Libra Man.*** Charming and very much the gentleman, the Libra man has a certain edge over men of other signs. Combine that with his compulsion to socialize, and you won't wonder why he usually has a generous supply of women in tow.

Take his charm, good looks, personal directory of attractive women's phone numbers, and natural psychological insight into others' desires and possibilities—and hook all this up to his disguised sexual predatory nature, and you will find a long history of horizontal women who have discovered what a ball the typical Libra man has, even when the ball is over.

However, the Libra man is romantic, as well as predatory, and if he has a predilection for standby women, it's probably because he wants a great deal more in the way of sensual pleasure than one woman is generally able to give him. He ultimately wants peace and harmony, and his home will be a reflection of this.

He may very well be comfortably situated financially, and he dresses well. He has a certain poise or presence, and is sexually suave. His apartment is tidy, casually colorful—somewhere between comfortable and luxurious. It's also a naturally elegant trap for a willing woman.

Libra is one of the four cardinal signs, which bespeak competitiveness (the others are Aries, Cancer, and Capricorn), but it is the only cardinal that is ruled by Venus, the planet of attraction. So the

Libra man attracts love, money, and status. He attracts whatever is beautiful—art, music, people, success, and the opposite sex. Women are drawn to Libra men; because of this, Librans do not often appear as grabbing, clutching men on the make.

One woman, recalling the method of operation of her Libran seducer, admitted, "I was finessed. It seemed the socially acceptable thing to do."

The Libra man thinks of sex as an art and his bed as the canvas. He may lapse into daydreaming of recruiting "newer models" who will be willing to assume any pose that might stimulate his artistic interest of the moment.

Oddly enough, with his well-run business, perhaps a family, hot-and-cold running mistresses at his beck and call, he'll rarely be involved in scandal. The Libra man takes the cake—he has it and eats it, too.

**The Libra Woman.** Women of other signs, eat your hearts out. The Libra woman, in mythology, is Aphrodite, goddess of love. She is worshipped and adored, yet she herself seeks a man to idolize.

She is a woman more blessed than others usually, with a great fig-ure and a beauty that goes beyond mere prettiness. Nothing is wrong with the typical Libra woman's physique—a dimpled loveliness with a keen touch of class. Her walk is sensually tantalizing, but does not detract from her image as a regal and ladylike woman of culture.

A Libra woman has a veneer of worldly wiseness that is the end product of much calculated study. She learns about life from books; she's learned about it from her friends; she's learned some things from music and art and philosophy. The rest she's learned from men.

She'll be facing constant decisions: to love this one or that one—or both? This is a recurring dilemma for Ms. Libra. While the Libra man may be the reverse sort of predator, in that he doesn't have to run very fast or far to get what he wants, the Libra woman is the quarry who doesn't feel up to a lot of running and dodging. Why fight them when you can join them? This is her motto.

The bad news, men, is that the same man who can afford a Rolls Royce may not buy it because he doesn't feel worthy of such a status vehicle. Your Libra woman may very well lean toward elevated social circles. At any rate, she will elude class, and in many cases a man who is desirous of meeting such a woman might be able to do so only at her invitation—after you've been on the waiting list.

Her preferences in men run from the virile, masculine types to the creative and executive types who are going places and doing things worthwhile and worth publicizing.

Whereas women of some signs invite you to tell the truth about how you feel about them (even to the point of accepting criticism), the Libra woman is a far different animal. With her, you may have to lie, and if you do, do it like a gentleman.

Like their astrological brothers, they like the social graces. A well-appointed table in an elegant restaurant, complete with flowers and champagne specially ordered, would be a perfect way to start the evening with your Libra date. Blend small talk with flirtation, and don't spare the compliments. Let her know you share in her taste for opulence, good company in general, and partnership in particular.

Libra is no prude. She lives for love and romance, and is not so in the clouds that she thinks sex is dirty. Quite the contrary; to her it is a ritual of beauty, sometimes approaching an act of worship. She feels no need to blush, act coy or hesitant about any erotic desires, whether they are hers or her lover's.

One of the social aspirations of both Libra men and women is their quest for partnership; they generally marry and become parents and participating members of their families.

The Libra woman (as well as her Libra brother) just can't make it as a loner, and life without love and romance for her would be like a living death.

## Scorpio (October 24–November 22)

♏ A relationship with a Scorpio is usually an unforgettable experience, one way or another. This is one of the most complex, quietly devious, unnecessarily secretive, magnetic, persistent, dynamic, intense, and smolderingly sensual of all signs.

Scorpio makes the most loyal of friends—provided you are considered worthy of their friendship, of course. On the other side of it, they can be the most implacable and dangerous enemies.

It's not strange that everyone—whether Scorpio or not—reads to find out what various writers on astrology have to say about this hardest-to-figure sign. Some of the qualities ascribed to Scorpio by different astrologers include resourceful, emotionally extreme, masters of pressure and sarcasm, intense, difficult to understand, deadly serious, reticent, uncommunicative, vengeful. The list could go on and on, and in the end there would be only one solid conclusion to draw: they are complex.

Scorpio has a certain gift (which they share with those born under Capricorn), that is, an ability to do, unhesitatingly and sometimes with relish, what those born under most other signs do not have the fortitude to do. They can bear pain; the sight of blood—yours or theirs—will not faze them. They have little fear of death. The powers of others do not impress them.

Scorpio's enemy has said, "He was a great hater!" Scorpio's parent has said, "He was never a little boy, really."

Scorpio's friends have said, "He never let me down, though he sometimes cut me to the quick."

Scorpio's lovers have said, "He loved many, but he loved me best; he wanted their bodies. I gave him mine, and he took my soul!"

***The Scorpio Man.*** No question about it, the Scorpio man has a passionate, obsessive love of his own body. A true sexual predator, he is a determined hunter, whose radar is rarely switched off. His prey is womankind—the long, the short, the curvaceous, and the lean. Sometimes he has to search for them. But he knows where game is to be found, and he knows how it can be snared.

Scorpio men have a try-anything attitude toward love and sex, and they possess a certain hypnotic mannerism with either sex. It wouldn't, incidentally, be at all unusual to discover a Scorpio man in the nude at an inconvenient moment—no sudden dropping in to say "Hi" with this creature.

But don't be misled—the Scorpio man can be quite loyal to the woman who can fascinate him totally. All the better for her if she can outsmart him at his own sensual and psychological games— without letting him realize he's being outsmarted, of course. It's not easy to outwit him in this arena, though. One of his supreme pleasures is playing with others' minds. He'll psyche you out and have you cooing—to his sensual and psychological benefit—if he thinks you are game. But if he becomes bored by the paucity of your responses, don't expect loyalty from him.

Cat-and-mouse games are one of his specialties, and he carries a form of these into the bedroom. He'll feel, touch, fondle, and caress every inch of you before the final business begins. So be prepared to be indulged—and to indulge—in foreplay.

If you are prepared to meet the Scorpio man on his own grounds, and to accept his sometimes inscrutable personality, you'll be rewarded with his generosity, as well as with his cooperation. But don't start any arguments with him, or you'll be out the door, pronto—and once thwarted, the Scorpio doesn't stop at mere rejection; rubbing salt into wounds can be one of his numbers.

And the sting issued by the scorpion is not to be thought of lightly. It hurts!

No matter whether he seeks you out or, for those who like to flirt with danger, you seek him out, you'll find it easier to get into bed with a Scorpio than to get out, unless, of course, you're kicked out. Once the Scorpio man has found his ideal woman, he will be loyal within his own frame of reference. This means that he can be tempted and will meet that temptation promptly by pursuing it. He won't view this as disloyalty—after all, he's the one setting the standards and rules of conduct for loyalty.

**The Scorpio Woman.** The femme fatale, the unforgettable woman—this is the Scorpio woman. When she says she has no intention of going to bed with someone tempting, you can figure that she's at least thinking about doing so, anyway. She's fantasizing on the when and where parts to the question. Her eyes flash, her eyelids narrow, her body moves in its sensual way; yet, with the vibrations she emits, she seems an erotic puzzle. Does she or doesn't she?

Like the Taurus woman, many Scorpio women have darker complexions, with dark eyes. Their look is appraising, mysterious, and it seems to see right through you, while revealing little of its own source—the fires within.

Meet a Scorpio woman and most likely you will meet a woman who has loved without holding back, one who has known disappointment and felt pain. Some Scorpio women seem to possess a masochistic streak; their desire for a bit of roughness and some suffering adds spice to the satisfaction of their deepest sensual needs.

They are potentially dangerous women to fool with or spurn. Subject to quick anger and jealousy, they are capable of physical violence. These are the women who carry grudges, who have long memories, and who often possess streaks of vindictiveness.

The young Scorpio woman—in her teens or early twenties—will tend to take remarks and actions of others too personally; she'll overreact to slights, whether real or imagined, and her hyperactive Scorpion power may, as a consequence, do both her and her mate much emotional injury.

Like her Scorpio brother, she radiates a certain erotic charm and charisma, and her smile may be taken many ways. This is the smile with humor, knowledge, and a hint of an invitation to indulge in unknown and potentially delicious wickedness. Let the man who accepts the challenge of this smile be strong, virile, and indefatigable. What will follow is a feast of the senses and a crash course in sexual education.

It may seem to her lover that her body is flexible in the extreme and has more erogenous zones than is standard for the average female—at least for the woman who has no planets in her native astrological chart in the sign of Scorpio.

Far from conventional, she can enter a certain hell-bent mood— a mood that may take her to such indulgences as "group gropes," wearing out one virile man after another, or experiencing more climaxes than seems earthly possible. A logical footnote to all this— Ms. Scorpio usually discovers the pleasures of sex early in life.

Scorpio women prefer emotionally and sexually experienced men who can appreciate women that like to tantalize to the utmost point of desire. If they are to be happy in any sort of permanent relationship, their mates must be vigorous and good providers. Ideally, the mate of the Scorpio woman should have a good self-image and be aggressive, with leadership qualities. Puritan men, incidentally, need not apply.

## Sagittarius (November 23–December 21)

♐ Adventurous Sagittarius is the problem child of the zodiac when it comes to matching him or her with others. Playmates are no problem, but a permanent partner may become one. They have a desire to be on the prowl, ever hunting new game.

Like Leos who prefer a little pleasure before or during business activity, the Sagittarian would break a date with the most desirable person in the world if it interfered with a hunting expedition or a business hurdle.

They are apt to call you long distance from another time zone and want to meet you at the airport at some ungodly hour of the night. They can feel at home anywhere they can change their clothes and freshen up a bit.

They, like Taureans, are first-cabin-complex people, generally, and have a gift for getting along with people who have lots of money to invest.

Notwithstanding their reputation as travelers and wanderers, many like to have a homebase, with a homebody of the opposite sex ever ready to prepare the fatted calf and start pouring drinks upon their return.

***The Sagittarius Man.*** When you try to total up the characteristics of the Sagittarian man, you may need an adding machine. Begin with tall, lucky, self-confident, laughing, impulsive, restless, and well traveled. Throw in born hunter, promoter, trader, philosopher, big spender, frequent winner, optimist, and a believer in truth who is capable of exaggerating and making extravagant promises.

He is the unintentional master of insult. It is somehow tied to his desire to be out front—truthful to a fault.

Sagittarian men place a high value on their freedom as well as on their products or services. They somehow consider the shade of the grass where they are now to be a little lackluster. Somewhere else it has a richer chlorophyll content, and somewhere, where this grass is so much more verdant, are lasses with their cheeks rosier, their bosoms bouncier, their psyches more willing and able. Somewhere are women more naive, yet less likely to want to slip the chains of commitment and responsibility on the reluctant Sagittarian wrists.

Their lives are evidence of the self-realizing prophecy: whatever they believe in happens, whatever they fear happens. If they fear marriage, they are drawn to it. They are often out of town, always noting the grasses and the lasses. The Sagittarian men have a talent for expanding their financial base, although they don't always know when to pull in their horns and consolidate.

Many Sagittarians do not see women as people so much as like trophies, creatures not quite tame who should be captured, enjoyed, and released back into their wild state when it is time for the big adventurer to head for other hunting grounds. They will keep track of their past lovers, however, and when they jet back into the same hunting preserve again, they feel they should feed you, feel you, and pour you quantities of the finest-quality liquors.

Weighted down with their expensive gifts picked up in remote corners of the world, you most likely will have a swinging day (at minimum, an hour or so between planes or conferences with money men). If they can't contact you or are indisposed, no big deal. A stewardess or chance acquaintance will do equally well.

They equate sexual enjoyment with celebration, and when there is no one with whom to share their frequent feelings of elation, they can always return to a more youthful habit: celebrating themselves.

Because they like to hold out for a better deal, Sagittarians often marry later in life, but because they are spontaneous and apt to take risks, some of them marry often and earlier in life.

The Sagittarian man's habits of freedom and independence may make him pretty hard to live with. No woman can stand to hear the truth about herself all the time, and living with someone with a short fuse, prone to tantrums, and continual wheeling and dealing can require a great deal of patience and tolerance. In times of crisis, they can be very, very trying. In good times, however, they are good sports, generous, and full of warmth and optimism. They entertain lavishly, dress extravagantly, and live with opulence and flair.

When too many things go wrong in a row, they can make a 180-degree turn, becoming extremely negative, petty, and overly emotional. Some head for the great outdoors again to renew themselves; some begin the chase again, feeling that the bodies of womankind contain some magical renewing wonder drug that turns back the clock, renews the worn, and cheers the grumpy!

Maybe they are the wisest sign, after all. What gentleman, what manner of man would not drink to those sentiments? Well, perhaps the more mature would not.

*The Sagittarius Woman.* Although the Sagittarian woman is not so hard to housebreak as her astrological brother, she does value her independence, sometimes to the point of obsession. She will not tolerate a man who wants her to account for every moment of her time or every dollar of her money.

Because of her capacity for big spending, she has been known to drive economy-minded men to distraction and divorce. Because of her need to live in the style she feels gives her freedom, she tends to remarry periodically for economic reasons.

Sagittarian women require a large home, spacious and not too close to the road. They relate to animals, in some cases better than to people. Men who do not enjoy the company of pets will probably enjoy the company of Sagittarian women even less, because they tend to have more than enough of their favored, four-footed friends in the way.

The woman of this sign who requires an annual trip out of the country is not unusual, and if the male member of the partnership can't get time off to go along, she'll go by herself or with a friend, or with one of her children in tow. Be careful with this type of Sagittarian, for she frequently starts feeling pretty sexy as soon as she feels the pressure of family responsibilities recede into the distance.

Her natural enthusiasm and her spontaneity in social intercourse often get out of hand. Before she knows what is happening, she is staring at the ceiling as her lover is peeling off her clothes and playing ride-a-cock-horse-to-Banbury-Cross. Sagittarian women, as well as men, often tend to remain single.

Sagittarius is an impulsive fire sign, more adaptable than Leo or Aries. In addition to a strong desire to be free spirits, Sagittarian women get angry or uncooperative if they are ordered about or restrictions are imposed upon them. Their strong sexual appetite, an expression of the joy of life, often comes into conflict with their inner desire to be straight-shooters and somewhat conventional.

As in the case of some Virgos, a few shots of *spiritus fermenti* tend to help them along in shedding their inhibitions. Not many Sagittarians, male or female, would even own up to having many inhibitions anyway.

Ms. Sagittarius really blows hot and cold. Her affairs tend to be of short duration because of her tendency to avoid long commitments. Yet once attached, she is such a positive thinker that if problems develop in the marriage, it is hard for her to go to a marriage counselor. "You may have problems," she'll say, but she would consider it negative thinking to consider the possibility that she has problems, too.

When marriage problems develop, the Sagittarian woman often makes personal, seemingly castrating remarks, which makes the problem worse, often leading to prompt parting, and, very likely, a substantial cash settlement.

Freedom almost automatically leads to another trip abroad. Once again, hunting season for fun and well-heeled males is open.

Her attitude toward life can be summed up by paraphrasing a popular old beer commercial: Live it up with gusto. You only live once and now is the hour. Go where the action is; find a target; go for the big game.

The Sagittarian woman who finds the right man, however, will follow him to the end of the Earth. She will hunt with him, fish with him, and alternately charm and shock his clients with her overly complete honesty.

A final word on the bedroom scene: Your lady Sagittarians are by no means sex fiends, but they really get into the spirit of the act and do not just lie there passively inert. They are high-spirited and highly athletic.

## Capricorn (December 22–January 20)

♑ Sometimes it's a little difficult to figure out Capricorns. What do they want of you? Are they using you? Are you simply a status symbol?

Ambitious, materialistic, dependable, responsible, a probable leader, duty-driven, and deadly serious—yet full of cunning wisdom. Don't misunderstand the Capricorn by any means. This is a sign with its moments of frivolity, and though people born under it seem to be workhorses, they do enjoy sex and they do look for love. Warmth and understanding are the two qualities they will look for in a mate. Short-term lovers will probably number few in their lives and often of a pay-for-play type.

In the area of permanent partners, they're looking for someone who won't embarrass them, won't become dull or tired, and will share their tasks and ambitions with them. In any relationship of a permanent nature with a Capricorn, you'll find that there will be money to spend—but Capricorn decides just what will be purchased and will sign the checks.

*The Capricorn Man.* Capricorn men get started early in life on the adult path of work and responsibility—earlier than others in their peer group. They seem to have learned quickly in life that the world is grim, life is earnest; and they may exhibit a fear of being brought to judgment for every idle thought.

Yet while they have the conscience of the severest Puritan, many have a lack of sexual morals. When their biological urges reach such a peak that it impairs their efficiency on the job, they are very apt to cast about the office for a likely and toothsome secretary or file clerk who wants to get ahead. Failing that, they may simply pay a call girl. More practical! Just pay and play, and you don't have to do anything for them later. Besides, it's more discreet, and image is important.

Then, of course, back to the task role.

For some Capricorn men, the problem is a little more complex, requiring even more secrecy and discretion. Some of them may prefer kinkier sex. Then there was the Capricorn man that claimed to have his own personal astrologer, who allegedly told him he had Greed rising and his Moon in the sign of Lust.

My personal feeling is that people should try to be nicer to Capricorns; Capricorns have had such a hard life, fraught with difficulties, defeats, losses, delays, and—for spice—roadblocks.

But they do have a lot going for them. They are hard workers. They are organized, shrewd, ambitious, dependable, and tend to dress expensively and neatly. They do have a sense of humor, running more to the grim or satiric.

Capricorn men are good providers, if a little tight-fisted. They are even given to buying presents for those who have done or could do them favors.

They can be cold, critical, suspicious, and sarcastic on the one hand, and warm, charming, friendly, and helpful on the other. They can be tender and they can be tough. They will never forget a favor and often feel obliged to return one to keep the balance sheet even.

Then again, the Capricorn man may display jealousy. He has a very long memory for slights and nonfavors, and those Capricorns not blessed with a forgiving nature (and there are many of them) are frequently tempted to avenge themselves long after the offender has forgotten the crime.

The planet Saturn rules Capricorns, and Saturn is Father Time. Capricorn men take their time. Their keywords are survival, use, and win. They bide their time. They wait. They have a way of winning in the end. Like fine wine, they improve with age. The frost in their nature melts and warmth glows as they mature.

This is the man who needs a woman who can contribute to his desire for greater social status, one who can be patient, enduring, and understanding, who can bear children he can be proud of, who can carry the weight and responsibility as hostess to friends and clients, and finally one who will make excuses for him for the many times he puts his job or business before the social and emotional needs of his family.

He needs a woman who will not wear out too early in life, because he'll need her when a subtle change of character sets in, at the point he decides he has put off fun and games long enough. He is a man who grows up in reverse—old as a child, with younger and younger feelings and actions as he mellows with age. He lives to a ripe old age provided he has not worked himself to death during middle age. Fortunately, he is still in shape to enjoy the fruits of his arduous years and incredible labors.

Whatever has been said about him negatively or positively, women will say, "When he took time out to do it, he was a great lover!"

***The Capricorn Woman.*** Women born to the sign of Capricorn are prone at certain points in their lives to a passive acceptance of the kinkier sides of sexual pleasure. At these times, they may be driven by an almost animal form of lust, which appears to lack depth, soul, and appreciation for their partners.

The true Capricorn woman will give you a come-up-and-see-me-sometime look, and then challenge you to warm her up. However, this is at least partly due to her fear of rejection—in place even before she finds hints of acceptance. In private, she may think about the glorious release of wholehearted indulgence in the loving sex act. In the presence of an obviously virile man, however, she tends to hang back.

Capricorn women seem reluctant, aristocratic, and worldly, but hesitant about surrender. She thinks, "What would be the outcome, status-wise?" "What is the likelihood of unwanted pregnancy; should I lower my defenses? What advantage could be gained by letting go and losing?" Inside this ice cube shaped like a most desirable woman is a burning flame that doesn't give a damn about any of these questions.

But the question "Will I be hurt?" persists at a level close to the exterior.

The really hot-blooded man must turn up the fire in her stove patiently, with reassurances, and gradually increased hand motion.

As in the case with the reluctant and inhibited Virgos, some fine, vintage potable will help cut through layers of defense and apparel. No presents, no flowers, and no vodka—no Zsa Zsa or Ivana!

Ms. Capricorn is usually very proud of her body, and you cannot go wrong by exclaiming with wonder at just how statuesque she is without all those expensive clothes hiding all that sculptural perfection. Run your hands over her body (after she's warmed to you, of course), but keep them away from her hairdo unless she is really on fire with passion.

Now here is the bad news: If you are a "whiz-bang-thank-you-ma'am!" type with a short, rapid peak time, you are going to be embarrassed, and she is going to be very disappointed and extremely annoyed with you. It usually takes her a lot longer to get into the spirit of the thing, and even once she does she is in no hurry to climax. She has probably delayed even agreeing to such liberties with other equally desirable males, and she does not think of the act as any kind of celebration.

To her, sex is a reward for virtue, long overdue. Just as she would be upset being cheated in a business deal, she would never forgive you cheating her with any premature ejaculation on your part. Think of the female attitude of the wife in *Who's Afraid of Virginia Woolf*: "Goof it and you're a houseboy!" she says. Take your time and you can make encore performances.

Don't take Capricorn women at face value. They may seem reserved and rather patrician, but under this brittle armadillo-like facade are hot, volcanic sexual forces ready to erupt and engulf their lovers in unbelievable waves of ferocious sexuality. Because many men are somewhat cowed by their beauty and apparent unapproachability, these women often endure long periods of sensual starvation. They have been disappointed often by the poor timing of their lovers. They need a man with a strong back who will not take "No" for an answer. They respect a man who knows what he wants and insists on getting it.

She is the woman who despises a man for considering her just another number in his address book, so don't call on her only when easier game is indisposed or otherwise occupied. Great loyalty is expected and great loyalty is offered by her; she relates to sincerity and dedication. She is not as grim as she appears to be.

In a husband she expects a worker and a good provider. As a wife she will help you meet the right people, and as the mother of your children she will insist that the little ones be obedient, respectful, and steered into practical paths educationally and vocationally. She has a certain no-nonsense approach to child rearing which the rebellious child will resent, but the more serious and more ambitious child will revere her, even when she resorts to punishment.

All Capricorns, male or female, warm up and improve with the experiences of partnership, good and bad. When the weaker signs desert you in times of trouble, the Capricorns will hang in there and struggle and fight against the forces of adversity.

Saturn, which rules the Capricorns, is the most dependable of all planets. It penalizes you when you goof and rewards you when you uncomplainingly pay your dues.

Show me a Capricorn and I'll show you someone who has had a difficult childhood and early adulthood, but who looks pretty darn good when the later years approach. These years are the most rewarding and satisfying to Capricorns, who have obsessively paid their dues as they go along.

# Aquarius (January 21–February 19)

If Librans are the "beautiful people," then Aquarians are the "fantastic, wild, and infuriating people." They have the worst track record for multiple marriage (serially, of course, except in cultures where monogamy is not the rule).

These are the sociable people, witty, well informed, well read, concerned about world problems—but not too concerned about your personal problems. They are original, independent, gifted, and often considerate.

The problem is that though they are romantic, charming, and delightful to be around, they are often utterly impossible. They were probably the inventors of the little black book. On another level, they are capable of making a 180-degree turn, from the bleeding-heart liberal to the pragmatic reactionary. Although they are often reformist or revolutionary at certain periods of their lives, and speak along the most idealistic lines, they may vote conservative all the way on election day.

The lover of an Aquarian may grow exasperated over the Aquarian's sense of obligation to friends. Now, this can be an an admirable trait—but not when it's exercised at the expense of the lover. People of this sign often attend to the problems of a friend before those of a lover or spouse.

However, in the words of a longtime spouse of an Aquarian: "One thing you can say about them—they'll never bore you."

*The Aquarius Man.* Among the most interesting and irritating men are the Aquarians. What may begin as a buddy-type relationship with an Aquarian could easily end as a partnership between the sheets. The seemingly unphysical friend is really a romantic with strong sensual needs.

He will have more than one lover, most likely, but if he's on the outs with everyone in his little harem, he will get morose and depressed. He needs his list of women's phone numbers to make him feel secure.

He may be obsessed with his wardrobe; he dresses to please himself, all the time thinking himself a fashion plate. An example of this is the famous 1930s Aquarian actor Adolph Menjou. For many years, he designed his own clothes and was on the list of the best dressed in Hollywood. However, he designed his clothes for himself, and continued designing them with himself—not fashion trends—in mind, until one day he took his place among the worst dressed. He hadn't changed his style—but the rest of the world had. Still Adolph didn't really mind.

Another Aquarian hang-up that manifests itself among the men of this sign is temperature. They are the ones who are constantly fiddling with the thermostat, setting it up or down. It's their circulation, most likely. They're either too hot or too cold. They tend to own more sweaters than people of other signs. Aquarian Presidents Lincoln and Roosevelt, if you remember, wore shawls.

Most astrology books say that Aquarian men make the kindest and most considerate husbands. This may be, but one Aquarian man is likely to make a kind and considerate husband to more than one wife. Statistically, Aquarian men enter short-lived marriages, only to marry again.

Aquarian men are most successful in corporate employment, especially if the company is run by loose reins. If the method of operation on the job includes chaos, or sudden interruptions or policy changes, the Aquarian man may be among the few who can handle things. He can respond to the unexpected with flair and originality, and he gets along with both subordinates and superiors, with unreasonable people and with uptight people, and he relaxes everyone with his resourcefulness at handling emergencies.

Another secret: These men are the ones who, though not out after applause or status, are the most represented sign in the sports, actor, and political halls of fame.

A certain type of woman may feel attracted to the maverick Aquarian man. She may be the woman who has problems and is seeking someone to solve them; or she may be a woman of intellect who is seeking a friend with whom to enjoy interesting conversations. However, remember that a friendship with an Aquarian may end in romance.

Most of these men have read all the sex manuals and know more on the subject than the authors. They may even have written some of these books, but their real interest is in the practice, not the preaching. Eccentric and exciting, sensual and intelligent, the Aquarian man will offer a good relationship—though the odds aren't all that great for its being eternal. "I know," as the typical know-it-all Aquarian man might say.

***The Aquarius Woman.*** The sexually liberated Aquarian woman: one side of her nature is cool, intellectual, independent, and quixotic, while the other side is romantic, friendly, understanding, and charitable—but sometimes a little strange.

The me-woman, you-man, we-go-to-bed attitude is hidden inside somewhere, and she's receptive to a reciprocal manifestation. Because Aquarians have a strong sense of past incarnations, and can project that sense to others, you might feel that you've known her somewhere before. Chances are you have—in a past life.

With her romantic, idealized picture of true love, fact and fiction tend to blend and blur into dreamy sensuality, the prelude to which often involves extended talk and discussion of literature or the arts.

If you are looking for wit and intelligence in a woman who is, in all honesty, a little weak on home economics and housekeeping, you will get the pleasant surprise of your life with Ms. Aquarius.

Expressing herself in the sensual encounter is her friendliest form of communication, and a way of exerting her independence of conventions.

She climaxes easily and early, relishing light caresses on her body before, and afterwards, when she goes into a state of languor.

Some of the Aquarian women like to slowly awaken their lovers in the small hours of the morning with light, tender, teasing movements of their fingers, lips, or tongues.

A woman poet wrote, "Let it arise and greet our dawn with ecstasy!" True Aquarian sentiments.

The Aquarian woman makes an exciting wife. She is not a nagger. She does not try to run her husband's business. She is neither suspicious nor jealous of him and is herself loyal.

She is refined and given to culinary experimentation. She often gives her children the feeling that they are super-special, and that they are here in this age as a part of some great cosmic design.

She is the woman who brings to marriage a refreshing sexual impishness—and friendship, that one ingredient missing in so many man-woman teams. If you told her this, however, she'd probably say, "I know"—just like her know-it-all astrological brother.

## Pisces (February 20–March 20)

♓ Among the less complimentary terms used to describe Pisceans are gullible, over-indulgent in drink and drugs, and out of touch with reality. Perhaps Pisceans are the only natives of the zodiac who see the world for what it really is. They quickly note that everyone seems to be marching together compulsively to the same drummer, yet the Piscean is always setting his or her foot down on another beat. Could it be that it is the right one?

One less spiritual and less in tune with universal rhythms might come to the conclusion that the mass perception is right and the individual perception wrong. But the Piscean has belief in self, if allowed to do so.

Soulful Pisces people do get emotionally, sympathetically, and empathetically involved in any unkind act. These are the people on the side of the underdog.

Pisceans have been called the terribly meek; they have, however, a gift of winning by losing. While the more aggressive signs attack, they retreat to victory.

These are often psychic people, believers in, and sometimes gifted with, ESP. They are well read, tend to be liberal, and though they may say that efficiency is their God, that deity may smile at the pronouncement. Practicality is something they need help with. They need an organizer for a mate, someone to get the mundane things in order and see that all the bills get paid and the checkbook stays uptodate.

Pisceans can inspire you or drag you down. They tend to give their love to the undeserving. They should get a better deal, but they tend to zero in on the wrong people and the wrong ideas.

**The Pisces Man.** Show me a man, slow of pace, a little round of shoulder, overweight, carrying a bottle of wine, a candle, and roses—a man with a sad, sensitive look on his face, a wishful, bed-roomy glint in his eyes, and I'll show you a Piscean with a sneaky approach to women.

"Women don't understand me," he says. "They take advantage of me," he complains, as he puts his clothes on again.

"He looked so unneeded, unwanted, and unloved, so vulnerable, that my heart reached out to him."

"In the most natural way, his arms reached for me, for comfort, I suppose...."

"As the sad words fell from his lips, I found my clothing falling from my body, as he reached for the kind of comfort few mothers can give!"

Piscean men may take this sort of approach: They may request a favor, often assuming negatively that it will not be granted. If you waver in deciding to help, they start their calculated retreat, with their tragedy mask on, littering words of humility, unworthiness, and self-abnegation, until you find yourself pulling their chestnuts out of the fire for them.

But let's look at the other side of the coin. Suppose you need some help and sympathy. Go to the Piscean man, reciting first your difficulties and your defeats.

Drink a little of his wine, and listen in turn to the story of his life. It is so depressing compared to your petty problems that you'll soon be feeling guilty for bothering him. But he may help you after he has gulped a few more goblets and shed a tear or two.

Regrettably for the peace of your conscience, such a Piscean man normally refuses to accept payment of any material nature for the kind of help that calls for it. Your gift must be tendered later. Don't send money. He has a rather unhealthy feeling about that commodity, feeling that it represents a payment against the helpless. His aptitude implies that he feels the paper pulp the dollar is made from was taken from the woodpile that was supposed to warm the poor blood of widows and orphans, from whose tears the dollar's ink was mixed.

Pisces men have an interest in sex that is difficult to put into words, although many words come to mind which approximate it: promiscuous, spiritual, poignant, poetic, loving, self-sacrificing, romantic, sentimental, and mystical.

He is the most introverted of the signs, probably the most vacillating, certainly the kindest, the organist par excellence of the emotions. He sees beyond the superficial beauty of clothing, cosmetics, and professionally set coiffures. If there is inner beauty, sensitivity, and a soul under the powder, perfume, and potions, his radar will tell him so.

He is most likely to become promiscuous after a rebuff or an emotional defeat—or under the influence. Bottle in hand and feeling out of hand, his radar guides him to a soft, warm, curved belly landing, and no matter how worthy the pickup or unworthy the lady of the evening may be, she will share the ritual drinks and the mutual autobiographical remarks, the inner aspirations and kisses, sometimes mingled with sentimental tears—in other words, the foreplay of his fantasies.

Although what follows may be action or fun for her, for him it was an act of love, no matter how transient the moments—and sweet revenge on the woman who upset him in the first place.

The habits of the Piscean man make him or maul him. He readily accepts great responsibilities, but he needs a practical helpmate to encourage and reorganize him, write the checks for utilities and other obligations, and steer him away from the liquor supply and the refrigerator when he is feeling depressed.

Being a dreamer rather than an action person, he often wonders why a person such as he, with such exalted ideas, is obliged to suffer in the corporate box while smaller-souled men are better compensated with prettier wives, more personal satisfaction, and more of the world's tinsel goods and ready cash.

Thrice blessed is the Piscean who does the kind of work he likes, who has tenure and retirement insurance. He's Mr. Nice all right, but the other side of his nature has earned him names worse than Mr. Naughty.

**The Pisces Woman.** Here is the woman who can play the emotional organ, from the sweetest music in the world to the most jangling, nerve-blowing discords. Her womanliness amplifies and exaggerates the duality of the Piscean nature.

She is an angel—a fallen angel.

She is a mistress of illusion, with power to draw you into the rose-colored realm of unreality. Some of the women of this sign have a glorious, fragile, but evanescent beauty in their early years. Many, while growing up, take ballet classes, dreaming of being whirled about by mad, passionate male dancers from theater to theater, world capital to world capital, receiving admiration, applause, champagne, and romance.

Ballet, however, requires great discipline and dedication, perspiration and effort. These words are nearly considered to be obscenities in the Piscean lexicon, along with that dirty four-letter word "work."

Acting, art, music, writing, poetry—these pursuits seem more like choices than obligations. While Capricorns get almost idealistic feelings when they contemplate the work ethic, Pisceans actually feel that it might degrade them in some way.

No matter what a bright start they make, the moment always comes when the Piscean woman starts feeling that she is and always has been some sort of victim, a prisoner in what, for others, is a freer world.

Is it possible that she is more gullible than the other signs? Could be. Does her track record include much wasted affection on the undeserving? Could be.

Have men asked her to do things, to submit to actions no Leo or Libra would put up with? Pour her a glass of wine and hear the story of her life. What this idealist has suffered in debasement, disgrace, and social ostracism, disappointments in familial, illicit, and even marital love would fill a five-foot shelf of books on romantic misadventures. Only the Marquis de Sade, you may begin thinking, could have thought up half of it.

Her sexual attitudes and habits can often be traced to what she went through as a child. Even if it was a comparatively happy childhood, she may not have realized it at the time. The villain in many of her childhood-originated problems was the father, who in some cases she idealized, but more often fed her feelings of being misunderstood, insecure, and unhappy. He may not have taken her seriously enough to find out who she really was as a person.

In other cases, her father may have imposed his iron will on her in an effort to make her into a different type of person because of some fear she would turn out the way she probably ends up turning out anyway. Shades of the Barretts of Wimpole Street!

That beautiful, tragic, and romantic (and surprisingly tough) poetess, Elizabeth Barrett Browning, was a Piscean's Pisces.

They seem weak, these Piscean women, but they can absorb quite a lot of punishment, and still be able to kiss their own blood off the hands of their tormentors. Some unsympathetic modern astrologers have dubbed them the poor little ol' me Pisceans, not realizing that these seemingly masochistic persons take pain and mistreatment only to wear out their sadistic oppressors.

They are as easily talked into doing the right thing as the inappropriate. The problem is that they distrust good advice and usually seek other opinions. The opinion they are most likely to take seriously is the one diametrically opposed to the most practical.

If they find themselves the prisoner of love or disdain, it takes them too many years to discover that they themselves have been carrying the key to their own prison, the key that could set them free.

If the Piscean woman could find a man (like Elizabeth's Robert Browning) who could take command over her life, understand her deepest emotional needs, forgive her when she was impossible, spoil her whether she deserved it or not, and love her with possessive, considerate violence, it would be her fantasy come true. Robert Browning was some special kind of Taurus with Sagittarius rising. He practically had to kidnap her to get her out of the prison she was in. He led her from physical and psychological invalidism to strength, wifehood, and motherhood. She needed his help to build the solid foundation under her poetic imaginings.

Ms. Pisces needs a strong, patient man who will put up with her temperamental outbursts and bar the exit when she seeks to escape into the pill bottle, the liquor decanter, or the wrong bed.

Sometimes he must padlock the door to the kitchen. She needs loving a lot more than she needs another helping of empty calories.

Pisceans are born under the twelfth sign, the last sign of the zodiac. This may mean that if they live on the positive side of their sign, perhaps all life's lessons can be happy and complete.

So, dear Pisceans, enjoy your ability to feel sympathy, your ability to create illusion, your awareness of the unseen, your warmth, your great strength in the face of adversity, all with your gentleness.

# $\mathcal{C}$OMPATIBILITY

## *chapter three*

*My idea of an agreeable person ...
is a person who agrees with me.*
—Benjamin Disraeli, *Lothair*

$\mathcal{N}$ow that the basic groundwork has been established, let's look over the chances the different signs have for getting on with each other in the realm of love. Some combinations are literally "made in Heaven," while others can spark the very fires of the Inferno. Then there's the area in between, where sweet and bitter meet to compose a romantic symphony of many different-sounding movements.

# $\mathcal{S}ign$ Combinations

This section moves from all the Aries pairs, to all the Taurus, Gemini, and so on, but Aries–Taurus will not be covered under Taurus as it was already covered under Aries. Likewise Gemini starts with Cancer, as Aries–Gemini and Taurus–Gemini were already covered. To find your combination quickly, first learn the order of the signs: Aries, Taurus, Gemini, Cancer, Leo, Virgo, Scorpio, Sagittarius, Capricorn, Aquarius, and Pisces. If your sign falls *after* the sign of your partner, then you must look under your partner's sign to find your combination. If your signs are the same, see pages 73-76 for the potential of your same sign relationship.

## Aries and Taurus

There would be some good romps in the beginning here, but tears and shouting may well follow. Taurus is a homebody and possessive, and Aries is a gadabout whose flirtations may ultimately unnerve Taureans' sense of the sacred hearthside.

## Aries and Gemini

So long as Gemini's jabberwockies don't get out of hand, this can be one of the best combinations. Warmth and love can grow here and be nourished by the stimulating natures of both people. Neither of these signs can tolerate boredom, so a match between them is sure to be without it. Exciting possibilities abound.

## Aries and Cancer

My feelings about this pairing run from mixed to negative, especially in terms of the long haul. Aries keeps a short fuse and irregular hours. How is the conservative and security-minded Cancer going to find ultimate reassurance here? Aries would have to stretch to be patient, and Cancer stretch to offer praise.

## Aries and Leo

Here's a red-hot combination, spiced with possible competition and power struggles in the beginning. If the impulsive Aries dares to rush into the lion's lair, the irresistible and delightful dagger he or she finds there could lead to the enjoyably dramatic side of love and romance. Of course, Leo will have to watch it, as Aries can take only so much Leonine braggadocio.

## Aries and Virgo

In the beginning it may seem like true love at last, and both would walk over hot coals for each other. However, their ultimate goals in life are not on the same track, and their differences in timing might throw the compatibility machinery into a state of stultifying strain. In the end, the relationship would become typified by impatience and disgruntlement, unless it mutates into a master-slave team.

## Aries and Libra

The old astrologers give this pair a top rating for success. I would add a caveat: flirtatious Libra could very well injure the ego of some Ariens whose "me first" attitude clashes with the "we first" of Libra. But when the first date stretches into months and years, this is the combination of Beauty and the Beast: Aries goes after, and Libra attracts. Aries will simply have to keep a rein on any feelings of jealousy about the others Libra attracts.

## Aries and Scorpio

Although they tend to have an almost frightening initial fascination for each other, pitched battles and emotional excesses are sure to follow. Aries likes to feel like a free agent, and Scorpio must control both body and soul of his or her lover. Compatible? I'd vote no.

## Aries and Sagittarius

The traits these two signs share could make a good basis for a long-term relationship. They're extremely compatible sexually; both are spontaneous and ambitious, and neither are strangers to hard work or long hours. Both like to eat out and love in. I give this a high rating for success, as long as Sagittarius resists the impulse to prick Aries' ego.

## Aries and Capricorn

Definitely not for the long haul. With Aries, "now" is too late; with Capricorn, a decade is too soon. The responsive and spontaneous needs of Aries probably can't be filled by Capricorn who, though sometimes lustful, is seldom truly romantic enough. Aries would feel too cramped and Capricorn too stretched.

## Aries and Aquarius

I'd call this match something between fantastic and incredible, so long as the compliments from both sides keep coming. If Aries is a sexual bonfire, Aquarius is the gasoline to make it spread. In the long haul, passion may blow hot and cold, but this is one of those finer long-term romances.

## Aries and Pisces

Sexually, the teaming here is quite interesting, since each knows how to satisfy the other's needs. But if the relationship lasts a long time—which it very well may—it will seem to lack a certain something, and that something will probably be joy.

## Taurus and Gemini

Here is a maybe for the short term. The main problem is that they have target trouble: Taurus shoots one at a time, while Gemini takes the scattershot approach, machine-gunning in too many directions for Taurus' taste. Then there's the possibility that Taurus may get shortchanged sexually. Further, their senses of timing are ill-matched—Taurus takes time and Gemini uses it (to change his or her mind too often).

## Taurus and Cancer

Another of those most favored unions. Both signs bespeak sensuality, and both need a certain amount of stability. Both are homebodies, both keep well-stocked kitchens, and both enjoy the hearthside with the family. Taurus and Cancer can offer each other the emotional security both crave, and their sex lives will only improve with the length of the relationship.

## Taurus and Leo

These are not really compatible signs, but put them together, and sparks will fly. On the good side, Taurus' first-cabin complex fits right in with Leo's dramatic flair for living life in style and with a bit of ostentation. On the other side, Leo is impulsive and spontaneous, veritable anti-matter for Taurus' contemplative, evaluative nature; besides, Leo's exhibitionist antics might anger or embarrass the more staid Taurus, leading to unsheathed claws and bared horns.

## Taurus and Virgo

Virgo is willing to cooperate and be considerate; Taurus would offer the rewards of being a good provider and a good partner. There would be areas of disagreement, however. On diet and drink, Virgo is happier with less—a little salad and a little juice—whereas Taurus is liable to want to feast often. Sex would be another problem area, with Virgo, again, wanting less than Taurus.

## Taurus and Libra

These two look pretty good in the beginning; they share a Venus rulership. But a permanent relationship would bring trials to both. Possessive Taurus is not going to care for Libra's social flirtations, and eventually that Taurean patience with the Libran social groupi-ness may turn into Taurean rage and temperamental outbursts. And Libra—perhaps before that point—may lose patience and feel hemmed in by Taurus' possessiveness.

## Taurus and Scorpio

The old astrologers say go to this combination. Here we have sensu-ality-plus, excitement-plus, and delicious dangers. Some of the dan-gers may not be so delicious in the long run. Scorpio is short on patience, where Taurus is long; Taurus' possessiveness and Scorpio's jealousy may, for some, work positively and keep the two together, but it could go in reverse and wreak havoc. Taurus needs a little more material comfort than Scorpio, but the earthy Taurean, who easily attracts attentions and gifts, can easily attract these from the attentively intense Scorpio.

## Taurus and Sagittarius

Although both signs are money- and sex-oriented, this is not the best of matches; the issue at stake is freedom vs. the hearthside shackle. Taurus' possessiveness can be transmuted to jealousy by the overtaxing nature of Sagittarius' appetite for the constantly new and different. Sagittarius is a flexible sign, however, and may be able to flex enough to avoid Taurus' vindictiveness, which appears if Sagit-tarius shows signs of infidelity.

## Taurus and Capricorn

An excellent match for those in their later years, although there have been successful ones of this color which started out early in life. Capricorn's sexual appetite may not be sufficient for sensual Taurus until maturity in the later years. Nonetheless, pleasure-loving Taurus and stable Capricorn represent a good balance. They both believe in taking their time, understand practical and material values, and pre-fer order and the very best (though perhaps for different reasons).

## Taurus and Aquarius

Idealistic Aquarius can be just as rigid and hard-headed as Taurus is stubborn and set. Although this is an unbelievably sensual combination, it is temperamentally problematic in the long run. For a short-lived sexual partnership, this is the match to look for. But do not, under any circumstances, become the most gruesome of twosomes by marrying. Sparks may get frozen in mutually stubborn ice blocks.

## Taurus and Pisces

If what Pisces needs is stability in order to free the inner spirit, and if what Taurus needs is someone who needs him or her, this can be among the best combinations. Sensually the relationship will thrive, since each is capable of fulfilling the other's desires. Pisces, too, will be free of earthly decisions, and Taurus will be free of wondering where his or her lover is.

## Gemini and Cancer

This can be a good relationship if it's allowed to end when it should—no long-lasting bells here. Cancers like to be touched while Geminis like to make mental riddles. Often, when Gemini would want to tell a brilliantly funny story, Cancer will be wanting more reassurance and deep feelings than a Gemini could counterfeit, certainly on a permanent basis.

## Gemini and Leo

There are more nays than ayes for this combo, at least in terms of long-lasting affairs. Leos are looking for followers, not devil's advocates, which Gemini, with its mental gymnastics, may become every now and again (even though it's just to keep in tune, intellectually). Besides, both love to talk, and while Gemini is elaborating on an idea, Leo is elaborating on how an idea relates to him or her and just waiting to steal the entire conversation and steer it ego-ward. With evenings spent this way, they may never see the bedroom.

## Gemini and Virgo

This is another talkative team, but their conversations would be more compatible, and more easily drawn to a conclusion. Gemini is full of ideas, and Virgo is full of facts, as well as an impeccable logic to help out Gemini with his or her ideas. However, this match gets no gold star for two reasons: first, Virgo may make Gemini look pretty shallow; and, second, their sexual incompatibility is great enough that, should they get together, they may build a house and forget the bedroom (and not even notice the oversight).

## Gemini and Libra

This is a strong potential bet for a long-term affair, an easy, adaptable pairing which is strong both spiritually and mentally. The one bug in this match could be Gemini's short attention span on any one topic, or the astrological twins' capacity to talk too much. But overall, these are signs that speak the same language.

## Gemini and Scorpio

Scorpio might endure the flashy mental somersaults for a while, but they had better lead somewhere, and the course had better not be complained about later. Gemini's fickle, flirtatious, freedom-loving, and argumentative style could be quite a trial to the jealous, control-oriented Scorpio; and once the battles begin, Gemini stands the risk of coming out too lightweight for the powerful, manipulative Scorpio. This pairing is not recommended, unless thorough astrological charts are cast for each person.

## Gemini and Sagittarius

Here is another of those matches that could be excellent if caution is exercised. Gemini's dread of boredom would not surface here, and the Sagittarian's love of travel would not be hindered; in fact, he or she may find Gemini a good travel companion. They also have a lot in common intellectually and philosophically, but they each possess different brands of fickleness, which on the surface are similar and may lead them to figure out the other's infidelities quickly, accurately, and with deadly results to the relationship.

## Gemini and Capricorn

This is a perfect match if all you're looking for is everlasting boredom. These signs can, however, get on together, but the type of getting-on is of a breed useful in business relationships, not romantic relationships. A solid friendship could be intellectually rewarding for both, as long as the unsuccessful try at romance and sex—where they are incompatible—hasn't soured things.

## Gemini and Aquarius

Here's a happy match—the Aquarian's surprises and Gemini's desire to be surprised. The sparks will fly here and they'll be sparks of romance if the setting is right. Gemini, with the need for a sounding board for ideas, will find Aquarius willing and able to discuss, discourse, and debate. And whenever Gemini's negative side shows, Aquarius will become all the more positive.

## Gemini and Pisces

Although some good sexual flings may attract these signs together, it's no go for the long run, generally. Pisces has too much emotion and Gemini may try to use discussion and logic as a solution to Pisces' admitted feelings of vulnerability. After a while, Gemini may go flitting off as a reaction to the Piscean's demands for more understanding.

## Cancer and Leo

Presumably, Leo's loyalty and generosity, combined with Cancer's thrift and love of children and home, bode a happy life together for these signs. However, I'm not so sure about this twosome's appropriateness. Although Cancer will offer support for Leo's proud flair and humor, the latter, ultimately, may not be able to come through with the kind of total reassurance that Cancer needs. Because of Cancer's intense need for reassurance, Leo may begin to feel even his or her own attention slipping away from the desired state of self-centeredness.

## Cancer and Virgo

This is a potentially great relationship, and it would also be a learning experience, especially for Virgo. The Moonchild is easily offended, so Virgo would have to learn how to soft-pedal his (or her) criticism and self-improvement programs. Too much criticism would be difficult for the "love me" Cancerian. On the other hand, when the Moon is in the wrong sign for a day or two, Cancer can become a terrible nag, but this wouldn't necessarily get into Virgo's craw, for Virgo often has "don't touch me" moods.

## Cancer and Libra

A combination of the over-emotional, changeable Cancer with the coolly rational Libra is not often a long-term proposition. Although the two may interest each other physically at first, there's no forever in the lexicon of this couple's vocabulary. Dullness and discord would be the most probable outcome after many emotional tangles, beginning when Cancer demands support—right or wrong—and judicious but fair Libra is unable to give it all the time.

## Cancer and Scorpio

Here's a combination with emotion and intensely personal feelings. Scorpio can act like a shot of vitamins to Cancer, and would help dispel some of Cancer's gloomy, moody moments. Both have strong sexual needs, and both are ultimately security oriented. As long as Scorpio's coldness and sarcasm don't hit Cancer when the Moon is passing through the wrong sign, things could go extremely well.

## Cancer and Sagittarius

In the majority of cases, this would be a pairing to avoid. Cancer, I'm afraid, could come out with less, and would end as just another of the Sagittarian's many ports of call. Sagittarius might be driven to distraction with Cancer's need for permanent love. Unless both partners have their complete astrological charts cast—in order to look more thoroughly into the possibilities of real romance—it's best for both signs to give each other wide berth, and avoid the sadness and anger that is likely to come.

## Cancer and Capricorn

Though these are polar opposites, the pairing is a could-be. It would take effort for both to be truly comfortable in the long run, however. Ambition's spur would push Capricorn to put business before the emotional needs of Cancer. Physical attraction would be strong, and if it's strong enough to get this pair through the hard times, their later years would be terrific together.

## Cancer and Aquarius

This would be quite a sensual and intellectual adventure, especially at the beginning. Both are romantics, and each would be able to fulfill the other's emotional needs for a short-to-medium-term fling.

## Cancer and Pisces

Both of these signs thrive on and generate enough emotional sparks and sexual energy to last for a lifetime of bliss and bluster. But the relationship would probably teeter between sexual exaltation and emotional gloominess or storms. Still the psychic, erotic, and ultimately emotional attraction should be strong enough for both to take their chances in the long term.

## Leo and Virgo

This isn't exactly one of those matches made in Heaven, but it has some good possibilities. The practical adaptability of Virgo, and the eye to fine detail—as long as it's used to good visual results—would attract Leo. And success-oriented Leo—prideful and kingly—may look very good for the Virgo who's been holding out for a better deal. Virgo would be a real challenge to the eat-drink-and-be-merry Leo, but ultimately, Leo would command; and Virgo, after some well-timed and cleverly critical remarks, would obey.

## Leo and Libra

If Leo can moderate the tone of command, this could be a perfect match. A problem could arise if Leo doesn't cooperate with the vows of loyalty expected by Libra. The latter will do the utmost to cooperate, but will be ordered about by no one. Both are romantic and potentially creative. Both enjoy luxury, so it would be best if both make enough to afford the good life.

## Leo and Scorpio

This pairing would make great material for a novel with intensely sensual scenes, jealous storms, recriminations, power plays, and periodic respites only during the fierce, unarmed combat in bed. The price for this relationship may seem too high for either sign.

## Leo and Sagittarius

This would be good for a short-term, exciting affair, but would run into troubled waters if it's carried on too long. At first, Leo would be giving orders, and Sagittarius would be running around as usual, if only to exert his or her independence. Sagittarius may begin to prick Leo's large ego if Leo's orders start getting too strong, but they can always make up in bed, where the real action is for this pair.

## Leo and Capricorn

A good business relationship, perhaps, but in the love and romance department, things could get a little weird with this duo. The energies are way off, and each is seeking a different pleasure and a different life from the other. I vote no on this, unless thorough astrological charts for both are cast and inspected.

## Leo and Aquarius

The old astrologers recommend a match between these two signs, perhaps because—aside from the romantic attraction—they have something to teach each other about methods of attaining life's goals, and thereby happiness. If neither is willing to learn, a relationship here could develop into something like tank warfare. They can be a creative and impressive couple, and they definitely desire each other, but Leo will have to tone down the orders. Aquarians can be very agreeable as long as they don't feel imposed upon or pressured.

## Leo and Pisces

This could end up being the odd couple. Both share interests in the artistic aspects of life, but it would take quite a sense of humor on both parties' parts to make this one last. A stimulating, exciting affair, if handled without delicacy (especially by Leo), could easily end up like shooting fish in a barrel.

## Virgo and Libra

It's possible that a relationship between these two signs could work, but problems may arise from Virgo's touch-me-not moods, especially if those moods strike when Libra is in a socializing mood. Virgo would have to take care not to get on Libra's back. It's not ideal, but it's workable.

## Virgo and Scorpio

These two may start out as admiring friends, until Scorpio's consuming need for self-gratification steers things to a horizontal turn. It would be fun at first, but for the long run Virgo would have to be a bit of a mind reader before laying on any criticism to the hypersensitive Scorpio. Silent fuming and nagging would be the worst to expect in this relationship.

## Virgo and Sagittarius

Ordinarily a strong initial attraction would not be enough to keep this couple together. They'd tend to bog down eventually, because both signs are happiest when they're single (for different reasons). Criticism and vituperation of a very personal nature tend to occur when the two signs are at cross-purposes. Virgo isn't going to like it very much when Sagittarius takes to the road, and Sagittarius isn't going to appreciate Virgo's nitpicking about it.

## Virgo and Capricorn

A pairing between these two would make a lot of sense, and would go far to melt the Capricornian sexual ice by spreading the fire that lies hidden inside Capricorn's frosty shell. Mutual admiration and respect, enhanced by Virgo's adaptability, would do much to make this a happy permanent relationship. Highly recommended.

## Virgo and Aquarius

Here are two intellectual types—one orderly and the other disorganized. It might end up as a mutual admiration society, or it might end up frustrating both. The changing moods of each make it difficult, so when their moods are off the same track, they should get away from each other. On the other hand, Aquarius, the fashion pacesetter (or so he or she imagines) would benefit by Virgo's good taste in this area.

## Virgo and Pisces

Another of those matches considered by the older astrologers to be very good. I'd have to agree here, as long as Virgo stays tender and works to keep Pisces in touch with the real world. As a reward, Pisces will not have to force order and organization, as Virgo will take care of this. Moods may clash at times, but overall the romance will be good for both.

## Libra and Scorpio

Not good for the long run, though a strong physical and mental attraction may make for a sensational short-term affair. Scorpio, in the end, would demand not only Libra's body, but the soul as well. A marriage here would be similar to mating a Sherman tank with a pink VW Rabbit. Short-fused and jealous, Scorpio would eventually exhaust Libra's supply of fairness.

## Libra and Sagittarius

Sexual fires will spark here between spontaneous Sagittarius and sociable Libra. Libra, however, likes commitment, and under the velvety sensual glove that attracts Sagittarius in the first place is an iron fist that demands loyalty; and commitment, as we know, is not the Sagittarian's style—it would cramp and annoy, ultimately. A rewarding short-term romance, but the future for the long run would be pretty tough for both.

## Libra and Capricorn

This could be a pleasant courtship which—depending on Capricorn's individual effort—may end up as a permanent relationship. It's the ownership thing with Capricorn: Libra is a luxury item to own. If it's okay with Libra, and if Capricorn is willing to give patience and a wide berth on some of those more social occasions, it could be a decent enough marriage. Still, this is another of those Sun sign combos wherein both parties should get themselves to an astrologer for an in-depth survey of complete charts before they get themselves to the preacher.

## Libra and Aquarius

Both of these signs have qualities that make for rather good communications; these are the terms in which I would describe this relationship. They would be proud of each other and would make a handsome couple. They have ambition and similar tastes, class plus romance. A snag may arise when Libra gets miffed at the Aquarian's unpredictability.

## Libra and Pisces

Both of these signs have qualities each relates to, so this is a pretty good romantic risk—if you like romantic risks. Sexually, it's right on. Perhaps this is a pairing best left to the short term, unless both parties are gamblers in love.

## Scorpio and Sagittarius

Don't look for lighthearted love in this pairing. Ecstatic sex, yes—gentle tenderness, no. Scorpio's jealousy and inscrutable fury would be seen by Sagittarius as a foe to freedom and wings. The price in emotional imbalance and philosophical friction is too high for the pure Scorpio and pure Sagittarius to try building a longtime match out of what could be a dramatic, sexy fling.

## Scorpio and Capricorn

Though these two are potentially compatible—if Capricorn's steadfastness quells Scorpio's passionate suspicions of cheating—both should dig thoroughly into the nitty-gritty of their astrological charts before making permanent moves. If both let their worst faults show at the same time, disaster may strike a relationship between them. A cautious possibility here.

## Scorpio and Aquarius

Two natural antagonists would be at work here, so be careful! Not even the initial good sex would be enough to prevent Aquarius from taking a very hasty leave after Scorpio issues the first sting. I'd vote nay on this combo, unless more is known of each individual than the Sun signs.

## Scorpio and Pisces

Strengths and weaknesses would be accented in this pairing. It would be a great romance for a while—lots of bangs in the beginning, but it would get tough, especially for vulnerable Pisces, who needs lots of tender loving care and emotional support rather than the constant intensity of Scorpio. The Scorpio's intensity might be a bit too strong for Pisces.

## Sagittarius and Capricorn

Here's a not-recommended match. The devil-take-the-hind-most Sagittarius probably never would convince earth-anchored Capricorn that the best is yet to come. Duty ridden and having perfected the art of waiting, Capricorn may be appalled by the apparent unreality of the Sagittarian's confidence with risks and prodigality with money. This one's an issue of "can down live with up?" Can a train run without tracks?

## Sagittarius and Aquarius

My blessings on this happy couple. It's one of the best combinations: A joining of two independents, two free souls seeking and finding excitement, shared travel, welcomed changes in lifestyle, indulgent love and sex, and, to top it all off, good mental and philosophical vibes as well.

## Sagittarius and Pisces

Off the bat, I'd say, "No go." This would be an attraction of opposites, ending with Pisces feeling he or she had been razzle-dazzled
and left holding an empty bag emotionally. Pisces doesn't want to
be a trophy, and doesn't always have the wherewithal to stand up to
the hunter.

## Capricorn and Aquarius

Temporary arrangements frequently develop between these two,
and each has considerable admiration for and a willingness to cooperate with the other. Temperamental incompatibilities would not
surface until later, so long-term arrangements shouldn't be antici-
pated too strongly. Aquarius is ultimately too unearthly for stable
Capricorn, and may begin to feel held back.

## Capricorn and Pisces

Here we have potential-plus for a fine romance: practicality wedded
to soul, respect to responsiveness. But conflicts will develop when
warmth-seeking Pisces meets, too often, the cold Capricorn.
Although a permanent affair may be made of the sexy child-adult
Pisces and the lover-parent Capricorn, the former's strain and pain
may frustrate Capricorn's need to be needed.

## Aquarius and Pisces

Sexy, but ultimately depressing for both, this should be kept in the
boundaries of the short romance. It would be a case of the sometimes positive, sometimes negative Aquarius being tripped out by
the unstable, poetic, unrealistic Pisces. Nonetheless, gratification is
possible for both, until the infuriating aspects become overwhelm-
ing. Pisces would come out ahead, and Aquarius would lose.

# $\mathcal{S}$ame Sign Combinations

## Aries and Aries

The Aries and Aries pairing, sharing the hasty Mars ruler, is the probable result of acting passionately. There will be impetuous, not leisurely, planning. Both will want to be in command. Both want to dominate. There is fire, excitement, emotion, and discovery with this lively couple. There will be moments of abandon and moments of intense quarreling. The blessing is that it is not in Aries' nature to remain angry very long. The big problem comes when deciding who is boss. Between taking care of business, with lots of irons in the fire, are interludes of passion's fiery inferno.

## Taurus and Taurus

The affectionate Venusian nature of Taurus sometimes leads to this pairing and there might be times when you both want to be silent, to reflect and contemplate. You are both fixed signs, not wanting change. At times almost becoming catatonic when big emotional problems come along. You both can be obstinate. You agree where money enters the picture. You are associated with income potential and personal possessions. You delight in obtaining a bargain but will spend willingly when it comes to comfort-producing luxury. This pair have in common a love of art, music, and top ticket lifestyle. Furnishings at home base are sumptuous. A well-stocked larder is a must and a liking for fine wines for cooking and drinking is indulged. In some cases singing publicly is in prospect. You are a beautiful couple.

## Gemini and Gemini

Can you picture a pair of Mercury-ruled Geminis in tandem? There certainly would be a lot of action, communication, and the beginning of but not necessarily the finishing of new projects. The pace would be fast with stimulating ideas transformed into action and what inventions these two could produce with some stick-to-it-iveness. We are viewing two people who are up on the latest gossip, two people having verbal, writing, or selling talents. Adept at bright conversation, they are invited to social gatherings because, together, they sparkle. In romance they are inventive, experimental, willing, and able. Let's hope one of them has an earth sign rising.

## Cancer and Cancer

This is not the most exciting relationship because these two may find much to criticize about each other and they could get tied down with red tape. Lunar-ruled Cancers are emotional, home and family inclined. When one of the pair is moody, the other is sympathetic. Cancers are touchers and huggers, not the worst traits for a couple who find security in loving. Homeownership and real estate investments are part of the picture. The kitchen as well as the bedroom are scenes of activity, pleasure, and joy.

## Leo and Leo

Full of charm, personality, and the ability to entertain are wonderful, but it is a matter of who will give up the spotlight. Each should realize the requirement of the other's need to show off. Fun-loving Leos are a love team, warmed by their mutual ruler—the Sun. They play jokes, they are creative and think of their home as their castle, a place to entertain friends royally. The perfect king and queen setup. Leo is a leadership and dramatic sign. Naturally, there will be some power struggles but lots of loving snuggles.

## Virgo and Virgo

You will both be discriminating and see in each other many sterling qualities. You certainly will both be well dressed and impeccably groomed. There would be a challenge of who would lead. You are eager to improve each other. You will expect much perfection in your children although you are very devoted and loving parents. In the bedroom you will be warm, supportive, and eager to please. You are both health and service oriented. You may wear yourselves out helping others because you feel you two are the mother and father to loved ones and friends. Even though you have so much in common, two under Virgo may not find it easy to harmonize in marriage. Why not run a hospital or nutrition-oriented resort together instead?

## Libra and Libra

Libra with Libra, the two partnership signs, could be interesting. Must be careful you both don't scatter forces. You will do much socializing. There will be the enjoyment of laughter in your lives. Lots of diversity. The pair of you will dress to complement each other. You will be quite a dashing couple in social situations. Both goal and leadership oriented, you will be before the public a great deal. Your home furnishings will be both comfortable and posh. It may not be a red-hot romance but privately, you are a couple of love birds. It could be, for each, amusing, pleasing, and elevating.

## Scorpio and Scorpio

With another Scorpio there would be a double amount of Pluto and a resulting struggle for power but an attainment of success in major objectives. There would be problems but they would not be apt to manifest in the financial area because both like to take on responsibilities and challenges. However, this smoldering, sensual pairing may be possessive of each other and need some happy-go-lucky laughter to ease the deadly seriousness. Both are mysterious, magnetic, psychic, and can be of tremendous aid to others in both a psychological and physical sense. Neptune-ruled fifth house Pisces gives an exceptionally romantic nature and with your superabundance of the vital force, you obtain the heights!

## Sagittarius and Sagittarius

Don't think that if your lover is another Sagittarian that you know all the answers and where all the buttons are to be pushed. You are connected to the same impulses but Sagittarians come in many models yet you will share similar interests. They include a celebration of life and a strong desire to head for the horizon, new languages, new places to be together. Enjoy.

## Capricorn and Capricorn

As a pair you are both organized, hardworking, and mean to make your mark in the world of business. You both know the value of good timing romantically and in the mundane world of making money. Ambition drives you and you are both indefatigable toilers. The shared earthiness of your character promises interludes of heavy-duty loving.

## Aquarius and Aquarius

The Aquarius with Aquarius sounds like a compatible team, great if the pair of you are involved in important humanitarian or scientific projects. Otherwise, you would do well to consult a good astrologer for a complete comparison of your horoscopes. Take time to know all of the implications before you jump the gun. This iffy romantic combination might or might not be permanent.

## Pisces and Pisces

Water and water, the Pisces and Pisces excursion into the mystical realm. With your two Neptunes dreaming up new fantasies, sharing poetic dreams, and finding spiritual rapture in each other's arms, you will do well to put your shoes on in the morning to go to work. With luck, your work will be as creative as your love life.

# TWELVE SECTORS OF

## chapter four

*It is something to be able to paint a particular picture, or to carve a statue, and so to make a few objects beautiful, but it is far more glorious to carve and paint the very atmosphere and medium through which we look—to affect the quality of the day—that is the highest of arts.*
—Henry David Thoreau

This chapter is devoted to the twelve sectors in your chart, as they relate to you personally: your talents, the persons in your life, the love sectors, the marriage sectors, the professional sectors, the money sectors, and the sectors of illicit relationships.

There are two basic charts that I'll discuss: the Solar Chart and the Natal Chart. These charts may be used for your Sun sign or your rising sign. If you do not know your time of birth, the Solar

LOVE, HEALTH, AND WEALTH

Chart is used (Sun sign), for it places the sign your Sun was in at birth in the first sector. The other eleven zodiacal signs are in logical sequence thereafter. No time of birth is needed for this chart; your birth date is all that is required.

The other type of chart *does* require both birth time and birth date; it is called the Natal Chart. If you know your time of birth, use it to look up your rising sign in the tables at the end of this chapter (see pages 144–174). Then, use that sign as your first sector.

If you do not know your time of birth, then use your zodiacal Sun sign as your first sector.

How can you put this information to work for you? We will begin with the first sector.

The first sector in the horoscope is the window through which others see you on a first-look basis. The first sector can give clues to personal appearance, the mask we wear in public, our apparent attitudes, and apparent personality.

After the first sector, you will read about the part that each of the succeeding eleven signs plays in your life, giving you an appreciation of how all the signs affect your chart.

Each sector is like a stage set, and the sign in the sector is the actor or playwright making things happen on this set.

If you want your life to abound with romantic moments and be filled with more exciting loving than you may be enjoying presently, then read on.

If by chance there's not enough poetry in your life, write a haiku. This Japanese verse form can spring from joy or sorrow, achievement or disappointment. The first line has five syllables, the second has seven, and the last line has five.

For extra insight, there will be a haiku when you come to the twelfth sector of each sign.

Haikus have neither rhyme nor rhythmic structure, for example:

*Not responsible*
*For promises uttered*
*When the full moon beams.*

Not all people are poets when they are enchanted by love's magic. But almost anyone can create a haiku and enjoy the feeling of expression through the written word. Perhaps you could send someone flowers and write something like this on the card:

*I'll write a haiku*
*without words on your pale skin,*
*in darkness, in joy.*

We will begin with Sun in Aries, or Aries rising, the first and pioneering sign of the zodiac.

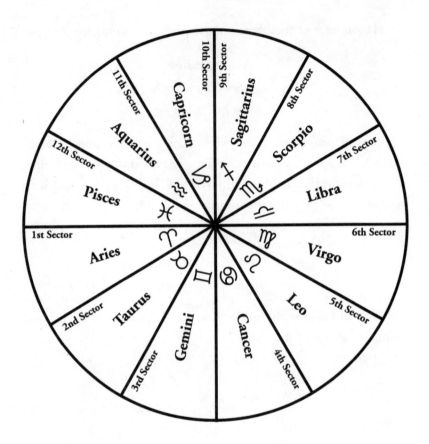

# *Aries*

## Sun Sign or Rising Sign

People with Aries in the first sector are personally aggressive, pushy, demanding to be at the head of any line, impulsive, impatient, fiery, ambitious, bold, dashing, enterprising, energetic, and interested in any new projects but not always staying with them.

Because Aries' second sector is Taurus, the artistic, financial, and practical sign, Aries people (March 21–April 20) are definitely interested in making and spending money, but they lose interest quickly if they are not making it fast enough; and because they are often involved in the many-irons-in-the-fire syndrome, they have many places to pay out and many sources of income.

Since their third sector is the dual-bodied mental sign Gemini, their ideas come in pairs, and seem able to be at two places at once. They are mentally flirtatious, able salespeople, and clever buyers.

They can be very emotional and real estate oriented because their base, the fourth sector, is Cancer. Many of them move and change residences often because the Moon, which rules change, is the planet with the most influence over the fourth sector.

The fifth sector is Leo, the sign of creativity, show business, and fondness for the bodies of the opposite sex. Even when Aries people are not employed in the profession of acting, they often put on a good show when they find themselves with an audience.

The Leo sign in the sector of children also relates to teaching or playing the leader or boss. If your boss is an Aries, he or she will pressure you by wanting everything done instantly or yesterday.

Aries people also treat lovers with the rush act, wanting to get them into bed on the first date. They need to develop patience.

The sixth sector for Aries, which is Virgo, includes servants, fellow workers, and employees. This sector also has a great deal to do with personal habits, and it is here we find the explanation of some of the strangeness of the sign. Because of this house, Aries people can be extremely difficult people to work for, inasmuch as they want everything done yesterday, but the bad news is that even the rush job must be done perfectly and one must not expect too much praise for doing it.

The Aries man could gain quite an enviable reputation as a ladies' man, while an Aries woman may be accused of being promiscuous, when she is only shopping around to find someone her speed, romantically or sexually.

In the seventh sector for Aries—partnerships, marriages, and open enemies—we find the sign of Libra, the sign of the peacemaker, artist, and the socially connected. This is very appropriate because the pushy, aggressive Aries individuals need someone who will cooperate even when they are not their most charming selves. Librans have a civilizing effect on hot-blooded Aries.

The eighth sector, the house for finance in the Aries-rising wheel, is ruled by Scorpio, a stop-at-nothing sign. Spendthrift Aries people who get behind in their payments, or neglect insurance premiums, or who get careless with tax matters will probably find this sector, which also deals with credit, to be a source of trouble and annoyances.

The eighth sector is the one where partnership money flows in and out. When partnership money is withheld, you can bet there have been poor public relations or unsatisfactory communications between the Aries partner and the other.

The ninth sector for Aries is Sagittarius, the sign of long-distance travel, philosophy, religion, man's law, nature's law, and God's law. This explains the positive mental philosophy of Aries individuals, their predilection for taking chances and gambles, and their periodic itchiness to travel. Sagittarius is the "good sport" sign, which accounts for the fact that, even after sudden anger, Arians seldom hold grudges, and forgiveness is automatic. These rages, however, are not always forgiven by the forgiven.

Why are Aries people business oriented and driven by ambition? The reason is partly because Aries is a cardinal sign, in itself synonymous with ambition, but the real reason is that the tenth sector for Aries is the practical, hard-working earth sign Capricorn.

This is also a reason for the double bind many Aries have to deal with: the eagerness and haste of Aries, combined with the necessity for Capricornian patience, organizational ability, and the willingness to wait for success while putting in long, productive hours.

The eleventh sector for Aries is Aquarius. This is the sector dealing with hopes, wishes, desires, and profit or loss in business (if the Aries individual is self-employed). It also deals with goals and participation in sororities, fraternal organizations, charitable activities, and humanitarian impulses.

The presence of Aquarius in the eleventh sector guarantees they will have friends who are unusual and unpredictable, some kindly and some boorish, some inventive, and some a little weird.

The twelfth sector for Aries is Pisces, and of all twelve this is one of the most interesting sectors. Astrologers long have given this sector a "black eye." Take some of the following attributes of this sector with a grain of salt. We will start out by giving the negative qualities of the sector, and then follow it up with the more positive ones.

This is the sector of self-undoing and confinement, and is suggestive of prison, mental institutions, monasteries, secret enemies, subversive activities, clandestine activity, ambushes, slavery, sorrow, persecutors, assassination plots, worry, secret fears, suicide, poorhouses, anguish, grief, and bad news in general.

Now for the good news. The twelfth sector, according to more modern astrologers, is the sector of unlimited resources, the sector of the subconscious, the "power house" of intuition, where quiet meditation and prayer take place. If you have beneficial planets in this sector, you are protected, given shelter and aid in times of trouble, a place to retire to or to hide in times of danger. The twelfth sector stands for spiritual qualities and attitudes, privacy, inner resources, hidden depths, imagination, poetry, abstractions, and duality, both good and evil.

On the negative or positive side, depending on your view of love and romance, the twelfth is also known as the sector of clandestine and secret lovers.

## *Haiku for Your Twelfth Sector*

*Mirages shimmer*

*We run toward Illusion*

*In search of untruth.*

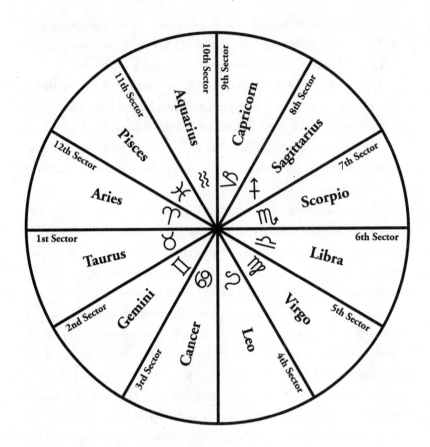

# Taurus

## Sun Sign or Rising Sign

When this sign is on the first sector, the window through which others first see you, people are inclined to see you as rather charming and not in any particular hurry to get your act into gear.

Though there can be tall and thin people with this sign on the first sector, you are more likely to be somewhere between muscular and stocky and rather plump. Many of you will have rather squarish, solid features and extremely sensual lips. Your complexion is rarely pale, more often olive-shaded.

You will gain a reputation for steadiness and probably are a person who does not make concessions. Let's face it, you are often called strong-willed, even stubborn. Taurus is a practical earth sign in the group of "fixed signs." (The other fixed signs include Leo, Scorpio, and Aquarius.)

Your speaking or singing voice is probably one of the first things that attracts others' attention because of its richness and range. Your expensive clothing and accessories set you apart as a person who has chosen to sit at the head table of life, among those who can appreciate wealth and luxury. You also exude a certain sexual and romantic vibration that is extremely stimulating to the opposite sex. Many of you consider the arts and music as a major interest—after money and loving.

The second sector for Taurus is Gemini, strongly indicating that your money-making talents are in the mental and verbal sphere, where head and hands team up to find and multiply cash resources. Gemini is a sign where writing, printing, talking, debating, traveling, and selling often show up side by side. The state of being prolific or able to duplicate your efforts is common to this sign, and it is reflected in your cash inflow and outflow sector.

The third sector for Taurus is Cancer, an emotional, cautious, and changeable sign influencing the sector of decisions and communication. Cancer is a cardinal water sign and, when it appears in this section of the chart, suggests that practical Taurus can be influenced by intuition and feelings about facts and figures. Cancer is considered a conservative sign and on this sector can promote unprogressive attitudes.

The fourth sector for Taurus is Leo, and it rules the home and all its furnishings. Because it is under the influence of the regal sign of Leo, the home tends to be spacious and expensively decorated with only the most impressive furniture, carpets, and drapery. Taureans like to live in better-class neighborhoods and tend to entertain rather lavishly. The cuisine is apt to be rich, with emphasis on fresh fruit and vegetables. Most of the sauces, soups, and other appropriate dishes are prepared with a proper wine.

The fifth sector, of romance and offspring, is Virgo. This knowledge can be helpful to anyone aspiring to be loved by the financially capable Taurean, for where Virgo falls in the chart a person is very particular and discriminating. The loved one's apparel must be neat and fashionable.

The Taurean expects few services above and beyond the mere filling of often insatiable sexual desires. Poor Virgos are always supposed to be at the head of the line of volunteers to serve.

The sixth sector for Taurus is Libra and indicates that the Taurean looks for, likes and expects cooperation, good manners, tact, and intellectual style in servants, fellow employees, and those hired to do work. Also preferred are employees who come from the upper echelons of society.

The sixth sector also rules health and good habits. Libra here would suggest that organic balance, balanced diet, and moderation in all things is the way to better looks and a better sense of well-being. Many people of this sign, however, are inclined to second helpings of rich foods, and sometimes a drink or two more than is advisable for proper balance.

The seventh sector, of marriage and partnership, is Scorpio, and often causes the potentially placid sign of Taurus to wind up with emotionally intense and extremely sensual spouses. Taureans are often overly concerned with meeting the payments they feel are due, and early in marriage are prone to be a little tight-fisted with their spouses. Scorpios, on the other hand, are pretty open-handed and feel that a bill paid late is not their problem, but the problem of the person kept waiting. This often causes some rather heated exchanges. As Taureans get older and richer, however, they lean in the other direction of more lavish spending.

The eighth sector for Taurus is Sagittarius, which often puts the Taurean into projects requiring the Sagittarian gift of promotion.

They like to make their money with other people's money and often go into money management. Sagittarius also is associated with publishing, and you will find Taureans in printing, publishing, or law, which both Libra and Sagittarius connote.

The ninth sector of travel for Taurus is practical Capricorn, which explains why some pleasure trips often involve a business hustle. Items bought on trips may become salable merchandise. New sources of export items or export buyers might be sought. Travel expenses are methodically logged and will appear as business expenses on their next tax form.

The tenth sector for Taurus, the professional sphere of operation, is the fixed sign Aquarius, which frequently indicates a business with fewer employees, occasionally a one-person business. Those Taureans who are employed by others will expect at least a junior executive position rather than an expendable-helper type of job. The work will be somewhat intellectual or mental, sometimes of a scientific nature, including engineering and artistic endeavors. Taureans like independence and personal autonomy in their work.

The eleventh sector, of friendships and associations, is Pisces and requires more discrimination in the choice of associates. Because Pisces is an emotional and changeable sign, Taurean friendships are often a source of unsteadiness and disappointment, but better communications can prevent misunderstandings. The Taurean needs to be careful in choices in this sector, and may need to learn to say no in a tactful way when put under emotional pressure to do something for a friend.

The twelfth sector points to the kinds of attitudes and activities that can land people behind the eight ball. For Taurus it is Aries. This sector is where enmity builds up, often resulting from a Taurean's attempts to change from a follow-through person to an aggressive innovator in situations where new ideas or methodologies are not acceptable.

We think of Taureans as family persons, but there is a sensual side to their nature that some find hard to control. The twelfth sector is where secret love affairs flourish, born out of impulse. This slipping and sliding around is not conducive to a stable marriage or parental image.

The more affirmative interpretation of Taureans' twelfth sector is that it is their house of inner resources, the subconscious mind. Here are born their pioneering ideas and independent souls. There must be a blending of opportunity and better timing. Sometimes it is wiser to study new ideas and think them out more carefully, awaiting an opportune time to spring them, so that what rises from the unconscious is welcomed instead of resisted.

### *Haiku For Your Twelfth Sector*

*We watch the hour hand,*
*Ignoring precious minutes,*
*Jewels of the now.*

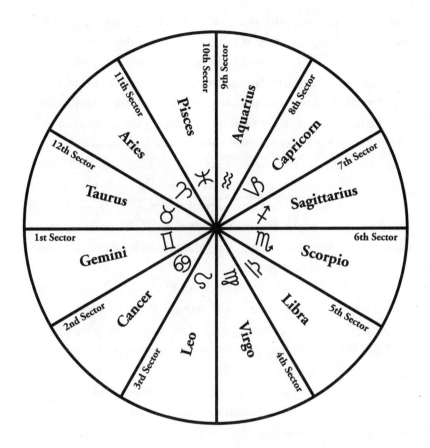

# Gemini

## Sun Sign or Rising Sign

The first sector for Sun in Gemini and for Gemini rising is, of course, Gemini, the sign of communication—an accommodating air sign that is adaptable, sometimes scatterbrained, literary, verbal and witty. Not all people with Gemini rising are persuasive and potentially sales oriented, but this sign is thought to give you the gift of gab.

In most cases, Gemini people have long, lean, willowy bodies, long piano-player fingers, attractive fingernails, and are given to rather large gestures with their hands and arms. Possessing clever-ness of mind and dexterity of hand, they are capable with typewrit-ers, adding machines, or hand tools. Because of their word-wiseness, Geminis often fascinate the opposite sex and find them-selves with more love companion potential than they can handle.

The second sector for Gemini is Cancer, the acquisitive sign given to saving souvenirs and other collectible or salable com-modities. This sector also reflects talents associated with food, shelter, and real estate. This creates a double bind: On the one hand, the person is driven to make or save money by buying and improving real estate, and on the other, he or she has a tendency to be a rolling stone, changing residences with higher frequency than the more stationary signs.

Because this sign of the family is on the financial sector, emo-tional uproars with spouse or offspring will tend to put you off your target of gain, and loss could follow. The better your feelings and the family harmony, the larger your profits and the smaller your losses through poor spending habits.

Your third sector is Leo, the creative, administrative, fixed fire sign. Leo is also a sign of pleasures and amusements, which will make you a great one for pleasure trips and holiday travel, more often by road than by plane or ship. People with this Leo place-ment are often thought to be drawn to hilly or mountainous areas rather than flat land, so you and any travel companions of the opposite sex should head for the high places for fun and games.

The third sector deals also with studies, and therefore, you should include among them drama, art, music, and creative writing.

The fourth sector, of living environments, is Virgo, a flexible, practical, and tidy earth sign, prone to changes and relocations. Wherever Virgo is by sector, there is apt to be criticism and desire to serve. The Gemini influence is often reflected in nervous energy and a high-strung nature. When the home is tidy and well organized, the strain on the nerves is lessened.

Because Mercury, your planetary ruler, also rules Virgo, your homesite sector ruler, you will probably have an office, studio, or workshop on the premises. You will have many books, records, and periodicals, ideally neatly arranged. You would actually feel more comfortable in proper rather than casual attire, even when relaxing around the house, because of the fashionable and particular Virgo influence here.

The love and sex sector for Gemini is Libra, the romantic, partnership-oriented, ambitious air sign, often thought to rule the upper classes and the luxury-life people. This indicates affectionate people who love parties, are often arty, and who are much given to attending plays, opera, and ballet. Expensive presents and considerable dining out are the usual required preliminaries preceding any loving.

The sixth sector, of habits, health, service, and the wardrobe for Gemini, is Scorpio, a fixed, intense water sign. Bad habits are harder to break and good habits are worth money to you.

Geminis are often sexually attracted to fellow workers or employees. Female Geminis are often very sexy dressers, striving for the sensual, streamlined look, which, in combination with their gift for wit and double-entendre remarks, makes them teases and flirts.

Gemini people are noted for a personal appearance that includes a dash of daring. Those who have kept their slender and svelte lines would look pretty exciting even in a potato sack, given the right costume jewelry and hairdo. Marilyn Monroe, a Gemini, was once photographed by William Mortenson, a famous Southern California photographer of beautiful women. He handed her a potato sack and, with a few stitches and pins, came up with a classic pin-up picture.

Because the sign of Scorpio is often prone to communicable disease, Geminis should avoid close contact with persons who are coming down with any infections. They should also avoid letting nervous tension about work overstimulate them, thus wasting their nervous energy. They should get plenty of rest when the pressures mount, and avoid excesses in food and drink.

The seventh sector for Gemini, the partnership and marital love sector, is Sagittarius, which explains the attraction these two signs have for each other. Sagittarius is a fire sign, and adaptable, much given to travel, overspending, overconfidence, philosophy, and generosity. The combination is compatible because the Geminis can permit the independent and freedom-loving Sagittarians plenty of space and relief from the possessiveness of some of the other signs.

Because Sagittarians often lack tact and social polish, however, the Gemini person needs to develop a certain toughness in order to deal with the occasional nonsupportive words of the Sagittarian. Sagittarians have an enthusiasm and spontaneity that is so strong it is sometimes tiring to others. They are great lovers, but sometimes prefer making love out of doors in a scenic setting—great, if it's not too cold or too damp! They also tend to travel a lot and not always with their spouses, more often with lovers.

The eighth sector for Gemini is Capricorn, and on this sector of life, death, legacies, taxes, and other people's money, the ambitious earth sign of Capricorn has the effect of promoting Gemini's longevity. The disappointing feature of having this sign on the house of legacies, however, is that many Geminis simply do not receive large legacies, or any at all, and must save for their future security, often continuing to work after retirement age, if not well married. This is often the sector of alimony or other divorce settlement monies and, here again, the Geminis sometimes have a hard time collecting or even being awarded sizable settlements, the way the Taureans seem to manage.

Aquarius is the ninth sector for Gemini, and it is the house of love enjoyed on trips or among strangers or foreigners. Geminis are idealists, with a streak of wanderlust, who want very much to please their lovers without being too conventional. They prefer loving to marrying, but are not impossible to land, given the right bait and no threat of coercion.

The tenth sector for Gemini, the love-at-the-office house, is Pisces, the bendable water sign. This is the house in which you will find your boss. He may be very sensitive, is probably misunderstood by his wife, and is often extremely charming around the opposite sex. Often he has a boat or other retreat where willing ones can be entertained in complete privacy.

You may have to do a lot of the organizing for your boss and persuade him to be more practical about paying bills on time and more determined about collecting accounts receivable.

Office relationships between people of this sign are often lacking in stability, as are the job records of many Geminis. They seem to do a lot of transferring or job-hopping, unless there are other steadying influences in the individual natal or solar chart.

The eleventh sector for Gemini, of goals, friendships, and memberships in associations, is Aries, the do-it-right-away sign. Here you will find fiery friendships that sometimes become sudden love affairs. You find friends who impulsively go to bat for you and encourage you to put ideas and words into profitable action.

People will tell you that you have fascinating friends who are doers and goers. You may see in them a primitiveness that complements your ideas and verbal orientation. You feel that you are in fast company. Whatever you lack in confidence, your friends will make up for, and their aggressive to-the-point nature could rub off on you in beneficial ways.

The twelfth sector for Gemini is Taurus, the financial sign, and since this is the house of secret machinations that could cause problems in your life, honesty in money matters is the only safe policy for you. Greed and possessiveness or jealousy and vindictiveness, on your part or on the part of secret adversaries, are qualities that work against you.

The positive side of this sector is that it provides you with unlimited subconscious resources. To develop these kinds of talents to their fullest, you should take courses in accounting, business administration, selling, or loans and escrows, and some of you might consider art and music, even interior decoration, all of which are possible vocations for Taureans.

### *Haiku for Your Twelfth Sector*

*Have a cup of tea*
*And then let's enjoy talking about*
*Books and art and love.*

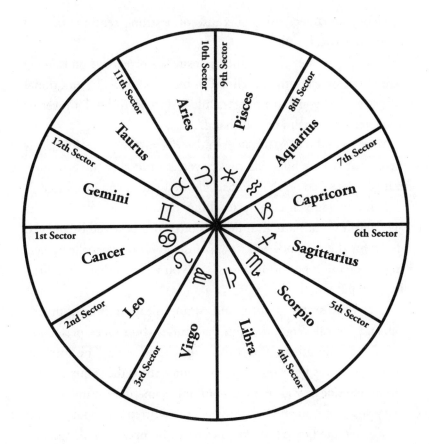

# *Cancer*

## Sun Sign or Rising Sign

If your solar Sun sign or natal rising sign is Cancer, your personality appears to others as warm, emotional, changeable, and often family or clan oriented. You tend to be conservative, home-loving, sensitive, and very much into touching and enjoying the touch of the one you love. You are probably very capable in the kitchen, and your living quarters are comfortable, but probably not large enough to accommodate all of your treasures, since you have a tendency to collect things because of a strong sentimental and acquisitive streak.

Your shy sexiness makes the opposite sex protective on the one hand, and on the other, inclined to be seductive. The emotional empathy that you can project could help you to hold a lover or audience in the palm of your hand.

Your second sector, of talent and moneymaking capabilities, is Leo. Your Moonchild side makes you a little close with money, but generous Leo on this sector will often tempt you to splurge.

Some of you will take up teaching, creative work, or the managerial role. Your natural timidity is often overpowered by the Leo desire for the audience and its applause. You may not take up acting or the other performing arts, but you will feel that something is missing if you don't.

Your third sector, of ideas and communication, is neat, practical, and critical Virgo, the sign that causes you to seek perfection in yourself and others. Virgo also nags you to serve. This intellectual sign in this position helps to balance the rather tempestuous emotional side of your nature—but only sometimes. Virgo is a literary sign, and on this sector of words, written and spoken, you may be tempted to sell or write novels, or become a public speaker.

The fourth sector for Moonchild is Libra, the sign of luxury. This is the sector of the home and real estate holdings, and with the home-loving character of Moonchild, combined with the desire for opulence of Libra, you will want to own your own home and constantly make it more and more beautiful. Many of you discover there is profit to be made in the buying and selling or renting of real estate, and you will go into the real estate business either full-time or as a sideline.

The fifth sector, of romance and children, is the sexy sign of Scorpio, a truly intense and sexually uninhibited sign. To the Moonchild, having a lover is an emotionally harrowing experience if there are any interpersonal problems. Losing the lover is an equally, if not more, emotionally harrowing experience. The Moonchild clings and romanticizes relationships, and often dreams about the return of a lover who has not the slightest intention of coming back or making any apology for the breakup. You need to know when to release people, be they lovers or children, and you need to be less sensitive to slights and criticism.

The sixth sector for Moonchild is Sagittarius, a sign noted for its affinity for animals. This sector is associated with pets, as well as health, work, and servants. Moonchildren are very likely to want a live creature in their homes. As children, and sometimes as adults, Moonchildren often like horseback riding. In the hinterlands, Moonchildren often farm or raise and breed livestock.

This sign often causes Moonchildren to be overstimulated by work and to use up too much energy, sometimes necessitating periods of longer rest hours to recuperate. There is a tendency toward excesses in food and alcoholic intake, which needs to be disciplined if the wardrobe is to fit comfortably.

Moonchild's seventh sector, of marriage and partnership, is Capricorn, the sign of hard work and ambition. Marriage therefore becomes a plausible ambition for family-oriented Moonchildren. Delays or a certain lack of demonstrativeness is sometimes a problem, since this sign is ruled by Saturn. A marriage house ruled by Saturn sometimes indicates a difference in age or maturity between the partners.

Saturn practicality is sometimes at odds with the sensitive and emotional Cancer. But Saturn's dependability and inclination to meet obligations, even at the cost of personal sacrifice, is a plus.

Capricorn is ruled by the lusty mountain goat symbol, which indicates some patient but exciting loving. Both signs have a frugal side, except in the horoscopes of unfortunate individuals, so the common goals of security and care and education of the children work well together.

Capricorn on the partnership sector is status conscious about the way the family is clothed, about the home, and also about the brand name/model of the family cars, a positive trait materialistically.

The eighth sector for Cancer is Aquarius, the partner's house of talents and resources, which sometimes indicates a strong desire on the partner's part to be the head of a business rather than always working in the corporate box.

This is also the house of mystic feelings and sensuality. With do-it-differently Aquarius ruling, you should have a rather unconventional sex life.

One note of advice for this placement: Pay your bills promptly and put some funds in savings.

Moonchild's ninth sector is Pisces, which makes you strongly inclined to travel either on water or over water. Since the sector also deals with strangers you meet abroad, some caution and discrimination should be exercised to avoid flighty or devious persons whose intentions are not entirely reliable. This sector also relates to in-laws of brothers and sisters, so observe the same care and caution in these relationships.

The ninth is the sector of religion and philosophy, and with the Pisces tone in this sector, there is often some mysticism and strong faith in your makeup.

Your tenth sector of professional efforts is Aries, the sign of the very independent and often aggressive executive. The sign of Aries is often associated with haste, and anyone with a boss of this sign will tell you that such a person wants everything done yesterday or on overtime. This person will often have many irons in the fire, so he or she needs someone adept at following up on things in which interest is temporarily lost.

If you have your own business, you'll probably have clients with similar characteristics. You will have to be on your toes and juggle many pending projects. Since the tenth house represents one of your parents, one may be the driving, aggressive type, whom you emulate.

The eleventh sector for Cancer, of friends, hopes, wishes, desires, and goals, is Taurus. Money is often a topic of conversation, as is stability and practicality. Taurean friends are friends for life, since they are slow to change but often possessive and set in their ways. They like to entertain and are often guilty of tempting you with delicious high-calorie foods and desserts or drinks. Resist. Refuse large helpings and seconds. Taureans often bring culture, art, and music into your life because of their Venusian interests. Many of them live rather extravagantly, but that is no reason for you to be less frugal.

The twelfth sector for Moonchild is Gemini, a sign often associated with gossip, friendly, witty, and otherwise. You would do well to avoid being too candid about your personal life and feelings, for this sector is associated with self-undoing. If you keep a diary, keep its secrets locked up, away from the prying eyes of those who would become envious or take too personal an interest in your emotional ups and downs.

Since Gemini rules paperwork and contracts, as well as letters, you need to be especially careful about anything you sign that could be legally binding.

The twelfth sector rules your subconscious mind, and with Gemini in this position, you are apt to have occasional internal dialogs in which there is some duality or double-blind thinking.

If you are a writer, you have the unlimited resources of your subconscious to help you plot and research what you write and publish.

## Haiku for Your Twelfth Sector

*I feel a feeling,*
*I think a thought…I touch you*
*You are soft, lovely.*

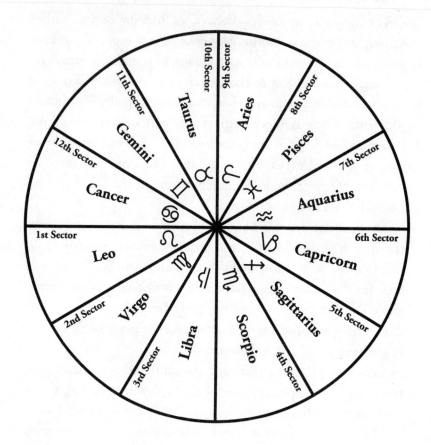

# *Leo*

## Sun Sign or Rising Sign

If your solar Sun sign or natal rising sign is Leo, your personality is dramatic, larger than life, creative, warm, generous, sunny, good-humored, and often a little bossy. We could throw in that you are commanding in appearance, proud, loyal, passionate, and seeking a position of leadership.

Acting and the field of teaching beckon some of you, and you are often the irresistible target of romantically driven persons of the opposite sex, sometimes for good, sometimes for ill. You have one potential character trait that some people will not admire. Many of you are overbearing and find it difficult to resist monopolizing conversations. However, if you have had an interesting life, your stories about yourself can be very humorous or entertaining.

To maximize your success potential, you should try to earn an official title before or after your name. Deserving Leos often attract many honors.

Your second sector of talent and monetary experiences is Virgo, the sign of the go-between, the agent, the healer, the quality control person, the person with clerical aptitude, including accounting. You would do well in medicine, the theater, the executive suite, and the fine or lively arts. Virgos are practical and work well with details and planning. You would do well in any kind of service trade, including personnel management.

Your idea and attitude sector, the third for Leo, is Libra, which makes you fair and just, and propels some of you into the law profession. Because the Libra attitude is social and socially connected, you probably can communicate very well with the so-called upper branches of society who prefer to live on the best side of town. Your talents include practicality and a sense of mental balance.

This sector has to do with transportation as well as communication, and makes it likely that you prefer prestigious and large cars.

Your fourth and residential sector is Scorpio, a fixed water sign, which gives you a reference for a house with privacy, located on a hillside or hilltop, or near water. The Leo tends to spend money on house and home, and because it is a royal sign, the Leo thinks of home as a castle.

The home is tied in with Leo pride. Servants are sometimes in evidence. Two of the most powerful money planets, Mars and Pluto, rule Scorpio. Since Scorpio is in the fourth sector, of real estate, many Leos are involved in buying and selling homes, apartments, or land. Home is where big-spender Leo entertains lavishly.

Leo's fifth sector, of speculation and love affairs, is Sagittarius, which describes persons of the opposite sex who may be foreigners, of a different religion, or persons who have traveled widely.

This sector describes the amusements that interest you, including horsemanship, trips to the track, and the great outdoors. Since there is an affinity between Sagittarius and wide-open spaces, you may find that you or your lover likes to make love on the top or side of a mountain, on the beach, on the shore of a pond, stream, or ocean, or in the hayloft of a barn (since that is where horses are kept). You are likely to be lucky in love when you are away from your town, state, or country.

The sixth sector, of your work, wardrobe, and better habits, is Capricorn, which is associated with status and a desire for prestigious clothes that are somewhat flamboyant yet quite conservative.

Since Saturn rules Capricorn and this sector, your health habits, exercise, and diet are of vital importance to your sense of well-being. Striving for the lean and slender look will add years to your life, while overindulgence at the table or bar will cause weight problems, taxing of your heart or back, or other illnesses associated with those who lack Saturnian discipline.

Your seventh sector, of marriage and partnership, is Aquarius, which could cause you to marry someone much younger or older than you, or much more or less mature. The two of you may be extremely fixed in your ways, but you will be stubborn about different things. Your spouse may be extremely interesting and unusual, with completely different goals from yours. Because this sector for Leo is ruled by Uranus, the planet of divorce, some of you will marry more than once unless you get lucky, have great rapport with your spouse, or consult an astrologer before tying the knot.

Uranians will not put up with taking orders from anyone. They are highly independent and freedom oriented, and full of original ideas that others may not be ready to accept right away.

Your eighth sector is Pisces, which requires you to take a very efficient and organized approach to your spouse's money, and requires some training of your spouse in this area. This sector also rules legacies. Leos often receive goods, property, and money as the result of the death of a person with whom communication was strained during his or her lifetime. The legacy may be the result of some personal denial and sacrifice on the part of the person whose goods are willed to you.

Your ninth sector of travel and philosophy is Aries, suggesting spontaneous decisions to board planes and head for the horizon, often to hot countries, or countries prone to rebellions or warfare. This is one of the most exciting sectors in the Leo chart, and it often leads to one-night or one-week stands abroad. Your characteristics often involve leadership, success, personal independence, and strongly articulated political views.

Your professional sector, the tenth, is Taurus, practical, artistic, sometimes musical, and often involved in corporate businesses, but sometimes involved in one-person businesses. Often your role is that of an executive and requires you to be able to keep things rolling along after they are started. You are capable of producing what is expected of you, no matter how much hard effort is required, especially if you get into the financial end of the business, where there are many details. Some of you may enter into lucrative businesses, but you will still be able to paint, sing, or play musical instruments in your spare time. Acting and public speaking are automatic talents for most Leos.

The more famous you are, the quicker you can attain material success. Your natural creativity is icing on your cake.

The eleventh sector of friendship, memberships in organizations, and goals is Gemini, a complex, intelligent, and restless sign. This describes your friends, who are apt to be witty, verbal, argumentative, and multitalented. Some will be writers, salespersons, lawyers, travelers, advertising folk, or public relations experts. They will be fascinating, controversial, and not always charming.

Your twelfth sector is competitive Cancer, and often indicates that members of your own family can be a source of some stress if you demonstrate a lack of empathy. It is the failures in communication from which your problems stem. Because of the Leo tendency to do all the talking, you may not even be listening for, or take seriously, the messages that others are trying to tell you, especially those messages of an emotional nature.

Try to avoid emotional embroilments that can work against you. You never know when what you think is amusing may be taken as a personal attack and remembered for years. Often someone is holding a grudge against you that you do not even know about. Be more public relations conscious and you'll have fewer detractors.

### *Haiku for Your Twelfth Sector*

*Delicate woman*
*Falls into clutches, escapes,*
*To find gentleman.*

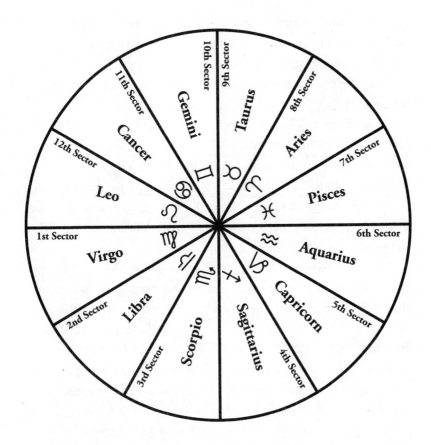

# Virgo

## Sun Sign or Rising Sign

If you have Virgo as your Sun sign or rising sign then your first sector shows that you have a love for fashionable clothing. Your features are fine, and your grooming is impeccable. You are choosy, health and self-improvement conscious, and tend to make helpful or critical suggestions to those people who do not realize they're not making the best of their appearance. Because you like to look your best, you tend to spend rather heavily on personal care, vitamins, clothing, and success seminars.

Your second sector, of talents and moneymaking abilities, is Libra, a mental sign that expresses itself as a gift for connections with important people. Many of you also have a gift for decoration and art direction, and your possessions reflect your desire for the best quality.

Some of you fall naturally into commercial jobs, clerical work, accounting, quality control, photography, teaching, reporting, writing, editing, nursing, and medicine. Some Virgos have a low tolerance for noise, and prefer to work alone because they find the chatter and clatter of other workers distracting. Virgos are seldom clock-watchers and, though they may arrive late sometimes, they are usually the last to leave the office.

Your third sector, of thoughts, ideas, and attitudes, is obsessive and sexy Scorpio, which often causes you to travel or make short trips due to obligations or reasons beyond your control. This can be a miserable sector for you if you do not have a car, or if you have one that is not dependable. When you have to ride with someone, you tend to get annoyed or frustrated by the impatience and conflicting desires of your driver. In order to get the ride, you may have to endure being imposed on by the other person.

This sector also influences your reading habits. Some of you prefer scientific material, while others like sensual romances, clever mysteries, or exciting intrigue stories.

This sector is also the strong driving force of those of you who write. The mystery writer and "queen of crime" was the Virgo, Agatha Christie, creator of Hercule Poirot, a textbook Virgo, and Miss Marple, who was more of a Gemini.

Your fourth sector is Sagittarius, which explains why so many Virgos leave home and move a long distance away to find a home which they prefer. People who have Sagittarius on the fourth sector often travel a great deal, either early in life or later on. Often they come from immigrant families.

Some of you would rather have an animal around the house than too many noisy people. Virgos need large homes because they like to collect beautiful things that need space to be displayed. The Sagittarian-type home is often on a hilltop, secluded from others, with large, spacious rooms and attractive landscaping. This means that only the affluent Virgo or the well-married Virgo can afford to have the kind of home that would be most to his or her liking.

Your sector of children, creativity, and love affairs is Capricorn, the sign of status, success, and dependability. This often causes you to be attracted to the older or more mature lover who has many business responsibilities. This is exactly the sort of person who needs the humanizing benefits of love and fun and associations with a practical person of the opposite sex. You often feel responsible for the health, clothing, and humor of your lover and try to keep him or her from acting too much like "an old stick."

Your recreational activities usually get you involved in organizational work, or "helper work," such as catering (if the social event is a party with food), and you may have to write and mail invitations.

Your sector of health, service, and good habits is Aquarius, a sign that implies intellectual work, sometimes connected with mechanical, scientific equipment—anything from typewriters to adding machines to computers to astrological charts. Many of you may have thought about doing work in the entertainment field.

Your health problems may be related to the condition of your blood—its circulation and your veins or nerves. Many of you keep your houses warmer than other people find comfortable, a sure sign of poor circulation or a lazy thyroid gland.

Because you have Aquarius in this sector, your service work may include some charitable or humanitarian activity.

The seventh sector, of marriage and partnership, is Pisces, an idealistic, dual-bodied sign. This sometimes indicates the probability of more than one marriage, ideally, the second one to a practical, affluent person.

This sector often requires you to make more sacrifices than you can manage in good humor. You need a protective, supportive, intelligent partner who is moderately frugal but with a dash of generosity and excitement. What you do not need is an emotionally unstable, unambitious person whom you couldn't depend on in a pinch. In a business partnership, you need an orderly, completely honest person who has no heavy drinking problems.

Your eighth sector, of money from partners and other people, is Aries, which makes you liable to some ups and downs due to impulsive spending and piling up of credit debt. This is the house of insurance, mortgages, and regular monthly payments, as well as taxes. One way of eliminating trouble in this sector is to avoid overuse of credit cards. Use your credit to buy and deal in property and to buy items that produce more money. Pay cash for the consumption purchases. Put money in savings.

Your sector of philosophy, religion, and travel is Taurus, which indicates a likelihood that early in life you abandoned the religion in which you were brought up, and a small likelihood of involvement in cult religions.

Travel is often connected with monetary matters, or the import or export business. If you wish to enjoy your travels to the fullest, try to go first class, because your natural critical tendencies appear when you get poor service and encounter dirt or untidiness.

Your professional sector and your boss are ruled by the sign of Gemini, a dual-bodied air sign, which indicates that occupations in which you use your head are the best for you. Your work will probably call for your doubling in brass and helping with someone else's work. Gemini is associated with the media—radio, television, newspapers, advertising, and the writing, speaking, and selling professions.

Your bosses tend to be charming one minute and Mr. Hydes the next. Virgos usually do good work, but they are too frequently not very adept at the manipulation skills needed for survival in the executive jungle. They often know exactly what is going on, but tend to cover for troublesome individuals on staff and wind up taking the blame for something that is not their fault. Some of you do find that nearly perfect job and stay for years, but the sign of Gemini, the rolling-stone-on-the-job house, causes you to serve in a variety of ways at many different places of employment.

At one time, nearly every Virgo has thought of becoming a nurse, teacher, doctor, fashion model, or the owner of a dress shop. Happy is the Virgo who finds the right place to light vocationally.

The house of friendships and goals is Cancer, and this house guarantees that you will have extremely emotional friends who can be very changeable, unrealistically romantic at times, and often prone to talking too much about their children or mothers.

This sector, which also encompasses your hopes, wishes, desires, and the profit or loss of the self-employed Virgo, brings into the picture other professional skills, real estate, food, drink, and the desire for one's own home or property. Jobs in which you are a go-between, an agent, a finder's fee person, or a consultant will bring you the money to make your materialistic goals easier to attain.

The twelfth sector for Virgo is Leo—often the sign you would rather be, if not Libra—your house of unlimited resources. It is also the sector that gives you a clue to what could cause enmity between you and others. Promiscuity is item one. Problems with those in authority is number two. Acting in a tyrannical way encourages those who would like to see your downfall.

The twelfth sector has to do with creativity, artistic abilities, and appreciation, and therefore includes show business. Many Virgos have distinguished themselves in this profession: Cliff Robertson, Sophia Loren, Ingrid Bergman, and Greta Garbo.

## Haiku for Your Twelfth Sector

*Let's go into mind*

*To search for wisdom, or wit.*

*Perchance to find Truth.*

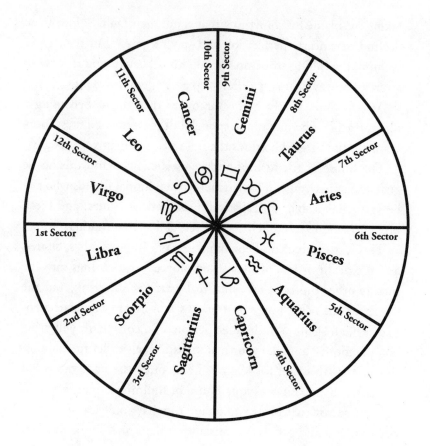

# $\mathcal{L}ibra$

## Sun Sign or Rising Sign

If you have Libra as your Sun sign or rising sign for your first sector, you are a romantic person in search of love and harmony through poise, good manners, and fairness. Partnership is one of the key words of your philosophy.

You are usually artistic, musical, attractive in appearance, and love social life and entertaining. Because you have taste, style, and a strong sense of color, you may feel that you are more special or better than many people that you meet in your daily rounds. Whether rich or in limited circumstances, Librans seem to have a special talent for making their living quarters beautiful and pleasant.

Your second sector, of talent and financial abilities, is the natural money sign Scorpio, a fixed sign that implies the money you make will stay with you because of your persistence and a degree of obsessiveness. You need to avoid losing your gains through unwise and unnecessary purchasing.

A fixed sign on this sector often indicates that follow-through is important in your work and that determination and great effort are a requirement for material success. Fortunately, these are some of your abilities.

Your third sector of ideas and mental abilities is Sagittarius, routing some of you into the study of law, for this sign is the one that rules man's, nature's, and God's law. This is one of the freedom signs, and on this sector, it has to do with relatives. In order to feel less restricted by their opinions, problems, and pressures, many Librans prefer to avoid too much contact with relatives.

The third sector concerns travel, and Sagittarius is a long-distance travel sign. This causes many of you to desire periodic flights or cruises to clear out the mental cobwebs.

Your fourth sector, of home and family, is Capricorn, which explains your desire to live in a prestigious area and to have your home a symbol of your status. You may have found that living with your parents was rather restricting because of the family regulations, but you probably love them, respect them, and try to visit them periodically, even when they live some distance from you.

Your fifth sector, of love affairs and children, is Aquarius. Your love affairs often are platonic friendships, until some planetary position pushes one of the buttons in your horoscope. Suddenly friend becomes lover. Aquarius is the sign associated with hopes, wishes, desires, and goals. This is why, in weighing the potential of a lover, you ask yourself if he or she fits in with your aspirations and life goals. As a romantic Libran, you won't be comfortable in a stormy love affair, especially if it is too one-sided, or ends with rancor.

Your children are apt to be quite unusual, and some of them may study a stringed instrument, drawing, or drafting. They could resent too much supervision or bossiness from their parents.

Your sixth sector, of work, wardrobe, good habits, and service, is Pisces. You are advised to stick as much as possible to protein, fresh vegetables, and fruit rather than processed foods, and avoid the temptations of stimulants or alcohol. Moderation or avoiding refined sugar will help you preserve your beauty, especially if you get a moderate amount of exercise. Your wardrobe should include evening clothes and sports outfits in yellow, gold, and pastel shades. Casual wear should include shades of your skin tone. Executive clothing should be expensive and fashionably conservative.

Avoid working in surroundings where there is too much tension, aggression, or hostility. Fortunately, Libra is an executive sign, so you have the power to create some harmony where you work.

One of the most important sectors for partnership-loving Libra is Aries, a go-getting fire sign of high volatility and impulsiveness. There is a tendency to clash over haste versus Libra's desire for moving at a slower, more studied pace. You like to think about doing and planning multiple choices of action, as well as the pros and cons, in order to choose the right course. Your partner may not want to talk or think about doing, preferring to act on the spur of the moment and without consulting your wishes. To find a harmonious balance, both of you will have to go through some retraining of old habits. You will need to act quicker, and your partner will need to think about joint wishes and goals and take a more leisurely pace. Failure to accommodate each other could cause angry clashes.

Your eighth sector of other people's money is the money sign Taurus, which frequently indicates that you will inherit money, goods, or property. You would probably prefer a socially acceptable marital partner, but some of you are attracted to the "diamond-in-the-rough" type that functions better in business than socially, and who from time to time lets words or tactless remarks slip.

On the plus side, on this sector of partner's talents and money-making abilities, Taurus usually has a practical approach to earning, saving, and providing funds for food, shelter, and drink.

Your ninth sector, of philosophy, travel, and communication with one's partner, is Gemini, an intellectual and verbal sign. Both you and your partner may have writing or public speaking abilities. Since you both use the telephone often, you probably need two or more phones and an answering service or message machine.

Your professional sector is Cancer, ruled by the Moon, which in turn rules the public in general and women in particular. Moonchild has connections with food, drink, shelter, and real estate, plus family and one of your parents and your partner's parents.

This sign on the professional sector often causes a strong inclination to deal or dicker in the sale and purchase of homes. Sometimes it causes you to have a study, studio, or workshop, so that you can bring work home with you, or even run a business from home base. This could apply to you, your partner, or both of you. With the two parental signs prominent in your chart and that of your partner, parents are, whether absent or present, often personally involved in your lives together, through visits, phone calls, or correspondence.

Your eleventh sector of hopes, wishes, desires, goals and memberships in organizations is Leo. This usually attracts creative, important persons into your circle, some with titles, professional, academic, or inherited. Often your friends are leaders, celebrities, in the arts, or in education.

Since the quality of your friends is tied up with your goals, a little practical discrimination is probably a good idea. You will be invited to join social organizations, which will probably put you under obligation to serve on action committees. You should learn when to accept and when to decline gracefully. Certain service activity leads to opportunities you will want to take advantage of, while other service responsibilities are counterproductive and a poor use of your energies and gifts.

Your twelfth sector is Virgo, the sign of service and research and the power of the subconscious. This is the sector from which you can draw the earthy practicality of Virgo and sound ideas about nourishment, exercise, and good habits. This sector can be the source of the one emotional experience that you may not be comfortable with—criticism.

This is also the sector of secret love affairs, and therefore is a potential source of notoriety or scandal. If self-restraint is not one of your strong suits, discretion had better be.

### Haiku for Your Twelfth Sector

*Their lips part, kissing.*
*Hearts beat, their rhythms speeding.*
*Arms embrace, loving.*

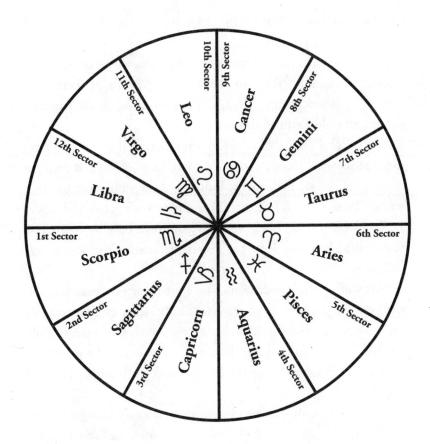

# *Scorpio*

## Sun Sign or Rising Sign

If you have Scorpio as your Sun sign or natal ascendant (rising sign) of your first sector, you are obsessively and intensely sensual and power oriented. You will not tolerate familiarity from subordinates, and you like to keep your private life very much to yourself. You have the potential to be manipulative in interpersonal relationships, whether familial, romantic, or corporate.

You are fascinating, enigmatic, dynamic, and a little scary to people who do not know the real you. Your desire for complete control often puts others on the defensive, so that you will not be on the defensive yourself.

You are resourceful and have great charisma, useful qualities for leadership or fame. You can charm the birds out of their trees when it suits you, or, in a change of mood, can scare the pants or panties off mild-mannered people.

Your second sector, of talent, moneymaking abilities, and attitudes about what money can and cannot do, is daring and dashing Sagittarius, the sign that often indicates deals with other people's money. Probably you feel that there is plenty of wealth and credit available, but you do not always pay your own bills on the first of the month. You may feel that this is the creditor's problem and not yours.

Many of you use your money or your talents as weapons, the way you use your strong emotions. You are either quite spartan in your tastes, or Sybaritic, desiring all the touches of luxury. Your life and your fortunes have their ups and downs, but thanks to your innate indomitability, you bounce back easily and can recoup your losses.

Your third sector, of attitudes, is pragmatic, cool, and calculating Capricorn, the sign of patience and persistence. You are constantly campaigning about something, important or not so important, and are like the chess player who knows what the adversary will do even before he or she does it.

Capricorn in this position infuses you with ambition and a deadly sense of timing, which is surprising and unsettling to those who act first and think afterward.

Your fourth sector, of home and parents, is Aquarius. This sign is associated with anything unusual, progressive, unpredictable, not to mention scientific. Your home base is where your visitors come, attracted by this sign. Your visitors are likely to be intellectual, humanitarian, and sometimes a little strange. Frequently, they are inventive or dedicated to causes. They, like you, are probably well read and in the higher intelligence brackets. They share your strong interest in sex and romantic intrigue, and they may have been through the mill of divorce and its attendant problems and irritations.

Your fifth sector, of love, fun and games, and creativity, is Pisces, the sign of dancers, mystics, actors, models, photographers, or those who indulge in the other arts, including poetry. Since this is your sector of recreation and art, many of you are quite accomplished, either professionally or unprofessionally. Pisceans are constantly in search of new and more stimulating emotional experiences, so it is not surprising that Scorpios have a rather prolific track record in the romantic conquest and seduction department.

Your sixth sector, of work, wardrobe, good habits, and health, is Aries, the sign of the now and the new. This sign often causes you to have more than one string in your bow, as far as business is concerned. Aries in this position causes you to drive your subordinates to speed up their work and is a source of much frustration when you have to work with incompetents who lack drive and direction. This work sector sometimes causes some job hopping until you find a place where your talents are appreciated and you feel emotionally satisfied with the work.

Your partnership sector is Taurus, a fixed earth sign of strong passions and somewhat spendthrifty tendencies. Your business or marital partner is apt to be just as fixed in his or her opinions as you are. Your partner is more than likely somewhat of a clothes horse and into designer originals in the higher-price markets. He or she may have a great speaking or singing voice, may play a musical instrument, paint, probably prefers fresh foods to processed, and will probably want a garden or orchard in addition to a fine home with very expensive furniture and original art on the walls.

Your partner's loving possessiveness will turn to extreme jealousy if you have a roving eye, a flirtatious nature, or if you treat him or her coldly or casually. With Taurus on this sector, sexual and financial compatibility are extremely important if the partnership is to be a lasting one.

Your eighth sector, of mortgages, insurance, and other long-term payments, is Gemini, a flexible air sign that often leads you to buy multiple or bulk purchases. You can often get a rate on bulk purchases, but buying two or more when you need only one can put financial pressure on you by straining your credit unnecessarily. When you feel overextended, there is a tendency for your nerves to fray, or for your natural optimism to sour. The self-destructive Scorpio will be apt to push him or herself into a financial corner by unwise and compulsive extravagance.

Your ninth sector, of higher education, travel, philosophy, and the higher mind, is sensitive and changeable Cancer. This causes you to change courses in college, change colleges, and even drop out—definitely not recommended. When possible, shoot for professional degrees in fields such as business, medicine, law, drama, or education. You function better when you are seated at the head table of life, and a good education can help you find your way there faster and hold your seat longer.

You tend to be family oriented, acquisitive, and conservative, yet concerned and progressive. Cancer on the ninth sector often indicates long journeys over water, both within and outside your country. Many of you will make sacrifices for both relatives and in-laws that involve some strain on your own financial resources.

The tenth or professional sector for Scorpio is dramatic, autocratic, and creative Leo, the sign of the boss, the celebrity, and the show biz personality. The Sun is the ruler of Leo; and whatever the Sun rules shows you where one of your important interests of the heart is. For you, it is in your work, if you have found the right place to devote your professional energies. Doing a good job, winning, and accomplishing gives you great personal satisfaction and ego balm.

Whether in the field of education or not, you are a born teacher and play the role, even in administrative positions. You do not appreciate flattery, but crave sincere compliments for a job well done. Honors go with the territory if your work is truly professional.

Your eleventh sector, of hopes, wishes, desires, goals, and friendships, is Virgo. This makes you particular, discriminating, cool, and interested in friends who are informed, modest, and usually experts at something. You can be a good and faithful friend, loyal to those you trust and who return your trust and loyalty.

From your seat of judgment, however, you can make false friends your enemy. You can cross your enemies off your list if you are mature, or you can plot their downfalls if you are petty and vengeful. One of the lessons you must learn is to be more tolerant and forgiving of other people's manners and weaknesses.

Your twelfth and karmic sector is Libra, the sign we associate with peace, love, harmony, balance, and togetherness. Karma has to do with payment or forfeit for acts or defaults committed in another lifetime. Scorpios have a special type of karma, called Kash-Karma, which brings almost immediate repayment for good or ill in this lifetime.

Libra on the twelfth sector indicates a balancing of payments or rewards as you go through life. Many people do not even believe in the Karmic Law of payment and reward, but since Scorpios have experienced it in this lifetime, they are continually experiencing this cycle of good and evil, doing or default, as Kash-Karma punishes them or rewards them for their wisdom or angers.

Your life will be more comfortable and pleasant if you align yourself with the straight shooters and the good guys.

### *Haiku for Your Twelfth Sector*

*Excitement your game,*
*Incitement is your measure,*
*And my pleasure, too.*

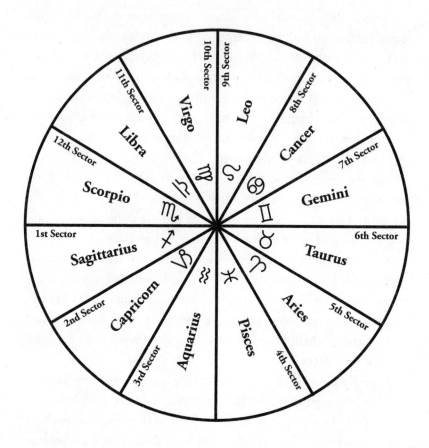

# *Sagittarius*

## Sun Sign or Rising Sign

With Sagittarius for your first sector, you may be above medium height and perhaps born with a well-built body suitable for an athlete. If you are as tall as some Sagittarians, you'll have to duck to get through the doorways of some older houses.

You are spontaneous, restless, a rover, a big talker, and thrive on risk taking. You were born to travel, and you find life an adventure, with each day bringing excitement and challenge.

When there are too many consecutive days that lack excitement or challenge for you, you are apt to start thinking about making major changes in your place of residence.

Most of you prefer the company of strangers or foreigners to the company of your own kin and the people with whom you grew up.

Because you think big and are natural gamblers, you sometimes bite off more than you can chew. This, combined with your rule by the planet Jupiter, said to be protective and to bring luck, causes you to win more often than you lose.

You are even forgiven your strong tendency to tactlessly tell the truth, even though it is poor public relations and often downright bad manners.

Much of the time, your eternal optimism and high spirits help you attain what others would think are impossible dreams more quickly than some of the slower-going signs. Many of you would be even more successful if you could hang onto your financial gains. You spend prodigally and just do not know how to be poor.

The thing that probably saves many of you from your own nature is Capricorn's rule of your second sector, of talents and money-making abilities. Capricorn is practical, tries to save for the morrow, and knows that financial ambitions can be realized only with cash in hand. You Sagittarians are great promoters and persuaders, and can often get someone with cash to get involved in your deals. As you become more mature, many of you become very responsible and hard working, often working at more than one job in order to get the financial freedom you dream of.

Your third sector, of ideas, travel, and mental attitudes, is Aquarius, the capricious, inventive, highly independent, freedom-loving, and scientific sign. This sign on your sector of communications often makes you indifferent to what others think of you, and nudges you periodically to say things that you know will shock the influential and conservative persons that you should be cultivating when you are involved in deals. It is what you say more than how you act that sometimes causes you to make enemies. There are some people that find your enthusiasm and bubbly energy tiring or unnatural. This probably doesn't bother you in the slightest, because like the Aquarians you don't give a damn about those you consider half alive or half dead. Most people consider you refreshing and full of fun, and admire your spirited ways.

Your fourth sector, of home and hearth, is Pisces, the spiritual and mysterious sign of dancers and those who act, paint, write poetry, or study music. If you have any of these talents, you may have learned some of them from your parents or visitors to your home or from forebears somewhere in your family tree.

Pisces can be a rather unstable sign on this sector, leading to many residential moves or absences from home due to travel and business ventures, or just plain restlessness.

Often one of your parents was not particularly the go-getter you are, and you are motivated to better yourself. You prefer to live in large, spacious places far from traffic, and with one or more animals. You resent intrusions on your privacy and the comings and goings of your guests and visitors. If you rent, you would strongly object to nosy apartment house managers and gossipy neighbors. You feel that what you do in your dwelling is your own business. Sometimes you conduct some of your business from where you live, especially if you work two jobs.

Your fifth sector of amusements and love affairs is Aries, the eager and impetuous sign of the hasty heart. People of the opposite sex whom you are not very interested in may consider you a tease because you can be very provocative. Although you are a loving person, you shun the possessive type as you would the jailor, because you like to feel you are a free spirit, and because you are reluctant to make strong commitments except to someone extremely special. The heat of your passions is quickly ignited, sometimes by inappropriate persons, as you will find out later. No matter, you are a good sport, and variety is the spice of your life.

Affairs that flame high and then eventually fade out often become friendships that last a long time. Some of your love affairs are brief, because you are traveling so much that you cannot stay around long enough to build lasting relationships.

A Sagittarian woman of my acquaintance told me that when she was younger her ambition was to be an airline stewardess. She suddenly got married instead and had three children. She is single again, and her children are grown and married. Would it surprise you to know that she has her own travel agency, and when she flies, she combines business with her pleasures?

Your sixth sector, of wardrobe, self-image, and service, is Taurus, the sign of luxury and riches, music, and art. Many of you will work with wealthy clients or employers. You tend to dress well and money is no object when you see clothing you want or jewelry that catches your eye. You are likely to have more sports clothes or travel outfits than some other people who are more stay-at-home types. You might need riding habits, if you are still interested in horses. In a moment of discontent with your present profession, you may even think about opening your own dress boutique. Whatever service you perform, you are not shy about asking top dollar for the product you sell or the time you spend on the job.

Your seventh sector of partnership and marriage is Gemini, a dual-bodied air sign, frequently indicating more than one marriage.

Take this astrologer's advice and avoid marrying a poverty-stricken suitor or a rich one who is a tightwad. Marriage to air signs promises companionship, interesting communication, a lack of stodginess, intellectual stimulation, and, of course, romance, but with a touch of idealism.

You may be one of those Sagittarians who marries out of impulse, and if you suspect that you are, slow down long enough to have an astrologer check out the horoscope of your prospect to make sure there is no Jekyll and Hyde in the chart. Make sure the partner has hobbies that you can share. Make sure the partner is not too rigid in his or her opinions or too set in his or her ways.

Also, try to be supportive and more tactful than you usually are. You need a fun-loving companion who is understanding, flexible but practical, aware, and not slow to compliment you when you need a morale boost.

Your eighth sector of inheritances, long-term payments, taxes, and insurance is Cancer, a sign associated with saving. One of your sources of windfall good fortune lies in the area of legacy. Many of you will inherit money and property. One reason is that members of your sign tend to live longer than other people. Your many acts of generosity and cheerfulness are remembered when wills are made out. Some of you will be named as executors of estates, whether or not you choose law as a career.

Your ninth sector, of travel, is Leo, the loyal, regal sign. Leo on this sector causes many of you to obtain professional degrees in college and you are inclined to teach, go into the healing arts, law, or philosophy. When you travel, you go luxury class, you explore, you mix with VIPs, and sometimes hunt and fish, climb mountains, ride elephants, and wade through marshes and streams.

The single Sagittarian will not want for romantic thrills while in foreign countries, because when you are abroad you meet the friendliest and most amorous people.

As I write these lines, I am glad that, though a Virgo, I am blessed with the sign of Sagittarius rising. As those of you realize who have read my book *The Love Boats*—from which I created the hit TV series "The Love Boat"—I have traveled a great deal as the cruise director for various luxury cruise lines.

Your tenth sector, related to your profession, is Virgo, the sign of service. This sign often has to do with food and drink, as well as agriculture and food processing. This is a very health-conscious sign, which is good, for the Sagittarian may be tempted to overeat or linger too long at the bar. One side of your nature knows that more temperate habits are better for the figure and self-image. Expensive clothes look a great deal better on the athletic body than on the paunchy frame that has lost its muscle tone.

Happy is the Sagittarian who is in a profession where there is no boss to harass him with orders he does not want to follow, or boring routines that become unbearable as the hours slowly pass.

Your eleventh sector, of friendships and goals, is Libra, the sign of beautiful people of wealth, style, and social acceptability. Your friends are often executives; they are well-mannered patrons of the arts, music, and theater.

You are known by the company that you keep, and, during your younger years, you may have received some scoldings about your tendency to be undiscriminating in the choice of your friends—some of whom may have been lacking in Libran qualities. Your natural ability to make friends quickly will put you in great stead and be advantageous if you are more choosy about their credentials. Librans often know the right people and can bring you together with people you might never meet otherwise.

Your twelfth sector is Scorpio, a sign that is known to be a little thin-skinned, never forgetting an injury or slight. Since this is a sector where secret enemies often lurk, think twice before ever insulting any person likely to carry a grudge. Your skill at flirtation can cause jealousies, and your ease in communicating with executives often produces envy among your fellow workers.

Lucky as you are, some of you have made an enemy here or there when your public relations were not the best. Try to mend interpersonal fences as you go along, turning the envious into admirers and your adversaries into friends.

## *Haiku for Your Twelfth Sector*

*Fresh vistas beckon*
*The eternal traveler.*
*A smile every mile.*

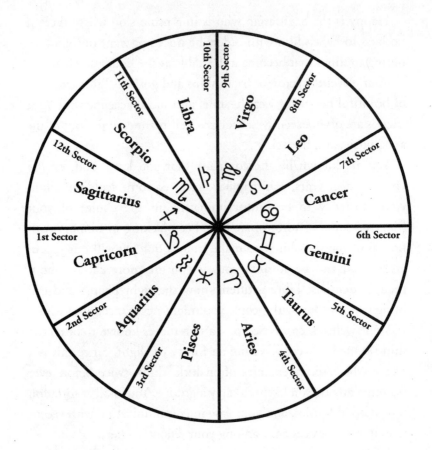

# *Capricorn*

## Sun Sign or Rising Sign

If you have Capricorn for your first sector, your face has a very strong bone structure, giving you a striking beauty or impressive appearance that tends to improve with age and maturity, as does your life and character.

You may feel you were born with adult ways and serious thoughts, and the older you grow, the younger you tend to feel. You went to work or shouldered some responsibilities too early in life. You are ambitious and realistic about your loved ones.

You are by nature a survivor and no stranger to setbacks and hard work. Duty and dependability are ingrained in you, and you desire recognition and status. You will earn both, not receive them on a silver platter. Because you have had to deal with problems, you are a problem solver and do not believe in taking the easy path, though you may have longed for it from time to time. You have a definite advantage over others with less motivated signs; you know what you want from life, can learn how to get it, and are much better organized than others.

Your second sector, of talent and cash inflow and outflow, is Aquarius, a fixed air sign that often telegraphs solutions to you just when you need them. It is an intellectual sign and a voracious reader of technical and vocational material. Aquarius is knowledgeable and one of the signs of the expert in useful fields of specialization and general knowledge, which, combined with your practical nature, can make you unbeatable. Whatever you set out to do may take a long time, but the benefits are lasting. You function very well in vocations where your ability to simplify the complex can make you an invaluable executive.

You can say no without hesitation or reluctance, and you can show the door to malingerers and unproductive employees. You can be strict and demanding, and you show others an example worthy to be followed. Many of you have a background in competitive sports, and some of you are extremely interested in corporate, state, or national politics, and the status possibilities of the successful officeholder.

Your third sector, of communication and mental aptitudes, is intuitive Pisces, ruled by the planet of the imagination, Neptune. This planet is the muse of writers and poets and is said to have some rule over the movie and television industry, not to mention those who go to sea or who find satisfaction in escapist moments of solitude and pleasant hours with a rod and reel by a quiet stream.

The third sector is the place in your wheel of life where you meet with relatives, brothers, sisters, and neighbors. Some of them will be creative, and more than likely some will come to you for advice or perhaps a loan (which may not later get repaid).

Your fourth sector is Aries, which rules the home and family. Aries is a sign of action, so there is likely to be high energy in your home, but you may not always be on time for dinner because of business obligations.

Though you may not relocate as often as Geminis or Sagittarians, you will find that moves do happen, often because of your work and changing fortunes. You Capricorns like to move into prestigious neighborhoods and often prefer to own your own property as a tax shelter to accumulate equity. The purchase and sale of property can be the source of revenue gain when your timing is right.

Many of you grew up in one-parent homes and helped with housekeeping or worked to help pay family expenses. This is often one of the spurs that drives you to be the best family provider you can be. You want your children to know the value of a dollar, of time, and of a good education.

Like Cancers, you make great sacrifices for your family and want to see them well housed, well clothed, and well fed. Also like Cancers, you tend to be a worrier, but you have a certain satirical sense of humor that provokes more thoughts than belly laughs.

Your fifth sector is Taurus, the sign associated with art, music, and the better things of life. This is your sector of love affairs, hobbies, and other recreations. Take away your fifth sector, and your life would be nothing but work, work, work, and duty, duty, duty.

You need to take time out for your children and for enjoyment, both simple and exciting. How many of you have taken time to paint, to take music lessons, or to study drama and dance? Those who have perform better, and if you choose any of these creative areas for your career, you will stay in it longer and continue to perform well, even after the age of retirement.

Your sixth sector of work, good habits, wearing apparel, and service is Gemini, the verbal-mental sign. You are the kind of person who is apt to read or study during meals and are very likely to keep books or magazines in the bathroom, so that no chance for improving your mind will go to waste. You do well in management work and, although you are often considered a slave driver by your subordinates, your department is likely to have bright, mentally stimulating people to work with, whom you should take a break to talk to every so often, as a relief from your self-imposed workaholic ways.

You are so particular about what you wear that you are even more likely than Virgos to make some of your own clothing. You feel that by choosing your own fabric designs, even threads, you can dress more impressively. Those of you who do not sew prefer tailor-made clothing or clothing from the finest shops, because what you wear contributes to your image and status.

Your sign is ruled by Saturn, the teacher and the symbol of Father Time. You believe in being prompt and become upset when you see time going to waste. Employees who come late or spend too much time talking seem expendable.

Your seventh sector of marriage and partnership is frugal Cancer—supportive, sensitive, and loving. You will probably find in your marriage partner a person who likes picnics, trips to the beach, river, lake, or the woods, and who has a way with foods and a penchant for desserts.

Your home will be kept spic and span, but will, as the years go by, fill up with memorabilia that you have lovingly collected. Besides the quality of the furnishings, your home will have a truly homey, comfortable atmosphere. Your children are apt to have better manners and be more civilized than your neighbors' bratty offspring, who show no respect for their parents.

Your eighth sector is Leo, which works well for some Capricorns and against others. We think of Leo as a money house of credit, as spending for show, in a negative way, and therefore having many overly large monthly payments to meet, making it difficult to save or have money for wise investing. On the positive side, Leo on this sector works to provide you with security by making you purchase wisely things that have value and last for years. The practical side of your nature makes you incline to put money into savings, in the knowledge that money as well as time is worth money.

The eighth sector, as well as the sixth, has certain medical implications, and many of you have had some problems with your knees, which Capricorn rules, and sometimes the back, which Leo rules. Leave heavy lifting to others.

The eighth sector also rules over the insurance business and tax matters. Capricorn's wide ranging reading habits often include learning about the ins and outs of tax law and the pros and cons of various insurance policies. Some of you become heavy buyers of insurance and prompt others to be prolific sellers of policies as a profitable vocation or as a sideline occupation.

Your ninth sector, of travel and philosophy, is Virgo, a practical earth sign. Some of you travel for business, health, or educational reasons. Many Virgos will acquire better habits while traveling and will abandon debilitating habits while they are under foreign skies. You will want to find accommodations with superior service and well-kept lodgings. You would love Holland and Switzerland for these reasons alone. Even if on business, you should take time out to visit villages and castles that still have a touch of medieval and historic charm. Avoid the noisy and garish in favor of the quiet and tasteful, for that is your cup of tea.

Your professional sector is Libra, a go-getter mental sign, well suited to the legal profession or political or industrial statesmanship. For example, the greatest Capricorn of them all was Benjamin Franklin: printer, storekeeper, hit song writer, public speaker, philosopher, soldier, legislator, diplomat, and master spy.

With all three of your vocational sectors ruled by air signs, ideas are your products and literary pursuits are not uncommon to your sign. You need to be in a profession in which you can gain personal satisfaction, good material benefits, and deal with enough problems to keep you stimulated and proud to serve.

Your eleventh sector, of friendship and goals, is Scorpio, which can lead to somewhat strained relationships because of the Scorpio tendency for possessiveness, jealousy, and sarcasm to creep into communications in this sector. When you lose a friend through misunderstanding, distance, or death, you can become very emotionally intense or even bitter.

Money and sexual matters are frequent subjects of conversation when you get together with friends, and, unless you are temperate, quite a lot of *spiritus fermenti* is ingested, and the humor is apt to get gamier and gamier. Just as you Capricorns really need that fun fifth sector, you also need your twelfth sector, which is Sagittarius, the sign of optimism, a quality that many of you lack.

The twelfth is the spiritual sector of unlimited resources. With helpful and forgiving Jupiter as its ruler, you should try to look on the bright side of life, and count and appreciate the blessings that come your way.

This sector also relates to retreats, places to go for quiet moments of renewal. Recommended are places where you can find wide-open space, the forest, the mountains, quiet or surging waters, or any other place where Mother Nature is putting on her best show.

The pleasure of good literature, biographies of achievers who began in modest circumstances and attained their goals, along with a few books of verse, renews your soul and unfrazzles your nerves.

### Haiku for Your Twelfth Sector

*Old doors are locked now*
*New doors swing open to you.*
*Your future is near.*

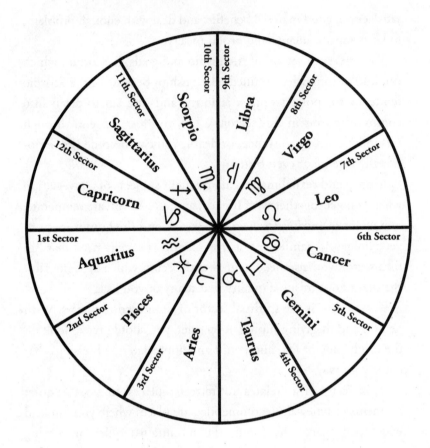

# $\mathcal{A}$quarius

## Sun Sign or Rising Sign

Aquarius in the first sector may bestow on you exceptionally handsome or beautiful features. In your face is a look of great intelligence, blended with the lines of the pixie. You stand out in a crowd because you are different, witty, and sometimes capricious.

You are a mental aristocrat with an uncommon ability to fit in among both the higher and lower echelons of society. You will not be ordered about or lectured to by those who know less than you do.

Your symbol is the Cosmic Man or Woman with arms out-stretched to embrace the world, feet in both the past and the future.

You feel more comfortable in the library than in the bank, but you do have a multitude of talents, which could make you rich in the world's material wealth, should you choose to use them.

You are literate, articulate, and persuasive. You are friendly, loving, and lovable, usually calm, confident, and poised, yet there are moments when you can be outrageous, shocking, eccentric, and downright disagreeable. You have both good and bad manners, but you are seldom temperamental. In your younger years, you may have knocked over a fair share of cups, glasses, and vases.

Even though you are naturally gregarious, you need to be alone to think, to study, to write, to explore the scientific marvels of books and projects, and to listen undisturbed to the great music of the past and present.

Your second sector, of talents and fiscal matters, is ruled by artistic, idealistic, and sometimes indolent Pisces. Pisces in this position often causes you to donate services instead of charging for them, to undercharge for services, or to fail to bill or collect for them. Even so, money flows to you, and you tend to have more than one savings account and more than one checking account, and you often forget how much you have in your reserves. You can be frugal or, periodically, quite the spendthrift.

You find that although you are good in sales, you would not want to make this your full-time work. We think of Aquarians as advisors and counselors, with many of the qualities needed by social workers, but the problem is that while your sympathies may be with the underdog some of the time, you can get very impatient with those who whine and lack skills or gumption to get out and work.

With all the vocational potentials you have, you can scatter your efforts unproductively unless you find the kind of work you like. You should treat each job as a learning experience, and if your self-starter is in good operating condition, you might consider having your own business. This way you can avoid clashes with authority figures. The happiest Aquarians I know have found work they love so much that they would be willing to work at it whether they got paid or not.

You are born in the one sign that can profitably turn a favorite hobby into a business. Some of you like to repair or modify things. Others get into a very Piscean occupation like photography, which has the side benefit of being gadget and appliance oriented, with a touch of the scientific. Another Piscean pathway that is seductive to some of you is acting or other creative pursuits such as writing and advertising.

Your third sector of thoughts, words, figures, and symbols is Aries, the sign of originality, quick-wittedness, independence, pioneering aggressiveness, and multiple interests. You like to live where there is action nearby and new things happening. This sign explains your frequent impatience and intolerance of delays. To think is to do, to act immediately. Your opportunity antenna is always working. You get so many ideas so quickly that you are apt to give the best of them away before you can get benefits from them. This doesn't bother you because you know that there are many more ideas where the others came from.

Your fourth sector of the home environment is Taurus, a sign of stability and security. You, like the Taureans, enjoy your possessions—some art in your home, a good sound system, and lots of books and periodicals.

One of your domestic skills is cooking, and you are likely to have some pretty inflexible ideas about diet, which you do not always practice. You may be able to live in a spartan environment when single, but as you accumulate more and more hard-to-throw-away possessions, you'll probably have to move into larger and larger homes. One of the domestic skills that you lack is housekeeping and neatness. You need domestic help or a spouse to pick up after you and to encourage you to dispose of beloved but often useless items you continue to collect.

You love to give and attend parties and can be a fantastic host or hostess. You probably fret less about social preparations than other people, and you may put off doing perfunctory tidying up and dressing until the last minute, so that guests who arrive early are liable to be pressed into service and obliged to greet other guests, while you finish up attending to your clothing and grooming.

Your fifth sector of children and love affairs is Gemini, the sign of fascination and communication. You are apt to make much conversation before it occurs to you that your companion may have more passionate ideas in mind.

Aquarians may have their mental moments and entertaining flirtatious ways, but they are not inclined to celibacy or to conventional attitudes about sex and love-making. Aquarians are full of pleasant surprises!

This is also the sector of offspring, and, though you love your children and enjoy communicating with them, they are frequently out of mind if out of sight. You are tolerant of your own children, but often not too fond of other people's little monsters, if monsters they are. You treat your children as if they were miniature adults and tend to be more pal than parent, allowing them and encouraging them to develop their individuality. You expect them to make good grades, but do not badger them excessively if they do not.

Your sixth sector, of clothing and service, is Cancer, the frugal and the sentimental sign. You are not above wearing old clothes around the house or even to work, but you hate to discard even out-of-style apparel that others would give to the Salvation Army.

You buy clothes in spurts and love to dress up, but your taste is not always the best unless you take someone along with you to restrain some of your funky impulses. You wear your new purchases for a while, then often return to your habits of wearing your older things. You are not inclined to regular appointments with either your doctor or your hairdresser, because you are not prone to sickness in the way that some of the more emotional signs are, and you feel that anyone who has to pay someone else to comb his hair has rocks instead of a brain. Your self-sufficiency in this area can make for some rather interesting but not impressive grooming.

Your seventh sector of marriage is also rather dramatic, for it is ruled by the sign of Leo, a potentially bossy sign.

There are exceptions to the rule about multiple marriage and divorce for your sign, but they are unusual. Aquarians make up a large part of the population that practices consecutive monogamy. There is something in your nature, choice of friends, and lifestyle that makes long marriages difficult for you or your spouse, or both.

Some astrologers have said, unkindly, that Aquarians love everybody. Partly true and partly canard. Certainly you crave intelligent and indulgent companions, but you are not looking for a boss or nagger.

Best you see your astrologer first before making that tempestuous voyage on the uncharted sea of matrimony. For some, it is a voyage to the isles of the blessed, and for others, a voyage without apparent end, on a ship of fools.

With Virgo on your eighth sector of other people's money and spending habits you have to tread that fine line between parsimony and practicality. To keep the checkbook balanced properly, you have to put it in order.

Your partner is probably a bigger spender than you can ever be, which is great if the earning potential is good, but is very disquieting to the Aquarian, who likes to be free of debt.

Your ninth sector, of education, travel, and philosophy, is the other luxury sign, Libra, with the touch of class. When you travel, you are often assumed to be more important than you are at home. Your social life and the caliber of people you meet when traveling is pleasing to your easy-going Aquarian temperament.

You make friends easily and receive more invitations to social events than you can accept. Others find you extraordinary and very interesting. It's your friendliness, good humor, and intelligence, no doubt.

The more peculiar people you meet in your travels will not shock you because you probably have in-laws just like them back home. You are not the typical tourist; you complain less and are enthusiastic even about privations. Your universalist philosophy helps you fit in and adapt to things that are different or a little unfamiliar. If snails, eels, or octopus are on the menu, you'll probably be willing to try them. You'll even learn to enjoy the flavor of French coffee and learn to like smoking Gauloise cigarettes (which I'm told are the world's worst tobacco product and unfit for burning even in greenhouses to discourage bugs).

Your tenth sector of profession and reputation is Scorpio, a sign often implying pressure. Aquarians do not require ideal working conditions, though they might prefer them. Noise and confusion do not bother Aquarians, and sudden changes of plans on the part of bosses do not bother them either. But they do balk about taking orders. Your best bet is to agree with the boss and say you'll do things his or her way. Then go right on doing your work your way, the right way.

Scorpio is ruled by Mars and Pluto, and Pluto's influence on your professional sector can make you abandon a paying job quite suddenly, sometimes to your temporary disadvantage. Sometimes, you even abandon your career in order to take up an entirely new endeavor, only to finally abandon corporate work to go into your own business.

You surprise everyone, even yourself, by your enterprise and resourcefulness in cutting corners and finding success and satisfaction with your off-the-wall methods.

Your eleventh sector of friends is Sagittarius. This is a most important sector for you, for it is here that you get encouragement from enthusiastic friends, and often business opportunities. If you need a loan, they come through for you. If you have had a falling out with your spouse, they'll drink with you. If you have had a falling out with your lover, they'll help you find another, pronto. If you are suffering from an inflated ego, they'll stick a pin in it and bring you down to earth with a few well-meaning insults.

Your twelfth sector, alas, is gloomy Capricorn, and you have to fight the old devil—worry—from time to time. He gets on your back when you are tired and alone. He tells you that you are not practical enough, that you are disorganized, and that you will never make it. When you have had enough of his negative cynicism, run, do not walk, back into your eleventh sector, to fun and friends, who will be only too willing to walk with you on the bright side.

After you have pulled yourself back together, you might do well to consider some self-improvement ideas, such as being more efficient, more dependable, and more organized.

Do what is expected of you and a little more. Get rid of the clutter in your life. Dress a little less flamboyantly, but do go on being yourself, your better self.

### Haiku for Your Twelfth Sector

*Happy the mortal*
*Not bound by ego or fears,*
*Content with what is.*

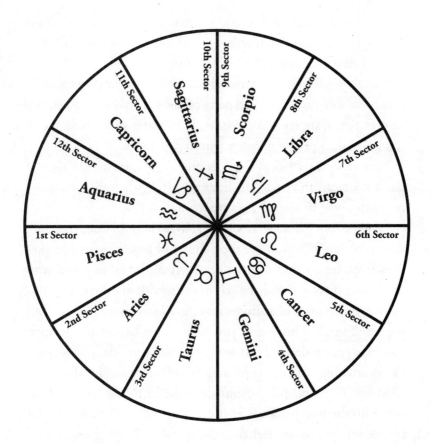

# *Pisces*

## Sun Sign or Rising Sign

With Pisces as your first sector, you are part softy and part dreamer, full of compassion and empathy for the unhappy rich and the unfortunate poor, for the orphans of the world, both four-legged and two-legged.

You were born to dance, romance, and to write great love letters and poignant poetry. You are in this world, but not entirely of this world, because of your mysticism and lapses in practicality, when your heart turns off your logic, in moments of high emotions (and there are many such moments). You can find a spark of goodness in people who have been rejected and misunderstood, and who have taken up bad habits and worse company.

Probably you have embarrassed your folks or your date on occasion by sobbing noisily at sad parts of plays and movies. Scientists suspect that Cancers and Pisceans, both water signs, have larger tear ducts than people of other signs of the zodiac.

Your second sector, of finances and talents, is Aries, a sign of quick decisions and haste, qualities you would do well to emulate, no matter how abhorrent they are to you.

While many Pisceans attain great wealth and fame, there are legions of you who consider these things of little importance, preferring spiritual riches and the obscurity of the solitary soul who goes about quietly sacrificing self in the service of others.

Your third sector of attitudes and ideas is stubborn, artistic, and musical Taurus. This means you have strong desires for security. You have your indecisive side and your stubborn side, and they are like alternating currents, confusing friends and enemies alike.

Many of the people in your life tend to lecture you and dis pense unsolicited practical advice, which you will probably not receive very graciously. Relatives come and go, helping sometimes, interfering often.

You are not always prompt. You may hate secretarial work and accounting, but there are still many useful things that you can do and like to do.

Your fourth sector of the home is Gemini, often indicating membership in a large family, many residential moves, or much travel, and sometimes involvement in a foster home or orphanage.

There is much discussion, debate, and many books in the Gemini's home. The escapist side of your nature is often the reason that some of your best friends are your books. The piano and the other stringed instruments are often of considerable interest to you, offering you hours of pleasure and enhancing your popularity.

You are more likely to find contentment in cities near an ocean or other body of water, and prefer a home that offers you quiet and privacy. Some of you fantasize about living on a boat or an island retreat, where you can run barefoot across warm sands and have less regular hours.

Your fifth sector, of lovers and children, is the romantic and sentimental Cancer. Your favorite illumination is candlelight and small colored bulbs. Most of you will bring out stemware and a bottle of wine on any romantic occasion, or when visitors drop by.

Being in love is a tremendously emotional experience for you, and your vulnerability and trusting nature have led you to do some pretty illogical things.

Cancer on this sector can lead to large families and much emotional wear and tear. With a water sign on the fifth house of pleasures, there is some possibility that you will eat sweets or drink in excess, which, as you know, dulls the senses and ruins the figure.

Your sixth sector is Leo. This is one of your vocational sectors, and it opens up prospects for teaching, the arts, theater, and administrative work. Many of you are not quite tough enough to make good bosses, but you could be the exception. The thing to watch out for on the job is letting yourself be imposed upon, taking too much time off, and coming in late.

You should try to avoid work that is too stressful or too routine. If you are on your feet a lot, you should wear sensible shoes. Many of you have special talents in the kitchen, and are attracted to work in the field of food. Chemistry, photography and personnel and social work are all in your area of competence.

Your seventh sector, of marriage and partnerships, is Virgo, and though this sign and your own are at polar extremes, they are complementary opposites, both quite adaptable and service oriented.

You may be rather casual about neatness and order, while Virgos can be quite obsessive about having the right things in the right place. The Virgo is logical, critical, and hard working, and you are more intuitive, less critical, and more indifferent to the work ethic.

The earth signs seem to think work is ennobling, while you may consider it boring. Realistically, you do have to pay your dues and put your shoulder to the wheel, and marriage is more than an eight-hour occupation and a non-union-pay job.

Your eighth sector, of other people's money and legacies, is Libra, the sign of partnerships. For your own security, in the event of the death of your business or marital partner, it is wise to invest in insurance policies when you are young, and to pay up your mortgages on property.

Your sign is dual-bodied and often indicates remarriage in the event of the loss of a partner through divorce or death.

Your ninth sector, of travel, philosophy, and religion, is Scorpio, the fixed water sign. You can be quite profound philosophically, and quite abstract in your attempts to explain your beliefs to others. You can be obsessively mystical, fatalistic, or militant about your religious opinions, to the point of seeming opinionated.

You love to think about travel, but may have problems making decisions because of obligations or financial concerns. When you do travel, circumstances tend to crop up to make it more than a mere transportation event.

Unforeseen circumstances that lead to high emotions and drama happen around you or to you. Your trip becomes an odyssey or series of tales that others feel are the fictional products of an overactive imagination. You should be a travel writer, not a travel consultant.

Your tenth sector of profession is Sagittarius, associated with colleges, churches, import-export businesses, and law offices. Sagittarian jobs may involve public relations, publishing, advertising, and the print or electronic media, and dealings with foreigners and companies with branch offices and franchise operations.

With the sign of Capricorn on your eleventh sector of goals, hopes, wishes, and desires, the realization of your cherished ambitions is apt to be tied in with the company you keep. You have in your circle of friends people dedicated to hard work and long hours. They talk to you of thrift and self-betterment. They sometimes try to use you by asking you to do favors, which they know you have difficulty refusing. If you take your time about complying, they are apt to criticize you or try to hurry you. You often feel embarrassed about asking them to pay you for work you have done for them. Sometimes they repay you in surprising or odd ways.

Your friends may recommend that you become a member of a club or organization in which you would feel quite uncomfortable. You often get involved in charitable organizations, but you are not always in agreement with the committee persons in charge.

Your twelfth sector, Aquarius, indicates you may have to mend some fences to keep your friends friendly. Friends with whom you lose rapport will tend to cut you off suddenly, and sometimes become not merely cool but openly hostile. The problem is often a failure in communication, leading to misunderstandings.

On the positive side, your warmth allows you to turn adversaries into supporters. You are periodically drawn into circumstances over which you have little control, and suffer losses that do not seem to be your fault. If you use your intuition positively, get out of the habit of singing the blues, and are as practical as your heart will let you be, you can live a life that has many high points. You will be able to handle responsibilities like a Capricorn and your love life like the heroines of romantic novels with happy endings.

You must give more of your energies to the positive and less to the negative, develop a sense of humor, and be choosy, like Virgos and Libras, in your choice of friends and lovers.

## Haiku for Your Twelfth Sector

*You wore but a rose,*
*Its petals dropped randomly*
*Over your body.*

# Tables to Determine Your Ascendant or Rising Sign

The following tables will show you your probable rising sign. These calculations are based on 40 degrees north latitude. You must have your hour of birth to determine your rising sign (Ascendant). If your specific birth date isn't shown, use the next closest.

## Interpretation of Symbols

| | | | |
|---|---|---|---|
| ♈ Aries | ⊗ Cancer | ♎ Libra | ♑ Capricorn |
| ♉ Taurus | ♌ Leo | ♏ Scorpio | ≋ Aquarius |
| ♊ Gemini | ♍ Virgo | ♐ Sagittarius | ♓ Pisces |

### JANUARY 1

| A.M. | | P.M. | |
|---|---|---|---|
| At 1 o'clock, | ♎ rises | At 1 o'clock, | ♉ rises |
| 2 | ♏ | 2 | ♊ |
| 3 | ♏ | 3 | ♊ |
| 4 | ♏ | 4 | ⊗ |
| 5 | ♐ | 5 | ⊗ |
| 6 | ♐ | 6 | ⊗ |
| 7 | ♑ | 7 | ♌ |
| 8 | ♑ | 8 | ♌ |
| 9 | ≋ | 9 | ♍ |
| 10 | ≋ | 10 | ♍ |
| 11 | ♓ | 11 | ♍ |
| 12, Noon, | ♈ | 12, Midn't, | ♎ |

### JANUARY 5

| A.M. | | P.M. | |
|---|---|---|---|
| At 1 o'clock, | ♎ rises | At 1 o'clock, | ♉ rises |
| 2 | ♏ | 2 | ♊ |
| 3 | ♏ | 3 | ♊ |
| 4 | ♏ | 4 | ⊗ |
| 5 | ♐ | 5 | ⊗ |
| 6 | ♐ | 6 | ♌ |
| 7 | ♑ | 7 | ♌ |
| 8 | ♑ | 8 | ♌ |
| 9 | ≋ | 9 | ♍ |
| 10 | ♓ | 10 | ♍ |
| 11 | ♓ | 11 | ♎ |
| 12, Noon, | ♈ | 12, Midn't, | ♎ |

## JANUARY 9

| A.M. | | | P.M. | | |
|---|---|---|---|---|---|
| At 1 o'clock, | ♎ | rises | At 1 o'clock, | ♉ | rises |
| 2 | ♏ | | 2 | ♊ | |
| 3 | ♏ | | 3 | ♊ | |
| 4 | ♐ | | 4 | ♋ | |
| 5 | ♐ | | 5 | ♋ | |
| 6 | ♐ | | 6 | ♌ | |
| 7 | ♑ | | 7 | ♌ | |
| 8 | ♑ | | 8 | ♌ | |
| 9 | ♒ | | 9 | ♍ | |
| 10 | ♓ | | 10 | ♍ | |
| 11 | ♈ | | 11 | ♍ | |
| 12, Noon, | ♉ | | 12, Midn't, | ♎ | |

## JANUARY 13

| A.M. | | | P.M. | | |
|---|---|---|---|---|---|
| At 1 o'clock, | ♎ | rises | At 1 o'clock, | ♉ | rises |
| 2 | ♏ | | 2 | ♊ | |
| 3 | ♏ | | 3 | ♊ | |
| 4 | ♐ | | 4 | ♋ | |
| 5 | ♐ | | 5 | ♋ | |
| 6 | ♑ | | 6 | ♌ | |
| 7 | ♑ | | 7 | ♌ | |
| 8 | ♒ | | 8 | ♍ | |
| 9 | ♒ | | 9 | ♍ | |
| 10 | ♓ | | 10 | ♍ | |
| 11 | ♈ | | 11 | ♎ | |
| 12, Noon, | ♉ | | 12, Midn't, | ♎ | |

## JANUARY 17

| A.M. | | | P.M. | | |
|---|---|---|---|---|---|
| At 1 o'clock, | ♏ | rises | At 1 o'clock, | ♊ | rises |
| 2 | ♏ | | 2 | ♊ | |
| 3 | ♏ | | 3 | ♋ | |
| 4 | ♐ | | 4 | ♋ | |
| 5 | ♐ | | 5 | ♋ | |
| 6 | ♑ | | 6 | ♌ | |
| 7 | ♑ | | 7 | ♌ | |
| 8 | ♒ | | 8 | ♍ | |
| 9 | ♒ | | 9 | ♍ | |
| 10 | ♓ | | 10 | ♍ | |
| 11 | ♈ | | 11 | ♎ | |
| 12, Noon, | ♉ | | 12, Midn't, | ♎ | |

## JANUARY 21

| A.M. | | P.M. | |
|---|---|---|---|
| At 1 o'clock, | ♏ rises | At 1 o'clock, | ♊ rises |
| 2 | ♏ | 2 | ♊ |
| 3 | ♏ | 3 | ♋ |
| 4 | ♐ | 4 | ♋ |
| 5 | ♐ | 5 | ♌ |
| 6 | ♑ | 6 | ♌ |
| 7 | ♑ | 7 | ♌ |
| 8 | ♒ | 8 | ♍ |
| 9 | ♓ | 9 | ♍ |
| 10 | ♈ | 10 | ♎ |
| 11 | ♈ | 11 | ♎ |
| 12, Noon, | ♉ | 12, Midn't, | ♎ |

## JANUARY 25

| A.M. | | P.M. | |
|---|---|---|---|
| At 1 o'clock, | ♏ rises | At 1 o'clock, | ♊ rises |
| 2 | ♏ | 2 | ♊ |
| 3 | ♐ | 3 | ♋ |
| 4 | ♐ | 4 | ♋ |
| 5 | ♐ | 5 | ♌ |
| 6 | ♑ | 6 | ♌ |
| 7 | ♑ | 7 | ♌ |
| 8 | ♒ | 8 | ♍ |
| 9 | ♓ | 9 | ♍ |
| 10 | ♈ | 10 | ♎ |
| 11 | ♉ | 11 | ♎ |
| 12, Noon, | ♉ | 12, Midn't, | ♎ |

## JANUARY 29

| A.M. | | P.M. | |
|---|---|---|---|
| At 1 o'clock, | ♏ rises | At 1 o'clock, | ♊ rises |
| 2 | ♏ | 2 | ♋ |
| 3 | ♐ | 3 | ♋ |
| 4 | ♐ | 4 | ♋ |
| 5 | ♑ | 5 | ♌ |
| 6 | ♑ | 6 | ♌ |
| 7 | ♒ | 7 | ♍ |
| 8 | ♒ | 8 | ♍ |
| 9 | ♓ | 9 | ♍ |
| 10 | ♈ | 10 | ♎ |
| 11 | ♉ | 11 | ♎ |
| 12, Noon, | ♉ | 12, Midn't, | ♏ |

## FEBRUARY 2

| A.M. | | P.M. | |
|---|---|---|---|
| At 1 o'clock, | ♏ rises | At 1 o'clock, | ♊ rises |
| 2 | ♏ | 2 | ♋ |
| 3 | ♐ | 3 | ♋ |
| 4 | ♐ | 4 | ♋ |
| 5 | ♑ | 5 | ♌ |
| 6 | ♑ | 6 | ♌ |
| 7 | ♒ | 7 | ♍ |
| 8 | ♓ | 8 | ♍ |
| 9 | ♓ | 9 | ♍ |
| 10 | ♈ | 10 | ♎ |
| 11 | ♉ | 11 | ♎ |
| 12, Noon, | ♊ | 12, Midn't, | ♏ |

## FEBRUARY 6

| A.M. | | P.M. | |
|---|---|---|---|
| At 1 o'clock, | ♏ rises | At 1 o'clock, | ♊ rises |
| 2 | ♏ | 2 | ♋ |
| 3 | ♐ | 3 | ♋ |
| 4 | ♐ | 4 | ♌ |
| 5 | ♑ | 5 | ♌ |
| 6 | ♑ | 6 | ♌ |
| 7 | ♒ | 7 | ♍ |
| 8 | ♓ | 8 | ♍ |
| 9 | ♈ | 9 | ♎ |
| 10 | ♈ | 10 | ♎ |
| 11 | ♉ | 11 | ♎ |
| 12, Noon, | ♊ | 12, Midn't, | ♏ |

## FEBRUARY 10

| A.M. | | P.M. | |
|---|---|---|---|
| At 1 o'clock, | ♏ rises | At 1 o'clock, | ♊ rises |
| 2 | ♐ | 2 | ♋ |
| 3 | ♐ | 3 | ♋ |
| 4 | ♐ | 4 | ♌ |
| 5 | ♑ | 5 | ♌ |
| 6 | ♑ | 6 | ♌ |
| 7 | ♒ | 7 | ♍ |
| 8 | ♓ | 8 | ♍ |
| 9 | ♈ | 9 | ♎ |
| 10 | ♉ | 10 | ♎ |
| 11 | ♉ | 11 | ♎ |
| 12, Noon, | ♊ | 12, Midn't, | ♏ |

## FEBRUARY 14

| A.M. | | | P.M. | | |
|---|---|---|---|---|---|
| At 1 o'clock, | ♏ | rises | At 1 o'clock, | ♋ | rises |
| 2 | ♐ | | 2 | ♋ | |
| 3 | ♐ | | 3 | ♋ | |
| 4 | ♑ | | 4 | ♌ | |
| 5 | ♑ | | 5 | ♌ | |
| 6 | ♒ | | 6 | ♍ | |
| 7 | ♒ | | 7 | ♍ | |
| 8 | ♓ | | 8 | ♍ | |
| 9 | ♈ | | 9 | ♎ | |
| 10 | ♉ | | 10 | ♎ | |
| 11 | ♉ | | 11 | ♏ | |
| 12, Noon, | ♊ | | 12, Midn't, | ♏ | |

## FEBRUARY 18

| A.M. | | | P.M. | | |
|---|---|---|---|---|---|
| At 1 o'clock, | ♏ | rises | At 1 o'clock, | ♋ | rises |
| 2 | ♐ | | 2 | ♋ | |
| 3 | ♐ | | 3 | ♋ | |
| 4 | ♑ | | 4 | ♌ | |
| 5 | ♑ | | 5 | ♌ | |
| 6 | ♒ | | 6 | ♍ | |
| 7 | ♓ | | 7 | ♍ | |
| 8 | ♓ | | 8 | ♍ | |
| 9 | ♈ | | 9 | ♎ | |
| 10 | ♉ | | 10 | ♎ | |
| 11 | ♊ | | 11 | ♏ | |
| 12, Noon, | ♊ | | 12, Midn't, | ♏ | |

## FEBRUARY 22

| A.M. | | | P.M. | | |
|---|---|---|---|---|---|
| At 1 o'clock, | ♐ | rises | At 1 o'clock, | ♋ | rises |
| 2 | ♐ | | 2 | ♋ | |
| 3 | ♐ | | 3 | ♌ | |
| 4 | ♑ | | 4 | ♌ | |
| 5 | ♑ | | 5 | ♌ | |
| 6 | ♒ | | 6 | ♍ | |
| 7 | ♓ | | 7 | ♍ | |
| 8 | ♈ | | 8 | ♎ | |
| 9 | ♈ | | 9 | ♎ | |
| 10 | ♉ | | 10 | ♎ | |
| 11 | ♊ | | 11 | ♏ | |
| 12, Noon, | ♊ | | 12, Midn't, | ♏ | |

## FEBRUARY 26

| A.M. | | | P.M. | | |
|---|---|---|---|---|---|
| At 1 o'clock, | ♐ | rises | At 1 o'clock, | ♋ | rises |
| 2 | ♐ | | 2 | ♋ | |
| 3 | ♐ | | 3 | ♌ | |
| 4 | ♑ | | 4 | ♌ | |
| 5 | ♒ | | 5 | ♌ | |
| 6 | ♒ | | 6 | ♍ | |
| 7 | ♓ | | 7 | ♍ | |
| 8 | ♈ | | 8 | ♎ | |
| 9 | ♉ | | 9 | ♎ | |
| 10 | ♉ | | 10 | ♎ | |
| 11 | ♊ | | 11 | ♏ | |
| 12, Noon, | ♊ | | 12, Midn't, | ♏ | |

## MARCH 2

| A.M. | | | P.M. | | |
|---|---|---|---|---|---|
| At 1 o'clock, | ♐ | rises | At 1 o'clock, | ♋ | rises |
| 2 | ♐ | | 2 | ♋ | |
| 3 | ♑ | | 3 | ♌ | |
| 4 | ♑ | | 4 | ♌ | |
| 5 | ♒ | | 5 | ♍ | |
| 6 | ♒ | | 6 | ♍ | |
| 7 | ♓ | | 7 | ♍ | |
| 8 | ♈ | | 8 | ♎ | |
| 9 | ♉ | | 9 | ♎ | |
| 10 | ♊ | | 10 | ♏ | |
| 11 | ♊ | | 11 | ♏ | |
| 12, Noon, | ♋ | | 12, Midn't, | ♏ | |

## MARCH 6

| A.M. | | | P.M. | | |
|---|---|---|---|---|---|
| At 1 o'clock, | ♐ | rises | At 1 o'clock, | ♋ | rises |
| 2 | ♐ | | 2 | ♌ | |
| 3 | ♑ | | 3 | ♌ | |
| 4 | ♑ | | 4 | ♌ | |
| 5 | ♒ | | 5 | ♍ | |
| 6 | ♓ | | 6 | ♍ | |
| 7 | ♓ | | 7 | ♍ | |
| 8 | ♈ | | 8 | ♎ | |
| 9 | ♉ | | 9 | ♎ | |
| 10 | ♊ | | 10 | ♏ | |
| 11 | ♊ | | 11 | ♏ | |
| 12, Noon, | ♋ | | 12, Midn't, | ♏ | |

## MARCH 10

| A.M. | | | P.M. | | |
|---|---|---|---|---|---|
| At 1 o'clock, | ♐ | rises | At 1 o'clock, | ♋ | rises |
| 2 | ♐ | | 2 | ♌ | |
| 3 | ♑ | | 3 | ♌ | |
| 4 | ♑ | | 4 | ♌ | |
| 5 | ♒ | | 5 | ♍ | |
| 6 | ♓ | | 6 | ♍ | |
| 7 | ♈ | | 7 | ♎ | |
| 8 | ♉ | | 8 | ♎ | |
| 9 | ♉ | | 9 | ♎ | |
| 10 | ♊ | | 10 | ♏ | |
| 11 | ♊ | | 11 | ♏ | |
| 12, Noon, | ♋ | | 12, Midn't, | ♐ | |

## MARCH 14

| A.M. | | | P.M. | | |
|---|---|---|---|---|---|
| At 1 o'clock, | ♐ | rises | At 1 o'clock, | ♋ | rises |
| 2 | ♑ | | 2 | ♌ | |
| 3 | ♑ | | 3 | ♌ | |
| 4 | ♒ | | 4 | ♍ | |
| 5 | ♒ | | 5 | ♍ | |
| 6 | ♓ | | 6 | ♍ | |
| 7 | ♈ | | 7 | ♎ | |
| 8 | ♉ | | 8 | ♎ | |
| 9 | ♉ | | 9 | ♎ | |
| 10 | ♊ | | 10 | ♏ | |
| 11 | ♊ | | 11 | ♏ | |
| 12, Noon, | ♋ | | 12, Midn't, | ♐ | |

## MARCH 18

| A.M. | | | P.M. | | |
|---|---|---|---|---|---|
| At 1 o'clock, | ♐ | rises | At 1 o'clock, | ♋ | rises |
| 2 | ♑ | | 2 | ♌ | |
| 3 | ♑ | | 3 | ♌ | |
| 4 | ♒ | | 4 | ♍ | |
| 5 | ♒ | | 5 | ♍ | |
| 6 | ♓ | | 6 | ♍ | |
| 7 | ♈ | | 7 | ♎ | |
| 8 | ♉ | | 8 | ♎ | |
| 9 | ♊ | | 9 | ♏ | |
| 10 | ♊ | | 10 | ♏ | |
| 11 | ♋ | | 11 | ♏ | |
| 12, Noon, | ♋ | | 12, Midn't, | ♐ | |

## MARCH 22

| A.M. | | P.M. | |
|---|---|---|---|
| At 1 o'clock, | ♐ rises | At 1 o'clock, | ♌ rises |
| 2 | ♑ | 2 | ♌ |
| 3 | ♑ | 3 | ♌ |
| 4 | ♒ | 4 | ♍ |
| 5 | ♓ | 5 | ♍ |
| 6 | ♈ | 6 | ♎ |
| 7 | ♈ | 7 | ♎ |
| 8 | ♉ | 8 | ♎ |
| 9 | ♊ | 9 | ♏ |
| 10 | ♊ | 10 | ♏ |
| 11 | ♋ | 11 | ♏ |
| 12, Noon, | ♋ | 12, Midn't, | ♐ |

## MARCH 26

| A.M. | | P.M. | |
|---|---|---|---|
| At 1 o'clock, | ♐ rises | At 1 o'clock, | ♌ rises |
| 2 | ♑ | 2 | ♌ |
| 3 | ♑ | 3 | ♌ |
| 4 | ♒ | 4 | ♍ |
| 5 | ♓ | 5 | ♍ |
| 6 | ♈ | 6 | ♎ |
| 7 | ♉ | 7 | ♎ |
| 8 | ♉ | 8 | ♎ |
| 9 | ♊ | 9 | ♏ |
| 10 | ♊ | 10 | ♏ |
| 11 | ♋ | 11 | ♐ |
| 12, Noon, | ♋ | 12, Midn't, | ♐ |

## MARCH 30

| A.M. | | P.M. | |
|---|---|---|---|
| At 1 o'clock, | ♑ rises | At 1 o'clock, | ♌ rises |
| 2 | ♑ | 2 | ♌ |
| 3 | ♒ | 3 | ♍ |
| 4 | ♒ | 4 | ♍ |
| 5 | ♓ | 5 | ♍ |
| 6 | ♈ | 6 | ♎ |
| 7 | ♉ | 7 | ♎ |
| 8 | ♉ | 8 | ♏ |
| 9 | ♊ | 9 | ♏ |
| 10 | ♋ | 10 | ♏ |
| 11 | ♋ | 11 | ♐ |
| 12, Noon, | ♋ | 12, Midn't, | ♐ |

## APRIL 3

| A.M. | | | P.M. | | |
|---|---|---|---|---|---|
| At 1 o'clock, | ♑ | rises | At 1 o'clock, | ♌ | rises |
| 2 | ♑ | | 2 | ♌ | |
| 3 | ♒ | | 3 | ♍ | |
| 4 | ♓ | | 4 | ♍ | |
| 5 | ♓ | | 5 | ♍ | |
| 6 | ♈ | | 6 | ♎ | |
| 7 | ♉ | | 7 | ♎ | |
| 8 | ♊ | | 8 | ♏ | |
| 9 | ♊ | | 9 | ♏ | |
| 10 | ♋ | | 10 | ♏ | |
| 11 | ♋ | | 11 | ♐ | |
| 12, Noon, | ♋ | | 12, Midn't, | ♐ | |

## APRIL 7

| A.M. | | | P.M. | | |
|---|---|---|---|---|---|
| At 1 o'clock, | ♑ | rises | At 1 o'clock, | ♌ | rises |
| 2 | ♑ | | 2 | ♌ | |
| 3 | ♒ | | 3 | ♍ | |
| 4 | ♓ | | 4 | ♍ | |
| 5 | ♈ | | 5 | ♎ | |
| 6 | ♈ | | 6 | ♎ | |
| 7 | ♉ | | 7 | ♎ | |
| 8 | ♊ | | 8 | ♏ | |
| 9 | ♊ | | 9 | ♏ | |
| 10 | ♋ | | 10 | ♏ | |
| 11 | ♋ | | 11 | ♐ | |
| 12, Noon, | ♌ | | 12, Midn't, | ♐ | |

## APRIL 10

| A.M. | | | P.M. | | |
|---|---|---|---|---|---|
| At 1 o'clock, | ♑ | rises | At 1 o'clock, | ♌ | rises |
| 2 | ♑ | | 2 | ♌ | |
| 3 | ♒ | | 3 | ♍ | |
| 4 | ♓ | | 4 | ♍ | |
| 5 | ♈ | | 5 | ♎ | |
| 6 | ♉ | | 6 | ♎ | |
| 7 | ♉ | | 7 | ♎ | |
| 8 | ♊ | | 8 | ♏ | |
| 9 | ♊ | | 9 | ♏ | |
| 10 | ♋ | | 10 | ♐ | |
| 11 | ♋ | | 11 | ♐ | |
| 12, Noon, | ♌ | | 12, Midn't, | ♐ | |

## APRIL 14

| A.M. | | P.M. | |
|---|---|---|---|
| At 1 o'clock, | ♑ rises | At 1 o'clock, | ♌ rises |
| 2 | ♒ | 2 | ♍ |
| 3 | ♒ | 3 | ♍ |
| 4 | ♓ | 4 | ♍ |
| 5 | ♈ | 5 | ♎ |
| 6 | ♉ | 6 | ♎ |
| 7 | ♉ | 7 | ♏ |
| 8 | ♊ | 8 | ♏ |
| 9 | ♊ | 9 | ♏ |
| 10 | ♋ | 10 | ♐ |
| 11 | ♋ | 11 | ♐ |
| 12, Noon, | ♌ | 12, Midn't, | ♑ |

## APRIL 18

| A.M. | | P.M. | |
|---|---|---|---|
| At 1 o'clock, | ♑ rises | At 1 o'clock, | ♌ rises |
| 2 | ♒ | 2 | ♍ |
| 3 | ♓ | 3 | ♍ |
| 4 | ♓ | 4 | ♍ |
| 5 | ♈ | 5 | ♎ |
| 6 | ♉ | 6 | ♎ |
| 7 | ♊ | 7 | ♏ |
| 8 | ♊ | 8 | ♏ |
| 9 | ♋ | 9 | ♏ |
| 10 | ♋ | 10 | ♐ |
| 11 | ♋ | 11 | ♐ |
| 12, Noon, | ♌ | 12, Midn't, | ♑ |

## APRIL 22

| A.M. | | P.M. | |
|---|---|---|---|
| At 1 o'clock, | ♑ rises | At 1 o'clock, | ♌ rises |
| 2 | ♒ | 2 | ♍ |
| 3 | ♓ | 3 | ♍ |
| 4 | ♈ | 4 | ♎ |
| 5 | ♈ | 5 | ♎ |
| 6 | ♉ | 6 | ♎ |
| 7 | ♊ | 7 | ♏ |
| 8 | ♊ | 8 | ♏ |
| 9 | ♋ | 9 | ♏ |
| 10 | ♋ | 10 | ♐ |
| 11 | ♌ | 11 | ♐ |
| 12, Noon, | ♌ | 12, Midn't, | ♑ |

## APRIL 26

| A.M. | | | P.M. | | |
|---|---|---|---|---|---|
| At 1 o'clock, | ♑ | rises | At 1 o'clock, | ♌ | rises |
| 2 | ♒ | | 2 | ♍ | |
| 3 | ♓ | | 3 | ♍ | |
| 4 | ♈ | | 4 | ♎ | |
| 5 | ♉ | | 5 | ♎ | |
| 6 | ♉ | | 6 | ♎ | |
| 7 | ♊ | | 7 | ♏ | |
| 8 | ♊ | | 8 | ♏ | |
| 9 | ♋ | | 9 | ♐ | |
| 10 | ♋ | | 10 | ♐ | |
| 11 | ♌ | | 11 | ♐ | |
| 12, Noon, | ♌ | | 12, Midn't, | ♑ | |

## APRIL 30

| A.M. | | | P.M. | | |
|---|---|---|---|---|---|
| At 1 o'clock, | ♒ | rises | At 1 o'clock, | ♍ | rises |
| 2 | ♒ | | 2 | ♍ | |
| 3 | ♓ | | 3 | ♍ | |
| 4 | ♈ | | 4 | ♎ | |
| 5 | ♉ | | 5 | ♎ | |
| 6 | ♉ | | 6 | ♏ | |
| 7 | ♊ | | 7 | ♏ | |
| 8 | ♋ | | 8 | ♏ | |
| 9 | ♋ | | 9 | ♐ | |
| 10 | ♋ | | 10 | ♐ | |
| 11 | ♌ | | 11 | ♑ | |
| 12, Noon, | ♌ | | 12, Midn't, | ♑ | |

## MAY 4

| A.M. | | | P.M. | | |
|---|---|---|---|---|---|
| At 1 o'clock, | ♒ | rises | At 1 o'clock, | ♍ | rises |
| 2 | ♓ | | 2 | ♍ | |
| 3 | ♓ | | 3 | ♍ | |
| 4 | ♈ | | 4 | ♎ | |
| 5 | ♉ | | 5 | ♎ | |
| 6 | ♊ | | 6 | ♏ | |
| 7 | ♊ | | 7 | ♏ | |
| 8 | ♋ | | 8 | ♏ | |
| 9 | ♋ | | 9 | ♐ | |
| 10 | ♋ | | 10 | ♐ | |
| 11 | ♌ | | 11 | ♑ | |
| 12, Noon, | ♌ | | 12, Midn't, | ♑ | |

## MAY 8

| A.M. | | | P.M. | | |
|---|---|---|---|---|---|
| At 1 o'clock, | ♒ | rises | At 1 o'clock, | ♍ | rises |
| 2 | ♓ | | 2 | ♍ | |
| 3 | ♈ | | 3 | ♎ | |
| 4 | ♈ | | 4 | ♎ | |
| 5 | ♉ | | 5 | ♎ | |
| 6 | ♊ | | 6 | ♏ | |
| 7 | ♊ | | 7 | ♏ | |
| 8 | ♋ | | 8 | ♐ | |
| 9 | ♋ | | 9 | ♐ | |
| 10 | ♌ | | 10 | ♐ | |
| 11 | ♌ | | 11 | ♑ | |
| 12, Noon, | ♌ | | 12, Midn't, | ♑ | |

## MAY 12

| A.M. | | | P.M. | | |
|---|---|---|---|---|---|
| At 1 o'clock, | ♒ | rises | At 1 o'clock, | ♍ | rises |
| 2 | ♓ | | 2 | ♍ | |
| 3 | ♈ | | 3 | ♎ | |
| 4 | ♉ | | 4 | ♎ | |
| 5 | ♉ | | 5 | ♎ | |
| 6 | ♊ | | 6 | ♏ | |
| 7 | ♊ | | 7 | ♏ | |
| 8 | ♋ | | 8 | ♐ | |
| 9 | ♋ | | 9 | ♐ | |
| 10 | ♌ | | 10 | ♐ | |
| 11 | ♌ | | 11 | ♑ | |
| 12, Noon, | ♌ | | 12, Midn't, | ♒ | |

## MAY 16

| A.M. | | | P.M. | | |
|---|---|---|---|---|---|
| At 1 o'clock, | ♒ | rises | At 1 o'clock, | ♍ | rises |
| 2 | ♓ | | 2 | ♍ | |
| 3 | ♈ | | 3 | ♎ | |
| 4 | ♉ | | 4 | ♎ | |
| 5 | ♊ | | 5 | ♏ | |
| 6 | ♊ | | 6 | ♏ | |
| 7 | ♋ | | 7 | ♏ | |
| 8 | ♋ | | 8 | ♐ | |
| 9 | ♋ | | 9 | ♐ | |
| 10 | ♌ | | 10 | ♑ | |
| 11 | ♌ | | 11 | ♑ | |
| 12, Noon, | ♍ | | 12, Midn't, | ♑ | |

## MAY 20

| A.M. | | | P.M. | | |
|---|---|---|---|---|---|
| At 1 o'clock, | ♓ | rises | At 1 o'clock, | ♍ | rises |
| 2 | ♓ | | 2 | ♍ | |
| 3 | ♈ | | 3 | ♎ | |
| 4 | ♉ | | 4 | ♎ | |
| 5 | ♊ | | 5 | ♏ | |
| 6 | ♊ | | 6 | ♏ | |
| 7 | ♋ | | 7 | ♏ | |
| 8 | ♋ | | 8 | ♐ | |
| 9 | ♌ | | 9 | ♐ | |
| 10 | ♌ | | 10 | ♑ | |
| 11 | ♌ | | 11 | ♑ | |
| 12, Noon, | ♍ | | 12, Midn't, | ♒ | |

## MAY 24

| A.M. | | | P.M. | | |
|---|---|---|---|---|---|
| At 1 o'clock, | ♓ | rises | At 1 o'clock, | ♍ | rises |
| 2 | ♈ | | 2 | ♎ | |
| 3 | ♈ | | 3 | ♎ | |
| 4 | ♉ | | 4 | ♎ | |
| 5 | ♊ | | 5 | ♏ | |
| 6 | ♊ | | 6 | ♏ | |
| 7 | ♋ | | 7 | ♐ | |
| 8 | ♋ | | 8 | ♐ | |
| 9 | ♌ | | 9 | ♐ | |
| 10 | ♌ | | 10 | ♑ | |
| 11 | ♌ | | 11 | ♑ | |
| 12, Noon, | ♍ | | 12, Midn't, | ♓ | |

## MAY 28

| A.M. | | | P.M. | | |
|---|---|---|---|---|---|
| At 1 o'clock, | ♓ | rises | At 1 o'clock, | ♍ | rises |
| 2 | ♈ | | 2 | ♎ | |
| 3 | ♉ | | 3 | ♎ | |
| 4 | ♉ | | 4 | ♎ | |
| 5 | ♊ | | 5 | ♏ | |
| 6 | ♊ | | 6 | ♏ | |
| 7 | ♋ | | 7 | ♐ | |
| 8 | ♋ | | 8 | ♐ | |
| 9 | ♌ | | 9 | ♐ | |
| 10 | ♌ | | 10 | ♑ | |
| 11 | ♌ | | 11 | ♒ | |
| 12, Noon, | ♍ | | 12, Midn't, | ♒ | |

## JUNE 1

| A.M. | | | P.M. | | |
|---|---|---|---|---|---|
| At 1 o'clock, | ♓ | rises | At 1 o'clock, | ♍ | rises |
| 2 | ♈ | | 2 | ♎ | |
| 3 | ♉ | | 3 | ♎ | |
| 4 | ♊ | | 4 | ♏ | |
| 5 | ♊ | | 5 | ♏ | |
| 6 | ♋ | | 6 | ♏ | |
| 7 | ♋ | | 7 | ♐ | |
| 8 | ♋ | | 8 | ♐ | |
| 9 | ♌ | | 9 | ♑ | |
| 10 | ♌ | | 10 | ♑ | |
| 11 | ♍ | | 11 | ♒ | |
| 12, Noon, | ♍ | | 12, Midn't, | ♒ | |

## JUNE 5

| A.M. | | | P.M. | | |
|---|---|---|---|---|---|
| At 1 o'clock, | ♓ | rises | At 1 o'clock, | ♍ | rises |
| 2 | ♈ | | 2 | ♎ | |
| 3 | ♉ | | 3 | ♎ | |
| 4 | ♊ | | 4 | ♏ | |
| 5 | ♊ | | 5 | ♏ | |
| 6 | ♋ | | 6 | ♏ | |
| 7 | ♋ | | 7 | ♐ | |
| 8 | ♌ | | 8 | ♐ | |
| 9 | ♌ | | 9 | ♑ | |
| 10 | ♌ | | 10 | ♑ | |
| 11 | ♍ | | 11 | ♒ | |
| 12, Noon, | ♍ | | 12, Midn't, | ♓ | |

## JUNE 9

| A.M. | | | P.M. | | |
|---|---|---|---|---|---|
| At 1 o'clock, | ♈ | rises | At 1 o'clock, | ♎ | rises |
| 2 | ♈ | | 2 | ♎ | |
| 3 | ♉ | | 3 | ♎ | |
| 4 | ♊ | | 4 | ♏ | |
| 5 | ♊ | | 5 | ♏ | |
| 6 | ♋ | | 6 | ♐ | |
| 7 | ♋ | | 7 | ♐ | |
| 8 | ♌ | | 8 | ♐ | |
| 9 | ♌ | | 9 | ♑ | |
| 10 | ♌ | | 10 | ♑ | |
| 11 | ♍ | | 11 | ♒ | |
| 12, Noon, | ♍ | | 12, Midn't, | ♓ | |

## JUNE 13

| A.M. | | | P.M. | | |
|---|---|---|---|---|---|
| At 1 o'clock, | ♈ | rises | At 1 o'clock, | ♎ | rises |
| 2 | ♉ | | 2 | ♎ | |
| 3 | ♉ | | 3 | ♎ | |
| 4 | ♊ | | 4 | ♏ | |
| 5 | ♊ | | 5 | ♏ | |
| 6 | ♋ | | 6 | ♐ | |
| 7 | ♋ | | 7 | ♐ | |
| 8 | ♌ | | 8 | ♐ | |
| 9 | ♌ | | 9 | ♑ | |
| 10 | ♌ | | 10 | ♒ | |
| 11 | ♍ | | 11 | ♒ | |
| 12, Noon, | ♍ | | 12, Midn't, | ♓ | |

## JUNE 17

| A.M. | | | P.M. | | |
|---|---|---|---|---|---|
| At 1 o'clock, | ♈ | rises | At 1 o'clock, | ♎ | rises |
| 2 | ♉ | | 2 | ♎ | |
| 3 | ♊ | | 3 | ♏ | |
| 4 | ♊ | | 4 | ♏ | |
| 5 | ♋ | | 5 | ♏ | |
| 6 | ♋ | | 6 | ♐ | |
| 7 | ♋ | | 7 | ♐ | |
| 8 | ♌ | | 8 | ♑ | |
| 9 | ♌ | | 9 | ♑ | |
| 10 | ♍ | | 10 | ♒ | |
| 11 | ♍ | | 11 | ♒ | |
| 12, Noon, | ♍ | | 12, Midn't, | ♓ | |

## JUNE 21

| A.M. | | | P.M. | | |
|---|---|---|---|---|---|
| At 1 o'clock, | ♈ | rises | At 1 o'clock, | ♎ | rises |
| 2 | ♉ | | 2 | ♎ | |
| 3 | ♊ | | 3 | ♏ | |
| 4 | ♊ | | 4 | ♏ | |
| 5 | ♋ | | 5 | ♏ | |
| 6 | ♋ | | 6 | ♐ | |
| 7 | ♌ | | 7 | ♐ | |
| 8 | ♌ | | 8 | ♑ | |
| 9 | ♌ | | 9 | ♑ | |
| 10 | ♍ | | 10 | ♒ | |
| 11 | ♍ | | 11 | ♓ | |
| 12, Noon, | ♍ | | 12, Midn't, | ♓ | |

## JUNE 25

| A.M. | | | P.M. | | |
|---|---|---|---|---|---|
| At 1 o'clock, | ♉ | rises | At 1 o'clock, | ♎ | rises |
| 2 | ♉ | | 2 | ♎ | |
| 3 | ♊ | | 3 | ♏ | |
| 4 | ♊ | | 4 | ♏ | |
| 5 | ♋ | | 5 | ♐ | |
| 6 | ♋ | | 6 | ♐ | |
| 7 | ♌ | | 7 | ♐ | |
| 8 | ♌ | | 8 | ♑ | |
| 9 | ♌ | | 9 | ♑ | |
| 10 | ♍ | | 10 | ♒ | |
| 11 | ♍ | | 11 | ♓ | |
| 12, Noon, | ♎ | | 12, Midn't, | ♈ | |

## JUNE 29

| A.M. | | | P.M. | | |
|---|---|---|---|---|---|
| At 1 o'clock, | ♉ | rises | At 1 o'clock, | ♎ | rises |
| 2 | ♉ | | 2 | ♎ | |
| 3 | ♊ | | 3 | ♏ | |
| 4 | ♊ | | 4 | ♏ | |
| 5 | ♋ | | 5 | ♐ | |
| 6 | ♋ | | 6 | ♐ | |
| 7 | ♌ | | 7 | ♑ | |
| 8 | ♌ | | 8 | ♑ | |
| 9 | ♍ | | 9 | ♒ | |
| 10 | ♍ | | 10 | ♒ | |
| 11 | ♍ | | 11 | ♓ | |
| 12, Noon, | ♎ | | 12, Midn't, | ♈ | |

## JULY 3

| A.M. | | | P.M. | | |
|---|---|---|---|---|---|
| At 1 o'clock, | ♉ | rises | At 1 o'clock, | ♎ | rises |
| 2 | ♊ | | 2 | ♏ | |
| 3 | ♊ | | 3 | ♏ | |
| 4 | ♋ | | 4 | ♏ | |
| 5 | ♋ | | 5 | ♐ | |
| 6 | ♋ | | 6 | ♐ | |
| 7 | ♌ | | 7 | ♑ | |
| 8 | ♌ | | 8 | ♑ | |
| 9 | ♍ | | 9 | ♒ | |
| 10 | ♍ | | 10 | ♒ | |
| 11 | ♍ | | 11 | ♓ | |
| 12, Noon, | ♎ | | 12, Midn't, | ♈ | |

## JULY 7

| A.M. | | | P.M. | | |
|---|---|---|---|---|---|
| At 1 o'clock, | ♉ | rises | At 1 o'clock, | ♎ | rises |
| 2 | ♊ | | 2 | ♏ | |
| 3 | ♊ | | 3 | ♏ | |
| 4 | ♋ | | 4 | ♏ | |
| 5 | ♋ | | 5 | ♐ | |
| 6 | ♌ | | 6 | ♐ | |
| 7 | ♌ | | 7 | ♑ | |
| 8 | ♌ | | 8 | ♑ | |
| 9 | ♍ | | 9 | ♒ | |
| 10 | ♍ | | 10 | ♓ | |
| 11 | ♍ | | 11 | ♈ | |
| 12, Noon, | ♎ | | 12, Midn't, | ♈ | |

## JULY 11

| A.M. | | | P.M. | | |
|---|---|---|---|---|---|
| At 1 o'clock, | ♉ | rises | At 1 o'clock, | ♎ | rises |
| 2 | ♊ | | 2 | ♏ | |
| 3 | ♊ | | 3 | ♏ | |
| 4 | ♋ | | 4 | ♐ | |
| 5 | ♋ | | 5 | ♐ | |
| 6 | ♌ | | 6 | ♐ | |
| 7 | ♌ | | 7 | ♑ | |
| 8 | ♌ | | 8 | ♑ | |
| 9 | ♍ | | 9 | ♒ | |
| 10 | ♍ | | 10 | ♓ | |
| 11 | ♎ | | 11 | ♈ | |
| 12, Noon, | ♎ | | 12, Midn't, | ♉ | |

## JULY 14

| A.M. | | | P.M. | | |
|---|---|---|---|---|---|
| At 1 o'clock, | ♉ | rises | At 1 o'clock, | ♎ | rises |
| 2 | ♊ | | 2 | ♏ | |
| 3 | ♊ | | 3 | ♏ | |
| 4 | ♋ | | 4 | ♐ | |
| 5 | ♋ | | 5 | ♐ | |
| 6 | ♌ | | 6 | ♑ | |
| 7 | ♌ | | 7 | ♑ | |
| 8 | ♌ | | 8 | ♒ | |
| 9 | ♏ | | 9 | ♒ | |
| 10 | ♏ | | 10 | ♓ | |
| 11 | ♎ | | 11 | ♈ | |
| 12, Noon, | ♎ | | 12, Midn't, | ♉ | |

## JULY 18

| A.M. | | P.M. | |
|---|---|---|---|
| At 1 o'clock, | ♊ rises | At 1 o'clock, | ♏ rises |
| 2 | ♊ | 2 | ♏ |
| 3 | ♋ | 3 | ♏ |
| 4 | ♋ | 4 | ♐ |
| 5 | ♋ | 5 | ♐ |
| 6 | ♌ | 6 | ♑ |
| 7 | ♌ | 7 | ♑ |
| 8 | ♏ | 8 | ♒ |
| 9 | ♑ | 9 | ♒ |
| 10 | ♍ | 10 | ♓ |
| 11 | ♎ | 11 | ♈ |
| 12, Noon, | ♎ | 12, Midn't, | ♉ |

## JULY 22

| A.M. | | P.M. | |
|---|---|---|---|
| At 1 o'clock, | ♊ rises | At 1 o'clock, | ♏ rises |
| 2 | ♊ | 2 | ♏ |
| 3 | ♋ | 3 | ♏ |
| 4 | ♋ | 4 | ♐ |
| 5 | ♌ | 5 | ♐ |
| 6 | ♌ | 6 | ♑ |
| 7 | ♌ | 7 | ♑ |
| 8 | ♍ | 8 | ♒ |
| 9 | ♍ | 9 | ♓ |
| 10 | ♍ | 10 | ♓ |
| 11 | ♎ | 11 | ♈ |
| 12, Noon, | ♎ | 12, Midn't, | ♉ |

## JULY 26

| A.M. | | P.M. | |
|---|---|---|---|
| At 1 o'clock, | ♊ rises | At 1 o'clock, | ♏ rises |
| 2 | ♊ | 2 | ♏ |
| 3 | ♋ | 3 | ♐ |
| 4 | ♋ | 4 | ♐ |
| 5 | ♌ | 5 | ♐ |
| 6 | ♌ | 6 | ♑ |
| 7 | ♌ | 7 | ♑ |
| 8 | ♍ | 8 | ♒ |
| 9 | ♍ | 9 | ♓ |
| 10 | ♎ | 10 | ♈ |
| 11 | ♎ | 11 | ♉ |
| 12, Noon, | ♎ | 12, Midn't, | ♉ |

## JULY 30

| A.M. | | | P.M. | | |
|---|---|---|---|---|---|
| At 1 o'clock, | ♊ | rises | At 1 o'clock, | ♏ | rises |
| 2 | ♊ | | 2 | ♏ | |
| 3 | ⊗ | | 3 | ♐ | |
| 4 | ⊗ | | 4 | ♐ | |
| 5 | ♌ | | 5 | ♑ | |
| 6 | ♌ | | 6 | ♑ | |
| 7 | ♍ | | 7 | ♒ | |
| 8 | ♍ | | 8 | ♒ | |
| 9 | ♍ | | 9 | ♓ | |
| 10 | ♎ | | 10 | ♈ | |
| 11 | ♎ | | 11 | ♉ | |
| 12, Noon, | ♎ | | 12, Midn't, | ♉ | |

## AUGUST 3

| A.M. | | | P.M. | | |
|---|---|---|---|---|---|
| At 1 o'clock, | ♊ | rises | At 1 o'clock, | ♏ | rises |
| 2 | ⊗ | | 2 | ♏ | |
| 3 | ⊗ | | 3 | ♐ | |
| 4 | ⊗ | | 4 | ♐ | |
| 5 | ♌ | | 5 | ♑ | |
| 6 | ♌ | | 6 | ♑ | |
| 7 | ♍ | | 7 | ♒ | |
| 8 | ♍ | | 8 | ♒ | |
| 9 | ♍ | | 9 | ♓ | |
| 10 | ♎ | | 10 | ♈ | |
| 11 | ♎ | | 11 | ♉ | |
| 12, Noon, | ♏ | | 12, Midn't, | ♊ | |

## AUGUST 7

| A.M. | | | P.M. | | |
|---|---|---|---|---|---|
| At 1 o'clock, | ♊ | rises | At 1 o'clock, | ♏ | rises |
| 2 | ⊗ | | 2 | ♏ | |
| 3 | ⊗ | | 3 | ♐ | |
| 4 | ♌ | | 4 | ♐ | |
| 5 | ♌ | | 5 | ♑ | |
| 6 | ♌ | | 6 | ♑ | |
| 7 | ♍ | | 7 | ♒ | |
| 8 | ♍ | | 8 | ♓ | |
| 9 | ♎ | | 9 | ♈ | |
| 10 | ♎ | | 10 | ♈ | |
| 11 | ♈ | | 11 | ♉ | |
| 12, Noon, | ♏ | | 12, Midn't, | ♊ | |

## AUGUST 11

| A.M. | | | P.M. | | |
|---|---|---|---|---|---|
| At 1 o'clock, | ♊ | rises | At 1 o'clock, | ♏ | rises |
| 2 | ♋ | | 2 | ♐ | |
| 3 | ♋ | | 3 | ♐ | |
| 4 | ♌ | | 4 | ♐ | |
| 5 | ♌ | | 5 | ♑ | |
| 6 | ♌ | | 6 | ♑ | |
| 7 | ♍ | | 7 | ♒ | |
| 8 | ♍ | | 8 | ♓ | |
| 9 | ♎ | | 9 | ♈ | |
| 10 | ♎ | | 10 | ♉ | |
| 11 | ♎ | | 11 | ♉ | |
| 12, Noon, | ♏ | | 12, Midn't, | ♊ | |

## AUGUST 15

| A.M. | | | P.M. | | |
|---|---|---|---|---|---|
| At 1 o'clock, | ♋ | rises | At 1 o'clock, | ♏ | rises |
| 2 | ♋ | | 2 | ♐ | |
| 3 | ♋ | | 3 | ♐ | |
| 4 | ♌ | | 4 | ♑ | |
| 5 | ♌ | | 5 | ♑ | |
| 6 | ♍ | | 6 | ♒ | |
| 7 | ♍ | | 7 | ♒ | |
| 8 | ♍ | | 8 | ♓ | |
| 9 | ♎ | | 9 | ♈ | |
| 10 | ♎ | | 10 | ♉ | |
| 11 | ♏ | | 11 | ♉ | |
| 12, Noon, | ♏ | | 12, Midn't, | ♊ | |

## AUGUST 19

| A.M. | | | P.M. | | |
|---|---|---|---|---|---|
| At 1 o'clock, | ♋ | rises | At 1 o'clock, | ♏ | rises |
| 2 | ♋ | | 2 | ♐ | |
| 3 | ♋ | | 3 | ♐ | |
| 4 | ♌ | | 4 | ♑ | |
| 5 | ♌ | | 5 | ♑ | |
| 6 | ♍ | | 6 | ♒ | |
| 7 | ♍ | | 7 | ♓ | |
| 8 | ♍ | | 8 | ♓ | |
| 9 | ♎ | | 9 | ♈ | |
| 10 | ♎ | | 10 | ♉ | |
| 11 | ♏ | | 11 | ♊ ♉ | |
| 12, Noon, | ♏ | | 12, Midn't, | ♊ | |

## AUGUST 23

| A.M. | | | P.M. | | |
|---|---|---|---|---|---|
| At 1 o'clock, | ♋ | rises | At 1 o'clock, | ♐ | rises |
| 2 | ♋ | | 2 | ♐ | |
| 3 | ♌ | | 3 | ♐ | |
| 4 | ♌ | | 4 | ♑ | |
| 5 | ♌ | | 5 | ♑ | |
| 6 | ♍ | | 6 | ♒ | |
| 7 | ♍ | | 7 | ♓ | |
| 8 | ♎ | | 8 | ♈ | |
| 9 | ♎ | | 9 | ♈ | |
| 10 | ♎ | | 10 | ♉ | |
| 11 | ♏ | | 11 | ♊ | |
| 12, Noon, | ♏ | | 12, Midn't, | ♊ | |

## AUGUST 27

| A.M. | | | P.M. | | |
|---|---|---|---|---|---|
| At 1 o'clock, | ♋ | rises | At 1 o'clock, | ♐ | rises |
| 2 | ♋ | | 2 | ♐ | |
| 3 | ♌ | | 3 | ♐ | |
| 4 | ♌ | | 4 | ♑ | |
| 5 | ♌ | | 5 | ♑ | |
| 6 | ♍ | | 6 | ♒ | |
| 7 | ♍ | | 7 | ♓ | |
| 8 | ♎ | | 8 | ♈ | |
| 9 | ♎ | | 9 | ♉ | |
| 10 | ♎ | | 10 | ♉ | |
| 11 | ♏ | | 11 | ♊ | |
| 12, Noon, | ♏ | | 12, Midn't, | ♊ | |

## AUGUST 31

| A.M. | | | P.M. | | |
|---|---|---|---|---|---|
| At 1 o'clock, | ♋ | rises | At 1 o'clock, | ♐ | rises |
| 2 | ♋ | | 2 | ♐ | |
| 3 | ♌ | | 3 | ♑ | |
| 4 | ♌ | | 4 | ♑ | |
| 5 | ♍ | | 5 | ♒ | |
| 6 | ♍ | | 6 | ♒ | |
| 7 | ♍ | | 7 | ♓ | |
| 8 | ♎ | | 8 | ♈ | |
| 9 | ♎ | | 9 | ♉ | |
| 10 | ♏ | | 10 | ♊ | |
| 11 | ♏ | | 11 | ♊ | |
| 12, Noon, | ♏ | | 12, Midn't, | ♋ | |

## SEPTEMBER 4

| A.M. | | | P.M. | | |
|---|---|---|---|---|---|
| At 1 o'clock, | ♋ | rises | At 1 o'clock, | ♐ | rises |
| 2 | ♋ | | 2 | ♐ | |
| 3 | ♌ | | 3 | ♑ | |
| 4 | ♌ | | 4 | ♑ | |
| 5 | ♍ | | 5 | ♒ | |
| 6 | ♍ | | 6 | ♓ | |
| 7 | ♍ | | 7 | ♓ | |
| 8 | ♎ | | 8 | ♈ | |
| 9 | ♎ | | 9 | ♉ | |
| 10 | ♏ | | 10 | ♊ | |
| 11 | ♏ | | 11 | ♊ | |
| 12, Noon, | ♏ | | 12, Midn't, | ♋ | |

## SEPTEMBER 8

| A.M. | | | P.M. | | |
|---|---|---|---|---|---|
| At 1 o'clock, | ♋ | rises | At 1 o'clock, | ♐ | rises |
| 2 | ♌ | | 2 | ♐ | |
| 3 | ♌ | | 3 | ♑ | |
| 4 | ♌ | | 4 | ♑ | |
| 5 | ♍ | | 5 | ♒ | |
| 6 | ♍ | | 6 | ♓ | |
| 7 | ♎ | | 7 | ♈ | |
| 8 | ♎ | | 8 | ♈ | |
| 9 | ♎ | | 9 | ♉ | |
| 10 | ♏ | | 10 | ♊ | |
| 11 | ♏ | | 11 | ♊ | |
| 12, Noon, | ♏ | | 12, Midn't, | ♋ | |

## SEPTEMBER 12

| A.M. | | | P.M. | | |
|---|---|---|---|---|---|
| At 1 o'clock, | ♋ | rises | At 1 o'clock, | ♐ | rises |
| 2 | ♌ | | 2 | ♐ | |
| 3 | ♌ | | 3 | ♑ | |
| 4 | ♌ | | 4 | ♒ | |
| 5 | ♍ | | 5 | ♒ | |
| 6 | ♍ | | 6 | ♓ | |
| 7 | ♎ | | 7 | ♈ | |
| 8 | ♎ | | 8 | ♉ | |
| 9 | ♎ | | 9 | ♉ | |
| 10 | ♏ | | 10 | ♊ | |
| 11 | ♏ | | 11 | ♊ | |
| 12, Noon, | ♐ | | 12, Midn't, | ♋ | |

## SEPTEMBER 16

| A.M. | | | P.M. | | |
|---|---|---|---|---|---|
| At 1 o'clock, | ♋ | rises | At 1 o'clock, | ♐ | rises |
| 2 | ♌ | | 2 | ♑ | |
| 3 | ♌ | | 3 | ♑ | |
| 4 | ♍ | | 4 | ♒ | |
| 5 | ♍ | | 5 | ♒ | |
| 6 | ♍ | | 6 | ♓ | |
| 7 | ♎ | | 7 | ♈ | |
| 8 | ♎ | | 8 | ♉ | |
| 9 | ♏ | | 9 | ♊ | |
| 10 | ♏ | | 10 | ♊ | |
| 11 | ♏ | | 11 | ♋ | |
| 12, Noon, | ♐ | | 12, Midn't, | ♋ | |

## SEPTEMBER 20

| A.M. | | | P.M. | | |
|---|---|---|---|---|---|
| At 1 o'clock, | ♌ | rises | At 1 o'clock, | ♐ | rises |
| 2 | ♌ | | 2 | ♑ | |
| 3 | ♌ | | 3 | ♑ | |
| 4 | ♍ | | 4 | ♒ | |
| 5 | ♍ | | 5 | ♓ | |
| 6 | ♍ | | 6 | ♓ | |
| 7 | ♎ | | 7 | ♈ | |
| 8 | ♎ | | 8 | ♉ | |
| 9 | ♏ | | 9 | ♊ | |
| 10 | ♏ | | 10 | ♊ | |
| 11 | ♏ | | 11 | ♋ | |
| 12, Noon, | ♐ | | 12, Midn't, | ♋ | |

## SEPTEMBER 24

| A.M. | | | P.M. | | |
|---|---|---|---|---|---|
| At 1 o'clock, | ♌ | rises | At 1 o'clock, | ♑ | rises |
| 2 | ♌ | | 2 | ♑ | |
| 3 | ♌ | | 3 | ♑ | |
| 4 | ♍ | | 4 | ♒ | |
| 5 | ♍ | | 5 | ♓ | |
| 6 | ♎ | | 6 | ♈ | |
| 7 | ♎ | | 7 | ♉ | |
| 8 | ♎ | | 8 | ♉ | |
| 9 | ♏ | | 9 | ♊ | |
| 10 | ♏ | | 10 | ♊ | |
| 11 | ♐ | | 11 | ♋ | |
| 12, Noon, | ♐ | | 12, Midn't, | ♋ | |

## SEPTEMBER 28

| A.M. | | | P.M. | | |
|---|---|---|---|---|---|
| At 1 o'clock, | ♌ | rises | At 1 o'clock, | ♑ | rises |
| 2 | ♌ | | 2 | ♑ | |
| 3 | ♌ | | 3 | ♒ | |
| 4 | ♍ | | 4 | ♒ | |
| 5 | ♍ | | 5 | ♓ | |
| 6 | ♎ | | 6 | ♈ | |
| 7 | ♎ | | 7 | ♉ | |
| 8 | ♎ | | 8 | ♉ | |
| 9 | ♏ | | 9 | ♊ | |
| 10 | ♏ | | 10 | ♊ | |
| 11 | ♐ | | 11 | ♋ | |
| 12, Noon, | ♐ | | 12, Midn't, | ♋ | |

## OCTOBER 2

| A.M. | | | P.M. | | |
|---|---|---|---|---|---|
| At 1 o'clock, | ♌ | rises | At 1 o'clock, | ♑ | rises |
| 2 | ♌ | | 2 | ♑ | |
| 3 | ♍ | | 3 | ♒ | |
| 4 | ♍ | | 4 | ♒ | |
| 5 | ♍ | | 5 | ♓ | |
| 6 | ♎ | | 6 | ♈ | |
| 7 | ♎ | | 7 | ♉ | |
| 8 | ♏ | | 8 | ♊ | |
| 9 | ♏ | | 9 | ♊ | |
| 10 | ♏ | | 10 | ♋ | |
| 11 | ♐ | | 11 | ♋ | |
| 12, Noon, | ♐ | | 12, Midn't, | ♋ | |

## OCTOBER 6

| A.M. | | | P.M. | | |
|---|---|---|---|---|---|
| At 1 o'clock, | ♌ | rises | At 1 o'clock, | ♑ | rises |
| 2 | ♌ | | 2 | ♑ | |
| 3 | ♍ | | 3 | ♒ | |
| 4 | ♍ | | 4 | ♓ | |
| 5 | ♍ | | 5 | ♈ | |
| 6 | ♎ | | 6 | ♈ | |
| 7 | ♎ | | 7 | ♉ | |
| 8 | ♏ | | 8 | ♊ | |
| 9 | ♏ | | 9 | ♊ | |
| 10 | ♏ | | 10 | ♋ | |
| 11 | ♐ | | 11 | ♋ | |
| 12, Noon, | ♐ | | 12, Midn't, | ♌ | |

## OCTOBER 10

| A.M. | | | P.M. | | |
|---|---|---|---|---|---|
| At 1 o'clock, | ♌ | rises | At 1 o'clock, | ♑ | rises |
| 2 | ♌ | | 2 | ♑ | |
| 3 | ♍ | | 3 | ♒ | |
| 4 | ♍ | | 4 | ♓ | |
| 5 | ♎ | | 5 | ♈ | |
| 6 | ♎ | | 6 | ♉ | |
| 7 | ♎ | | 7 | ♉ | |
| 8 | ♏ | | 8 | ♊ | |
| 9 | ♏ | | 9 | ♊ | |
| 10 | ♐ | | 10 | ♋ | |
| 11 | ♐ | | 11 | ♋ | |
| 12, Noon, | ♐ | | 12, Midn't, | ♌ | |

## OCTOBER 14

| A.M. | | | P.M. | | |
|---|---|---|---|---|---|
| At 1 o'clock, | ♌ | rises | At 1 o'clock, | ♑ | rises |
| 2 | ♍ | | 2 | ♒ | |
| 3 | ♍ | | 3 | ♒ | |
| 4 | ♍ | | 4 | ♓ | |
| 5 | ♎ | | 5 | ♈ | |
| 6 | ♎ | | 6 | ♉ | |
| 7 | ♎ | | 7 | ♉ | |
| 8 | ♏ | | 8 | ♊ | |
| 9 | ♏ | | 9 | ♊ | |
| 10 | ♐ | | 10 | ♋ | |
| 11 | ♐ | | 11 | ♋ | |
| 12, Noon, | ♑ | | 12, Midn't, | ♌ | |

## OCTOBER 18

| A.M. | | | P.M. | | |
|---|---|---|---|---|---|
| At 1 o'clock, | ♌ | rises | At 1 o'clock, | ♑ | rises |
| 2 | ♍ | | 2 | ♒ | |
| 3 | ♍ | | 3 | ♒ | |
| 4 | ♍ | | 4 | ♓ | |
| 5 | ♎ | | 5 | ♈ | |
| 6 | ♎ | | 6 | ♉ | |
| 7 | ♏ | | 7 | ♊ | |
| 8 | ♏ | | 8 | ♊ | |
| 9 | ♏ | | 9 | ♋ | |
| 10 | ♐ | | 10 | ♋ | |
| 11 | ♐ | | 11 | ♋ | |
| 12, Noon, | ♑ | | 12, Midn't, | ♌ | |

## OCTOBER 22

| A.M. | | | P.M. | | |
|---|---|---|---|---|---|
| At 1 o'clock, | ♌ | rises | At 1 o'clock, | ♑ | rises |
| 2 | ♍ | | 2 | ♒ | |
| 3 | ♍ | | 3 | ♓ | |
| 4 | ♎ | | 4 | ♈ | |
| 5 | ♎ | | 5 | ♈ | |
| 6 | ♎ | | 6 | ♉ | |
| 7 | ♏ | | 7 | ♊ | |
| 8 | ♏ | | 8 | ♊ | |
| 9 | ♏ | | 9 | ♋ | |
| 10 | ♐ | | 10 | ♋ | |
| 11 | ♐ | | 11 | ♌ | |
| 12, Noon, | ♑ | | 12, Midn't, | ♌ | |

## OCTOBER 26

| A.M. | | | P.M. | | |
|---|---|---|---|---|---|
| At 1 o'clock, | ♌ | rises | At 1 o'clock, | ♑ | rises |
| 2 | ♍ | | 2 | ♒ | |
| 3 | ♍ | | 3 | ♓ | |
| 4 | ♎ | | 4 | ♈ | |
| 5 | ♎ | | 5 | ♉ | |
| 6 | ♎ | | 6 | ♉ | |
| 7 | ♏ | | 7 | ♊ | |
| 8 | ♏ | | 8 | ♊ | |
| 9 | ♐ | | 9 | ♋ | |
| 10 | ♐ | | 10 | ♋ | |
| 11 | ♐ | | 11 | ♌ | |
| 12, Noon, | ♑ | | 12, Midn't, | ♌ | |

## OCTOBER 30

| A.M. | | | P.M. | | |
|---|---|---|---|---|---|
| At 1 o'clock, | ♍ | rises | At 1 o'clock, | ♒ | rises |
| 2 | ♍ | | 2 | ♒ | |
| 3 | ♍ | | 3 | ♓ | |
| 4 | ♎ | | 4 | ♈ | |
| 5 | ♎ | | 5 | ♉ | |
| 6 | ♏ | | 6 | ♉ | |
| 7 | ♏ | | 7 | ♊ | |
| 8 | ♏ | | 8 | ♋ | |
| 9 | ♐ | | 9 | ♋ | |
| 10 | ♐ | | 10 | ♋ | |
| 11 | ♑ | | 11 | ♌ | |
| 12, Noon, | ♑ | | 12, Midn't, | ♌ | |

### NOVEMBER 3

| A.M. | | | P.M. | | |
|---|---|---|---|---|---|
| At 1 o'clock, | ♍ | rises | At 1 o'clock, | ♒ | rises |
| 2 | ♍ | | 2 | ♓ | |
| 3 | ♍ | | 3 | ♓ | |
| 4 | ♎ | | 4 | ♈ | |
| 5 | ♎ | | 5 | ♉ | |
| 6 | ♏ | | 6 | ♊ | |
| 7 | ♏ | | 7 | ♊ | |
| 8 | ♏ | | 8 | ♋ | |
| 9 | ♐ | | 9 | ♋ | |
| 10 | ♐ | | 10 | ♋ | |
| 11 | ♑ | | 11 | ♌ | |
| 12, Noon, | ♑ | | 12, Midn't, | ♌ | |

### NOVEMBER 7

| A.M. | | | P.M. | | |
|---|---|---|---|---|---|
| At 1 o'clock, | ♍ | rises | At 1 o'clock, | ♒ | rises |
| 2 | ♍ | | 2 | ♓ | |
| 3 | ♎ | | 3 | ♈ | |
| 4 | ♎ | | 4 | ♈ | |
| 5 | ♎ | | 5 | ♉ | |
| 6 | ♏ | | 6 | ♊ | |
| 7 | ♏ | | 7 | ♊ | |
| 8 | ♏ | | 8 | ♋ | |
| 9 | ♐ | | 9 | ♋ | |
| 10 | ♐ | | 10 | ♌ | |
| 11 | ♑ | | 11 | ♌ | |
| 12, Noon, | ♑ | | 12, Midn't, | ♌ | |

### NOVEMBER 11

| A.M. | | | P.M. | | |
|---|---|---|---|---|---|
| At 1 o'clock, | ♍ | rises | At 1 o'clock, | ♒ | rises |
| 2 | ♍ | | 2 | ♓ | |
| 3 | ♎ | | 3 | ♈ | |
| 4 | ♎ | | 4 | ♉ | |
| 5 | ♎ | | 5 | ♉ | |
| 6 | ♏ | | 6 | ♊ | |
| 7 | ♏ | | 7 | ♊ | |
| 8 | ♐ | | 8 | ♋ | |
| 9 | ♐ | | 9 | ♋ | |
| 10 | ♐ | | 10 | ♌ | |
| 11 | ♑ | | 11 | ♌ | |
| 12, Noon, | ♑ | | 12, Midn't, | ♌ | |

## NOVEMBER 15

| A.M. | | | P.M. | | |
|------|------|------|------|------|------|
| At 1 o'clock, | ♍ | rises | At 1 o'clock, | ♒ | rises |
| 2 | ♍ | | 2 | ♓ | |
| 3 | ♎ | | 3 | ♈ | |
| 4 | ♎ | | 4 | ♉ | |
| 5 | ♏ | | 5 | ♊ | |
| 6 | ♏ | | 6 | ♊ | |
| 7 | ♏ | | 7 | ♋ | |
| 8 | ♐ | | 8 | ♋ | |
| 9 | ♐ | | 9 | ♋ | |
| 10 | ♑ | | 10 | ♌ | |
| 11 | ♑ | | 11 | ♌ | |
| 12, Noon, | ♒ | | 12, Midn't, | ♍ | |

## NOVEMBER 19

| A.M. | | | P.M. | | |
|------|------|------|------|------|------|
| At 1 o'clock, | ♍ | rises | At 1 o'clock, | ♓ | rises |
| 2 | ♍ | | 2 | ♓ | |
| 3 | ♎ | | 3 | ♈ | |
| 4 | ♎ | | 4 | ♉ | |
| 5 | ♏ | | 5 | ♊ | |
| 6 | ♏ | | 6 | ♊ | |
| 7 | ♏ | | 7 | ♋ | |
| 8 | ♐ | | 8 | ♋ | |
| 9 | ♐ | | 9 | ♋ | |
| 10 | ♑ | | 10 | ♌ | |
| 11 | ♑ | | 11 | ♌ | |
| 12, Noon, | ♒ | | 12, Midn't, | ♍ | |

## NOVEMBER 23

| A.M. | | | P.M. | | |
|------|------|------|------|------|------|
| At 1 o'clock, | ♍ | rises | At 1 o'clock, | ♓ | rises |
| 2 | ♎ | | 2 | ♈ | |
| 3 | ♎ | | 3 | ♈ | |
| 4 | ♎ | | 4 | ♉ | |
| 5 | ♏ | | 5 | ♊ | |
| 6 | ♏ | | 6 | ♊ | |
| 7 | ♐ | | 7 | ♋ | |
| 8 | ♐ | | 8 | ♋ | |
| 9 | ♐ | | 9 | ♌ | |
| 10 | ♑ | | 10 | ♌ | |
| 11 | ♑ | | 11 | ♌ | |
| 12, Noon, | ♒ | | 12, Midn't, | ♍ | |

## NOVEMBER 27

| A.M. | | | P.M. | | |
|---|---|---|---|---|---|
| At 1 o'clock, | ♍ | rises | At 1 o'clock, | ♓ | rises |
| 2 | ♎ | | 2 | ♈ | |
| 3 | ♎ | | 3 | ♉ | |
| 4 | ♎ | | 4 | ♉ | |
| 5 | ♏ | | 5 | ♊ | |
| 6 | ♏ | | 6 | ♊ | |
| 7 | ♐ | | 7 | ♋ | |
| 8 | ♐ | | 8 | ♋ | |
| 9 | ♐ | | 9 | ♌ | |
| 10 | ♑ | | 10 | ♌ | |
| 11 | ♒ | | 11 | ♌ | |
| 12, Noon, | ♒ | | 12, Midn't, | ♍ | |

## DECEMBER 1

| A.M. | | | P.M. | | |
|---|---|---|---|---|---|
| At 1 o'clock, | ♍ | rises | At 1 o'clock, | ♓ | rises |
| 2 | ♎ | | 2 | ♈ | |
| 3 | ♎ | | 3 | ♉ | |
| 4 | ♏ | | 4 | ♊ | |
| 5 | ♏ | | 5 | ♊ | |
| 6 | ♏ | | 6 | ♋ | |
| 7 | ♐ | | 7 | ♋ | |
| 8 | ♐ | | 8 | ♋ | |
| 9 | ♑ | | 9 | ♌ | |
| 10 | ♑ | | 10 | ♌ | |
| 11 | ♒ | | 11 | ♍ | |
| 12, Noon, | ♒ | | 12, Midn't, | ♍ | |

## DECEMBER 6

| A.M. | | | P.M. | | |
|---|---|---|---|---|---|
| At 1 o'clock, | ♍ | rises | At 1 o'clock, | ♓ | rises |
| 2 | ♎ | | 2 | ♈ | |
| 3 | ♎ | | 3 | ♉ | |
| 4 | ♏ | | 4 | ♊ | |
| 5 | ♏ | | 5 | ♊ | |
| 6 | ♏ | | 6 | ♋ | |
| 7 | ♐ | | 7 | ♋ | |
| 8 | ♐ | | 8 | ♋ | |
| 9 | ♑ | | 9 | ♌ | |
| 10 | ♑ | | 10 | ♌ | |
| 11 | ♒ | | 11 | ♍ | |
| 12, Noon, | ♓ | | 12, Midn't, | ♍ | |

### DECEMBER 9

| A.M. | | | P.M. | | |
|---|---|---|---|---|---|
| At 1 o'clock, | ♎ | rises | At 1 o'clock, | ♈ | rises |
| 2 | ♎ | | 2 | ♉ | |
| 3 | ♎ | | 3 | ♉ | |
| 4 | ♏ | | 4 | ♊ | |
| 5 | ♏ | | 5 | ♊ | |
| 6 | ♐ | | 6 | ♋ | |
| 7 | ♐ | | 7 | ♋ | |
| 8 | ♐ | | 8 | ♌ | |
| 9 | ♑ | | 9 | ♌ | |
| 10 | ♑ | | 10 | ♌ | |
| 11 | ♒ | | 11 | ♍ | |
| 12, Noon, | ♓ | | 12, Midn't, | ♍ | |

### DECEMBER 13

| A.M. | | | P.M. | | |
|---|---|---|---|---|---|
| At 1 o'clock, | ♎ | rises | At 1 o'clock, | ♈ | rises |
| 2 | ♎ | | 2 | ♉ | |
| 3 | ♎ | | 3 | ♉ | |
| 4 | ♏ | | 4 | ♊ | |
| 5 | ♏ | | 5 | ♊ | |
| 6 | ♐ | | 6 | ♋ | |
| 7 | ♐ | | 7 | ♋ | |
| 8 | ♐ | | 8 | ♌ | |
| 9 | ♑ | | 9 | ♌ | |
| 10 | ♒ | | 10 | ♍ | |
| 11 | ♒ | | 11 | ♍ | |
| 12, Noon, | ♓ | | 12, Midn't, | ♍ | |

### DECEMBER 18

| A.M. | | | P.M. | | |
|---|---|---|---|---|---|
| At 1 o'clock, | ♎ | rises | At 1 o'clock, | ♈ | rises |
| 2 | ♎ | | 2 | ♉ | |
| 3 | ♏ | | 3 | ♊ | |
| 4 | ♏ | | 4 | ♊ | |
| 5 | ♏ | | 5 | ♋ | |
| 6 | ♐ | | 6 | ♋ | |
| 7 | ♐ | | 7 | ♋ | |
| 8 | ♑ | | 8 | ♌ | |
| 9 | ♑ | | 9 | ♌ | |
| 10 | ♒ | | 10 | ♍ | |
| 11 | ♒ | | 11 | ♍ | |
| 12, Noon, | ♓ | | 12, Midn't, | ♍ | |

## DECEMBER 23

| A.M. | | | P.M. | | |
|---|---|---|---|---|---|
| At 1 o'clock, | ♎ | rises | At 1 o'clock, | ♈ | rises |
| 2 | ♎ | | 2 | ♉ | |
| 3 | ♏ | | 3 | ♊ | |
| 4 | ♏ | | 4 | ♊ | |
| 5 | ♐ | | 5 | ♋ | |
| 6 | ♐ | | 6 | ♋ | |
| 7 | ♐ | | 7 | ♌ | |
| 8 | ♑ | | 8 | ♌ | |
| 9 | ♑ | | 9 | ♌ | |
| 10 | ♒ | | 10 | ♍ | |
| 11 | ♓ | | 11 | ♍ | |
| 12, Noon, | ♈ | | 12, Midn't, | ♎ | |

## DECEMBER 28

| A.M. | | | P.M. | | |
|---|---|---|---|---|---|
| At 1 o'clock, | ♎ | rises | At 1 o'clock, | ♉ | rises |
| 2 | ♎ | | 2 | ♉ | |
| 3 | ♏ | | 3 | ♊ | |
| 4 | ♏ | | 4 | ♊ | |
| 5 | ♐ | | 5 | ♋ | |
| 6 | ♐ | | 6 | ♋ | |
| 7 | ♐ | | 7 | ♌ | |
| 8 | ♑ | | 8 | ♌ | |
| 9 | ♒ | | 9 | ♍ | |
| 10 | ♒ | | 10 | ♍ | |
| 11 | ♓ | | 11 | ♍ | |
| 12, Noon, | ♈ | | 12, Midn't, | ♎ | |

# $\mathcal{T}$HE FACE

## OF LOVE

### *chapter five*

*The world is a looking glass and gives back to every man the reflection of his own face.*
—William Makepeace Thackery

$\mathcal{W}$hy is it that we can always tell two new lovers by the way they gaze into each other's faces? What is it that each is seeing in the other's face? How magnetic the attraction between two faces!

The first thing most of us see in another person is his or her face. As we get to know someone, we begin noticing the expressiveness of the face, the finer details. As we get to know each other, we learn how to gauge each other's mood by finer and finer changes in expression: the partly raised brow, the slight twitch of the lips. Yet, it can take years before we can read these fine expressions for what they mean emotionally.

Since you spend a good deal of time looking into your lover's face, it would seem almost logical that here is an apt place to begin to learn more about him or her, and you don't have to apply that sometimes costly trial-and-error method learning the whence of the changes in expressions. The face itself, in repose, offers untold depths of information about your lover's character, and learning to read the face of your lover is as important as learning to match your lover's face with your own.

The ancient Chinese art of face reading, known to us as physiognomy, has been practiced in one form or another throughout the ages and in different parts of the world. According to the original Chinese school of thought, facial characteristics reveal a person's entire personal history, temperament, and destiny. One of the masters of physiognomy, Timothy Mar, states, "The face is a map of the past, present, and future." An expert in face reading will never mistake the loved for the unloved, the virtuous for the wicked, or vice versa. What each face reveals is there for the world to see.

Let's take a look at some of the basics of this art, to see how it can help us in our search for a more perfect lover. In the face lies not only a person's history, but character and temperament as well—those individual traits so necessary to know about one we would love.

# *Basic* Face Shapes

There are five basic shapes to faces; each shape says something about the general character of a person.

*Round Face.* This usually indicates an easy-going, good-natured individual who loves the comforts of life: physical comforts, the touch and feel of things, good food. People with round faces, generally speaking, are good lovers. This face shape corresponds to the endomorph type.

*Square Face.* This shape reflects a rugged, firm personality, and perhaps a temper. People with this shape of face are possible leaders and fighters; they are generally frank in both business and love affairs, and have strong drives for success. A square face corresponds with the mesomorph type.

*Semitriangular Face.* With a wide forehead and narrow (but not pointed) chin, the semitriangular face indicates a nonaggressive personality, a person with superior intelligence and artistic capacity. As a lover, this would be an affectionate person.

*Triangular Face.* Especially if the individual is thin and does not have an excess of flesh between the cheekbones and the chin, this shape reflects a sensitive personality. The tighter the skin, the more sensitive the person may be. This type of individual may become introverted, but he or she is extremely intelligent. People with triangular faces can be dreamers or they can be cunning; they can be jealous of and without loyalty to their lovers, or their sensitivity can work to overcome such traits. This shape corresponds to the ectomorph type.

*Oblong Face.* An oblong face is indicative of a lover who will be a success in life; this shape is often seen among aristocrats and those in positions of power. These are strong characters, powerful, often with an attitude that seems to say, "I deserve the best."

The more deeply you delve into your loved one's facial characteristics, the more detailed your knowledge of his or her true personality. So let's dig a little more deeply, and look at the areas of a person's face which must be analyzed.

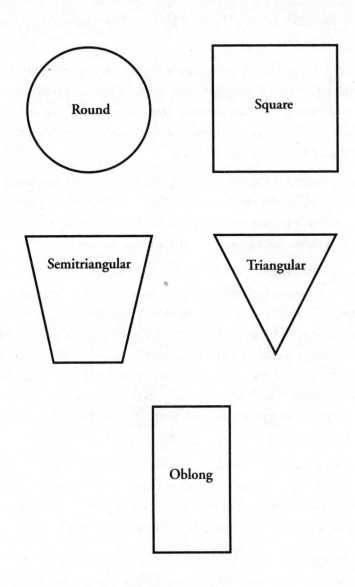

**Five basic face shapes**

# *B*asic Zones of the Face

Each person's face has three basic zones; ideally, these are in proportion and balanced, although the "ideal" seldom exists in fact.

Zone 1, the upper zone, is the area from the original hairline to the eyebrows. Zone 2, the middle zone, extends from the eyebrows to under the nose. Zone 3, the lower zone, takes in the area from under the nose to the bottom of the chin.

*Zone 1: The Upper Zone.* The forehead indicates the intellectual facilities. If the forehead is well developed, the person is generally bright. Ideally, the ears should be wide apart and the forehead long and high.

*Zone 2: The Middle Zone.* If this zone is long, in a face with a high forehead and a long lower zone, the individual possesses noble qualities. If the middle zone is too long in comparison with the other zones, the individual may be arrogant, but would be gifted with an adventurous spirit. If the zone is in ideal (equal) proportion with the other zones, the individual probably possesses a long life span.

*Zone 3: The Lower Zone.* If this zone is longer than the other zones, and is strong, wide, and perhaps fleshy, it indicates success and prosperity later in life. Now, if the chin is long but pointed, the individual probably needs to reorganize his (or her) outlook on life and learn to get along with others. People with this sort of lower zone characteristic should turn to science or philosophy and the arts, where they may find more spiritual awareness. A long and broad lower zone indicates a physically oriented person; a too narrow lower zone, a more mental than physical person who would have a great imagination where love is concerned.

**Three zones of your face**

Each part of each zone of the face has its own signals and signs; each has significance and bearing on the emotional life. Let's go even deeper in our search through the face's map, looking first at the eyebrows.

## *Eyebrows*

In some ways the meanings we attach to the old expressions "highbrow" and "lowbrow" are similar to the Chinese face readers' interpretations of the high or low-browed person. The higher the brow, the stronger the interest in higher things; the lower the brow, the stronger the interest in purely physical things, and the less the attraction to the abstract and the aesthetic.

The ideal eyebrow would be long and elegant, forming a gentle arch over the eye (above).

When the outer, thinner end of the brow turns upward, a great deal of courage and strength of heart are indicated. This lover will stick with you during bad times.

If the outer, thinner end is long and curves downward from an arch, the person is very probably a peaceful individual, long-lived and with a prosperous future. Life would be rich and free from strife with such a lover.

A short and thick eyebrow indicates a personality that expresses loyalty to family, filled with an aggressive spirit.

If the eyebrow hair tends to grow in two directions, beware—this may well indicate an inflexible, uncompromising lover.

Imagination, foresight, and courage are indicated if the eyebrows slant upward from the outer eye. An exciting love affair is indicated.

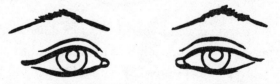

The "boomerang" eyebrow shows a person who has good ideas and the capacity to execute them. A dominant person with strong sexual magnetism is indicated here, as well as someone who is self-confident and follows his or her own advice, including advice on affairs of the heart.

Eyebrows that meet very closely often mean a personality filled with determination and resourcefulness—the lover who will invent ways to woo you once his or her mind is made up about you.

If the eyebrows are actually joined together and run in a straight line, the personality is forceful and unconcerned about society's opinions. These are usually straightforward people.

## *Eyes*

Now to the eyes—the most telling aspect of anyone's face. We'll dwell a bit longer here, for the eyes are the most important single aspect of the face, truly the mirror of our hearts and souls. It was during my studies on face reading with my brilliant teacher Dr. Charles V. Kuntz that I learned the importance of the eyes. In a healthy body, the eyes' brilliance—or lack of it—can reveal more than a thousand pages on a person's life and loves.

First, look for the glitter in the eyes. The look often called "starry-eyed" says, "I possess *joie de vivre*." This glitter varies in all of us, depending upon our states of awareness, for it is a reflection of what the ancients called the "Divine Spark." Perhaps you've noticed that when you've fallen in love on a deep and pure level, when you become interested in broadening your horizons, or when you become more desirous of improving your self and developing a wider awareness of your world, your life has ceased its dullness and the jewels in your eyes begin to show themselves.

Our eyes reflect the alertness we have toward life on all its varied and exciting levels. Lackluster, sparkless eyes in an otherwise healthy body show a lack of enthusiasm toward living and loving.

Perhaps you've encountered someone with magnetic eyes that seem to have power over you and over entire groups of people at once. Look more closely at that person's eyes; they have that sparkle, and the stronger their magnetic attraction, the brighter they shine and sparkle.

It seems that once we are truly interested in improving our consciousness, an interest in our health develops. We have become aware that our bodies truly are the temples of our souls. This new respect for our bodies starts to show immediately in the form of added luster in the eyes.

If you want a lover who will not only be the life of the party, but who will be a happy person and an inspiration to you and others as well, look for the person whose eyes glitter.

Dr. Wayne Brown, another master of face reading, points out an additional important aspect of the eyes: their steadiness. The more control a person has over his or her ability to maintain a steady glare, the more dependable that person is. We've all heard of the shifty-eyed person, and we all understand the implications of that expression. There is a truth behind almost every cliche, and this is not one of the exceptions. Shifty or unsteady gazes indicate that the person needs to develop more confidence and dependability.

Shifty-eyed people, even those who have developed that mirrored-soul glitter, need to direct their inner vitalities toward more constructive use, and need to avoid impetuous actions against others.

Try to discern whether the glitter in the eyes of your lover is controlled or uncontrolled. Controlled (steady gazing) glitter is ideal; but if it is completely uncontrolled, it could reveal a person who is a potential (or actual) fanatic. Controlled glitter exudes peace and is possessed by those who seem to own a hidden, happy secret.

The size of a person's eyes are a third important aspect.

*Large Eyes.* The larger your lover's eyes, the more sensitive he or she is.

*Smaller Eyes.* On the other hand, smaller eyes indicate steadfastness in your lover.

Pupil size is another sign of emotional difference. Under equal light conditions, the pupils of different individuals vary in size.

*Large Pupils.* These generally indicate warmth, kindness, gentleness, and devotion to loved ones. The person with larger pupils is more open to others' feelings.

***Smaller Pupils.*** These indicate that the person's actions toward others are based in primitive power, and that he or she is discontented.

The size of one's irises—the colored part of the eye surrounding the pupil—reveal as much as the size of the pupils about a person's emotional capacities.

***Large Irises.*** These may show a lack of an adventurous spirit, but they also reveal a sympathetic and conservative character. The affections of this person are less trapped; these are the people who laugh and cry more easily.

***Small Irises.*** This person is matter-of-fact and expects little demonstrativeness. This is the person who may need encouragement to show emotion, or he or she will feel awkward in such an exhibition.

When you look at someone's eyes, you can determine if the person has the same general outlook on life as you have, if his or her eyes are set similarly to yours. Are your eyes set more closely together than average, or more widely apart? How about your lover's? As a gauge, think of the average distance between eyes as approximately the length of one eye.

***Close Eyes.*** These people tend toward specificity in their lives—focusing on the details of the objective world in order to draw their conclusions. In the negative extreme, these can be people who are narrow-minded.

***Eyes Far Apart.*** Do you and your lover see eye to eye? In general, the more widely spaced the eyes, the more broad-minded the individual. Widely set eyes may indicate a person with the capacity to dramatically broaden his or her horizons without too much effort.

All the eyes' elements must be understood together to be meaningful. But once you have mastered this art, you will be able to tell much of a person's individuality and capacity for the kind of romance you seek.

Eye contact—the look you give and receive when meeting another person—says far more than the words of greeting that are exchanged. A smile is priceless in its communicative powers, too, and one is able to smile with the eyes as well as with the lips.

Whether or not we have studied face reading, we are all aware of that indefinable something which passes between two people's eyes when they meet. This first contact can spark an interest and attraction between two people, or it can do the opposite. Practice paying attention to this inner sensitivity that may tell you more about the people you meet than all the conversation that follows.

No matter what kind of eyes you may have, you can use them for so much more than merely looking at the obvious physical world. Learn to listen with them. Train them to "talk." Eyes can be our most effective means of communication.

Remember to treat yourself to the thoughts of your most cherished wishes and desires—instead of your fears. These thoughts are reflected in your eyes, and your eyes will tell your happy story. Who ever was attracted to gloom?

As we've said, you'll find that as your thoughts begin to change toward more positive emotions and desires, you will most likely begin to take better care of your body. As you follow good eating habits—avoiding junk foods, refined table sugar, white, refined, bleached flour, artificial stimulants, and preservatives—your eyes will take on a healthy appeal and a new attractiveness. Your skin condition will improve and your hair will take on an added gleam, no matter what your age.

After all, there is truth in the cliche, "We are what we eat." Behind that is the truth that we are what we think. Remember: "*Mens sana in corpore sano*—In a healthy body dwells a healthy mind." All this is reflected in your eyes.

# Nose

Knowing the nose is another valuable guide from the art of face reading. Again, we must use this in conjunction with all the features of the face in order to get a true picture. Just as in graphology and palmistry, the whole story of a person's character cannot be read into one feature alone. Right now, we are gathering together the clues in a person's face—the clues that will help build the complete picture.

What are some of the clues which the nose can provide? The ideal length of the nose is said to be one-third the length of the face. For convenience's sake, we'll use this as our starting point, terming anything less than this a short nose, and anything over this a long nose.

The ideal—which is almost impossible to find—is one that is not only one-third the length of the face, but is straight, with the inside of the nostrils unseen when it is viewed directly from the front. The tip of the ideal nose would be well rounded, with the wings (outside of the nostrils) perfectly formed—not too wide for the face shape.

It seems that noses have more varieties in shape than any other single feature. This obviously means a great deviation from the ideal in nature, and this alone tells us much about the importance of individual noses as guides to differences in character.

Let's look at the two extremes in length first.

**Short Nose.** Indicates a person who is more flexible, more naturally likeable and open-hearted, and sometimes impetuous. People with short noses perform their work on the basis of emotional impulse. They thrive on strokes, and in love they should be given pats on the back as well.

**Long Nose.** Here is the person with a good temperament and a strong sense of authority. It's not surprising to find that a long-nosed person is sexually overactive. These are a proud and mercurial people, with seriousness and refined tastes, as well as with a strong sense of responsibility and conscientiousness in work habits. Inflexibility is another trait of the person with an extremely long nose.

If the nose is very large, as well as long, and if it extends high above the eyes, the person is self-willed, perhaps stubborn, and most likely will insist on having his or her own way in the relationship—and on being obeyed.

The nose's shape is a more detailed indicator of the basic character underneath. There are convex noses, concave noses, narrow ones, and flat ones. Each tells a different story.

*Convex Nose.* This person is business-like and generally must make an effort to express inner joy and emotion. He or she may have to try harder to express the happiness he feels when he does a lover a good turn. If your lover has a convex nose, you'll have to help him or her by expressing your own happiness at his efforts in making your relationship a better one. Incidentally, this shape also indicates someone who has the capacity to be aggressive in chasing the dollar—an important point to keep in mind if material things are of value to you.

*Concave Nose.* Just as concave is the opposite of convex, the character reflection of this nose is the opposite to that of the convex nose. Here is someone who will gladly offer help when it is needed. He or she will express emotions and perhaps lavish them on a lover. Perhaps this generosity of self is also overextended in the realm of spending money.

**Narrow Nose.** An indication of a hard worker, both in business and love, especially when the bridge seems to have a sharp ridge.

**Flat, Large Nose.** If the bridge of the nose is flat and large, the person is a more calculating individual, capable of real coldness, especially when it comes to material gain. He or she can be a good and loyal lover if love has formed an integral part of his or her life and values.

## *Lips*

We've saved the most sensuous detail of the face for last: the lips. More than the words that pass between them, the lips can say volumes about your lover's inner self. And just like the words that pass between them, the lips symbolize the meeting of the inner and outer worlds. Both the shape and movement of the lips silently express inner love, and silently receive it from the outside. Our lips are actually structured by our thinking.

Let's look into some of the secrets of the two basic lip shapes.

**Thin Lips.** People with thinner lips tend to be more taciturn. Thin and tightly held lips—that is, lips pressed together when at rest—indicate someone who gets right to the point. Don't expect a lot of extra love play from this person, but when he or she says, "I love you," it will pack a wallop. It is the single arrow shot to hit the mark, free of flowery prose and flattery. In general, thin-lipped people do not like to have their time wasted. They get to the point in conversation and bed.

**Thick Lips.** More talkative and more giving of time and self, the full-lipped person is the one whose spoken sentiments will be polished with expressions. These are more generous people, capable of extending a helping hand to friends in trouble or need. A listener as well as a talker, this is the person to turn to for a sympathetic ear, a comforting word, and affection. Fuller lips are indicative of a more sensual person, who can take time in love and in bed.

No matter whose face you are reading, there are two important psychological points to keep in mind: first, whatever the face seems to be saying to the world—no matter how gloomy it looks—inside, its owner wants to feel loved and worthwhile; and, second, everyone wants, needs to feel important. So, when you greet someone, especially for the first time, use your own face language by expressing your attention and interest. Your attentiveness will show up as magnetism in your facial features, and will draw toward you the person with whom you are speaking. You'll find that people will warm to you much more quickly and will express their inner emotions much more clearly in their faces.

When you have developed your ability to direct your attention to the other person, it will automatically be expressed in your face. Practice focusing on the other person until it becomes second nature to you, and express your attentiveness not only upon greetings, but upon farewells, too. What you express will be sensed and what you read in the other's face may tell of the love you seek.

Robert L. Whiteside, noted author and authority on face reading, reminds us that after studying the face, not only are you more cognizant of what other faces tell you, you are also more aware of what your face tells them! You know ways to satisfyingly improve your appearance and image, eliminating worry lines and being sure you have a happy mouth! Either intuitively or consciously, people are busy every day taking you at face value. The value of the dollar may be skidding out of your personal control, but you can deliberately increase the face value of your own countenance. Talk to the other person's key trait and work on your own.

When you are approaching your lover, look at his or her face, first as an individual, and secondly, as a member of the opposite sex. This is the key to face reading. Watch the manifestations of nature as they appear on the face; here we have proof of the Maker, and within each part of the face, a piece of the Maker's wisdom; and in each piece of wisdom, the tune of life.

Rules to face reading have developed over the centuries since the art was first practiced in ancient China. You can discover much more about this fascinating study and add it to all the other available ways that help us know each other.

As you begin to master face reading, you'll surprise yourself with your growing ability to express your own love and to determine the love of others. Enrich your own life and destiny with your ability to judge another's personality and destiny. But keep in mind that each of us is, indeed, the captain of our own "ship," and that ultimately it is *we* who shape our destiny, though we often misname it "fate."

# THE GRAPHOLOGY OF LOVE

*chapter six*

> *Handwriting bears an analogy to the character of the writer, as all voluntary actions are characteristic.*
>
> —Disraeli

*W*ho is so bereft of words or of poetry in his soul that he has never written a love letter? From the shy country boy etching his love's initials into a great oak tree, to Casanova, penning dulcet phrases to his lady love on scented parchment, everyone will turn to the written word when swaddled in love's silken chains.

As love can scale mountains, so too can its written expression draw forth aspects of our personalities. These aspects go beyond the endearing words or those little *XOXOX* symbols we append to our love missives. Within the very style of your lover's handwriting—the shape of the script—are to be found the deepest signs of his or her emotion and passion.

From earliest times, scholars have been fascinated by the study of handwriting as a key to character. Aristotle taught that just as no one's speech sounds like anyone else's, so no one's handwriting looks like anyone else's. The Roman emperor Justinian observed in his memoirs that a person's script changes with the state of his health and with age. It has been a common observation that individuals produce variations in even so simple a graphic process as drawing two parallel lines.

If we are taught the same letter formations but end up writing differently—as we do—there has to be a good reason. That is because our handwriting reflects everything we are consciously, subconsciously, emotionally, morally, and physically.

Handwriting analysis has been practiced both seriously and as entertainment since the seventeenth century, and it has been considered a science in some parts of the world for over a hundred years. Today in some European countries, it is treated as a branch of psychology and has been found useful by medical students and criminologists, as well as members of the psychiatric community.

Certainly, graphology is a complex study, since it deals with human nature's infinite variety and combinations of traits. I do not aim to make expert graphologists out of readers in one chapter. However, I can introduce those handwriting traits that reflect the nature of human love, as well as some of those traits which are useful to know before making emotional commitments to your lover. If you are already committed to someone, graphology can be useful for you and your mate, in enlightening both of you toward a more complete understanding of yourselves and each other. Understanding goes a long way toward coping with love problems.

To analyze the traits necessary to understand your lover in depth, we'll look at the *slant* of a person's writing, the *pressure* of the writing, the overall *movement* of the handwriting style, the *openness* of key letters, and the *spacing* between letters and words. We'll also analyze the shape and size of the letter *I* and what it indicates.

Love, according to most standard dictionaries, is "a strong, complex emotion or feeling." But the dictionary doesn't tell us a thing about determining if someone is capable of this strong, complex emotion, or how much anyone is governed by emotions. In graphology, these things can be discovered.

First, you'll need at least a half page of your potential or present lover's handwriting. (Now you know why you saved all those love letters.) Then, you'll start by looking at both the direction of the writing's slant and the pressure, or force, with which the words were written.

# Slant

Slant tells us whether a writer is ruled by his or her feelings, whether he or she is able to control them reasonably, or repress them unreasonably. Ultimately, from the direction of a person's writing slant, we can determine if one possesses a lot or little capacity for expressing true love.

*I feel I show my emotion my heart rules my head*

**Specimen 1**

When handwriting slants to the right (see Specimen 1), the writer responds to his or her feelings and is susceptible to sentiment. When the right slant is pronounced (as it is in this specimen) the writer may tend to be too emotional and too inclined to let his or her emotions rule actions. Impulsive commitments for love everlasting may come from the lips of a person with this sort of extremely right-slanted writing; passion probably plays an important role in this person's love life. Impulsive anger is another potential for the extreme right-slanted writer. Specimen 1 is not too extreme.

*This is a sample of my handwriting I hope you like it.*

**Specimen 2**

Vertical handwriting reflects a personality that is deliberate and self-restrained. The writer of Specimen 2 has the capacity to be obstinate and to refuse to be hurried into anything. A person who writes vertically listens to his or her head, rather than heart. This is a person who may postpone serious romantic commitments while pondering the pros and cons, weighing logic against affection, and ultimately being more responsive to the logical arguments. This is someone who hesitates at becoming romantically involved with another, who is capable of walking through a crowd of people perfectly erect, looking neither left nor right; who, when present at the scene of a conflict will stand aloof and express little emotion. Both passion and temper may be held back by this lover.

*I wish I were not so self conscious*

**Specimen 3**

A left-slanted writer, as shown in Specimen 3, is quite capable of resisting his or her feelings. This resistance ranges from mere self-restraint to complete repression, depending upon the degree of the slant. Also known as backhand, this type of writing reflects a person who has a natural difficulty being spontaneous; often, when such a person attempts to be spontaneous, his or her appearance comes off as affected. Other tendencies of the backhanded writer are self-interest, lack of charity, rebelliousness, and defensiveness. Adolescents often adopt this slant because, on the threshold of life, they feel inadequate and are constantly ready to draw back; or they are digging in their heels in a fight against authority. The teenager who today writes with a backhand may, in the future, write with a different slant. Overall, the left slant, especially when extreme, reflects undesirable and negative capabilities, and a struggle against moving forward.

What sort of capacities are you looking for in your lover? Look to the slant of his or her handwriting for a clue. Ardor and passion will tilt it to the right; reason and rationality draw handwriting to a vertical position; resistance and opposition push it back toward the left.

**Specimen 4**

There is yet another type of slant—perhaps we should say a combination of slants—which reflects the writer's capacity for emotion.

This is the erratically slanted handwriting, script that slants first one way and then the other. Emotional instability is reflected in this style; the writer of handwriting such as in Specimen 4 (page 199) tends to be undisciplined, unreliable, changeable, insecure, nervous, and quite unpredictable. In some cases, an erratic slant is a temporary thing, caused by an emotional upset. But when someone consistently writes in this style of slant, he or she has a naturally difficult time making decisions about anything, including whether the relationship is real love or just a little foolishness.

# *Pressure*

The pressure or force applied to the pen as one writes gives us clues to the measure of the writer's vitality and depth of emotion. Great pressure shows up as heavy writing (unless, of course, the width of the pen tip, or its material, produces heavier writing; have your lover present samples written with a medium point ball pen, not a felt-tip).

When heavy writing results not from a particular type of pen but from pressure, it reveals a writer who puts ardor and much feeling into whatever he or she does. This person's emotion has depth and endurance if the pressure is uniform throughout, and not spotty. People with heavy handwriting tend to be active, courageous, and persuasive—in all arenas, including the bedroom.

Heavy writing with a right slant says that the person is expressive and of great emotional depth, someone who absorbs life's and love's experiences like a sponge, and is probably a fantastic lover.

Extremely heavy script reveals a love of food and an artistic appreciation of color, music, and literature. However, a script that looks as if it had been written by a pen dipped in mud—thick and splotchy from too much pressure, with oval letters closed and filled in—warns that the person is capable of sadistic, sex-driven sensuality. This is a person who may drink to excess and take on other dangerous habits.

If your lover writes with very little pressure, to produce light script, he or she is a naturally quiet person with modest tastes and little desire for luxury or material pleasure. The less force that is applied to the pen, the more spiritually inclined is the writer. This, of course, does not mean that the person is a church-going religionist; it does mean that this person has an ethereal quality, an intouchness with nature and the finer qualities of life. This may be the person who is the believer—a trusting, trustworthy individual—as long as his or her trust is met with truth. Love, to this person, is not an idle subject.

Very light pressure in combination with a vertical or left slant reveals a person of low vitality and a cold nature—not the person who is apt to burst out with "I love you!"

Moderately light handwriting with a right slant indicates that the writer is an affectionate but temperate person who may go on an occasional emotional spree. This is a person who will not erupt like Mt. Vesuvius over disturbing incidents, although he or she may bluster about for a while and become dramatic, but he or she will soon forget the outburst and assume others will be equally forgiving.

Slant and pressure of a script, as we've seen, tell much about the general emotional climate of a person. But it doesn't determine whether or not a person is able to freely express that emotional climate. In order to find this out, we have to look more closely at the finer points of the script.

# Movement

Movement is one measure of a person's truthfulness to self and emotions—and by extension, to others. The more spontaneous the handwriting, the more truthful the writer. The more complex, or studied the movement of the handwriting, the less honest the writer.

*was good to hear from you again*

**Specimen 5**

Specimen 5 shows a script that is spontaneous (unstudied) and natural, and reflects an honest, expressive hand. This is a person who communicates easily with others.

*How are all of you?*

**Specimen 6**

Another example of spontaneous script appears in Specimen 6. Here, the handwriting is as simplified, with as easy a forward movement as the script in Specimen 5, but it is distinguished by a firmer, or straighter base line. The base line is another indication of a person's expressive ability, and of confidence in self-expression.

In Specimen 6, the straightness of the line of script reveals a person who knows he is expressing his true emotions when he expresses them. He means it when he says, "I love you."

# Openness

Another measure of frankness and honesty in script is the openness of the oval letters. These are the letters *a, o, d, g,* and *q.* In both Specimens 5 and 6, the ovals are slightly open and free of loops and other decorations. This kind of openness in the ovals suggests a personality that is free to express itself, a person who is not reticent or quiet about feelings. If, however, the ovals were more open than they are, the person would be overly talkative and perhaps too frank.

*We love you!*
*Let's wipe up the floor with*

**Specimen 7**

Look at the difference in the ovals in Specimens 5 and 6, and in Specimen 7. The tightly closed and looped ovals in Specimen 7 indicate a person who keeps his thoughts and feelings to himself. This may be a secretive and introverted person, one who leaves his lover to guess his feelings. A lover who writes in this kind of closed-ovals script may be the difficult-to-understand one. The script in Specimen 7 does not necessarily indicate a dishonest person, but it does reveal someone who has a hard time talking about his feelings.

*all things, eternal good and
need proof. I don't know*

### Specimen 8

Loops where they don't belong, especially on the right side of certain ovals, indicate dishonesty in expression. A compulsive liar would write in the extreme of this "looped and closed" style. Specimen 8 is a moderate example of this clue to dishonesty. In this case, a lover may say, "I love you," and not mean it at all; he or she may be saying it only because it's what you want to hear, or for other even less savory ulterior motives. Note also the unevenness of the base line in Specimen 8: no confidence in self-expression for this writer.

You'll want to know, of course, if your lover is faithful. You may suspect hypocrisy, which is revealed in handwriting by a left slant in combination with ovals that are tightly closed and looped. Again, the writing in Specimen 8 tends to slant to the left, and it possesses those giveaway tight ovals.

*and I love you.*

### Specimen 9

Downright dishonesty is reflected by ovals that are open at the bottom, or base, and by lower extensions of letters (the portion of a letter such as *y, g,* or *p* that extends below the base line) formed in clawlike shapes. For a good example of both these traits in combination, see Specimen 9.

When dishonesty is reflected in handwriting, we often have to look a little further to see how that dishonesty will manifest itself, and where the dishonesty comes from. Generally, it comes from an insecure personality. A lover who lacks confidence is a lover who may resort to pettiness, jealousy, bitterness, sarcasm, and negativity, as well as faithlessness. Know the signs to look for in handwriting that point to personal insecurity, for insecurity leads to those day-to-day problems that can spell ruin for a love affair.

# Spacing

Very closely related to the degree of a person's emotional security, and his ability to express it, is the state of the ego. Does he or she have a secure ego? Is he or she a complete person, capable of fulfillment? This is a vital question when it comes to a long-term relationship, because a person with an insecure ego is not likely to respect a lover's privacy; this is the kind of lover who will be unable to spend time alone or be self-sufficient. You may feel hemmed in by such a person, who literally will be on your heels. Your own freedom will be taken away by this constant dependency on you.

**Specimen 10**

The unsure ego is reflected in script by words that are written in a huddle across the page—very little spacing between the words. Take a look at Specimen 10. Here is a writer unable to leave others alone; he or she is forever with other people, and as a lover would want to be around his sweetheart twenty-four hours a day, the type that would make you feel claustrophobic.

*This vitamin is widely distributed in foods
of both animal and plant origin.*

**Specimen 11**

The spacing of script also reflects a person's generosity (or lack of it). In Specimen 11, it is not the words that are crowded, but the letters. Here is a writer who is penurious. Crowded letters, cut short with hooks at the ends of words (as in Specimen 11), reveal a naturally tight-fisted individual; this person may be able to overcome the trait now and then, but repeatedly succumbs to the strain of keeping up a false appearance.

Penuriousness may seem to be a petty problem at the outset of a steamy love affair—but it'll play an important part in the long run.

Another indication of this, in combination with crowded letters, is writing that has no respect for margins—crowded pages. However, crowded pages without crowded letters shows enthusiasm in emotions and all areas of life. The less crowded the letters, the more generous the personality.

# *Letter I*

One last handwriting trait—the one most commonly known and talked about—is the shape and size of the letter *I*, especially when this letter is used as the first person pronoun.

*India and I Edgar
Leroy said that I*

**Specimen 12**

Look at the size of the *I* in Specimen 12. The *I* here is smaller than the other capital letters (look at the *E* and *C*). This writer has a poor self-image as reflected by the smaller capital *I*. Notice also how the capital *I* turns in on itself, and how the final strokes of each word tend to curve back to the left.

Both the design and size of the capital *I*, in combination with those leftward-turning end strokes, indicate a self-defensive person whose own lack of self-esteem leads him or her to overreact to criticism. This is the kind of person who is constantly building an automatic rearguard protection. The slightest comment on his or her behavior—the slightest question, perhaps—could result in a storm of angry protest. As a lover, this kind of person should be handled, as they say, with kid gloves. There will be no lack of problems in a relationship with a person who has a combination of low self-image and inability to accept criticism, if you are not willing to be the primary giver and the understanding one. (Sometimes the love and the devotion of another will help such a person develop a good self-image; knowing we are loved does untold wonders for our images of ourselves. Keep this in mind when you inspect the I part of "I love you" in your lover's letters.)

*is quite interesting*

**Specimen 13**

As long as we're on the subject of the letter *I*, let's take a quick look at the lowercase *i*. In Specimen 13, we have the handwriting of someone who is best off not getting into a romantic relationship with the writer of Specimen 12. Why? Look at the way the small *i* is dotted; it's more of a reversed accent than a dot—it slants downward and toward the left. Here's a writing characteristic that reflects an overly harsh and critical personality. This personality trait of the writer shows up again in the way the letters are connected within a word; the lines are more pointed than curved. In the word "quite," especially, look at the connection between the letter *i* and the letter *t;* in the word "interesting," you'll see the trait most clearly between the letters *i* and *n*, and again between the letters *r* and *e*.

So, looking back over the ways in which emotion, affection, and honesty are reflected in handwriting, we can make a few educated generalities about the graphology of love. Are you looking for a naturally emotional lover who is capable of expressing his or her love to you, but who is not an emotional Vesuvius either? Do you want an honest lover, someone who is not tight-fisted or overly harsh, yet who will state feelings if it's appropriate and won't use words to hurt you? Do you want a lover who will express affection without mothering you, who will be generous without using generosity as a tool to build his or her own ego? Look to the handwriting. A right slant, written with moderate lightness, uncrowded letters and words, and simplified but legible letters whose ovals (*a, o,* etc.) are slightly open and whose capital *I* is at least as large as other capital letters, indicates a person who can be this kind of lover.

Look at the handwriting again; do you see a left slant—a backhand—written extremely lightly? Are the letters and the words crowded? Do you see far too many loops in the script—especially where they don't belong? Are the oval letters tightly closed? Is the capital *I* much smaller than the other capital letters? Does the *I*-dot look like a line more than a dot? Are the ovals open at the bottom, and do lower extensions look angular and clawlike? Here is someone who cannot express love, even to himself. Honesty is not in this person's vocabulary; neither is affection. This is a lover who would never give but only take, someone who would be dependent on the lover for all things of the heart and would not be able to return these gifts.

Of course, these are two stereotypical portraits; rarely does anyone have only negative or only positive handwriting traits. It's ultimately up to you to decide on your lover after you've seen his or her strengths and weaknesses reflected in script. But remember, the love you take, as the Beatles once sang, is equal to the love you make; what you put forth to assure your lover of your love can change your lover, and those changes may one day show up in handwriting.

Two people in love, whose handwriting reveals opposite emotional traits and moral behavior, may discover a sex life on an expressive basis, but they will be incompatible in other areas. Good bedfellows do not necessarily make good life partners, for each may have emotional paths that conflict with the other's.

It *is* important to have a sensuality that is similar to your lover's; the bedroom does exist in lasting relationships, but it is not going to be the site where other incompatibilities in a relationship are resolved. So look carefully before you leap. Inspect those love letters; compare them to your own. Not just for the sentiments you express in words, but for the potential sentiments which are expressed in the way each of you write the words. Handwriting analysis shows clearly which character traits and combinations would be apt to result in discord and which would be conducive to harmony. It can also point the way to bring harmony into a less-than-happy relationship.

Even when similar characteristics draw two people together, there can be problems. Let's say that two people write with approximately the same slant; there's a pretty good chance that they will be congenial to each other—but only if each has an agreeable disposition. If each of two expressive people has a quick temper (heavy pressure reveals this, to a degree), you may have real fireworks in the relationship. On the other hand, if handwriting shows that one is emotionally volatile and the other is emotionally subdued, the one will dominate the other into submissiveness; outward peace may be maintained, but this is a far cry from true harmony or fulfillment for either partner; it's a one-sided situation.

When disharmony arises in a long-term relationship, it's a good idea to remember each other's positive qualities, instead of focusing on each other's shortcomings and on your mutual incompatibilities. Understanding, patience, giving, and good will are necessary exercises in all affairs of the heart; if we weren't all somehow capable of exercising these things, we'd all have been created identically—and what a bore that would be!

How beautiful it must be when two different, but complementary, people find each other and are big enough to love and encourage each other's uniqueness. It takes real wisdom to love without trying to own and manipulate the object of that love, to allow the other freedom to evolve according to his or her own needs and inclinations, to be joined as one, yet remain independent (though never hurtful in this individual freedom, for "freedom" should never be confused with license).

Love is a two-way street. More happiness can be achieved by understanding than by tolerance, because both people have to know the "why" of their differences and be motivated by good will to make their relationship an enduring success. A one-sided marriage simply cannot make the grade.

A graphologist can help two people understand each other better and can relieve tension by pointing out how to modify characteristics that adversely affect a marriage, as well as by pointing out good traits that may have long gone unrecognized and unnourished.

Graphology is widely accepted today; but in case there may be a few skeptics still around, permit me to quote from the late Paul de Sainte Colombe's book, *Grapho-Therapeutics Pen & Pencil Therapy* (de Sainte Colombe Foundation, 1966).

> *The act of writing is in part physiological movement, involving brain, nervous system, muscles, and supporting vital organs, but it also involves the subconscious*

*and the emotional nature of the writer. Thus the indi-*
*viduality of handwriting is an index to the character,*
*personality, mentality, psychology and physical condi-*
*tion of the writer.*

A person, he contends, has three characters: the one he exhibits, the one he actually has, and the one which he thinks he has; and few people can accurately discover all the truth about themselves without help. As his authority for the graphologist's ability to give this help, he quotes Dr. Carl Gustav Jung: "A half hour with a good graphologist can do more to analyze a person's psychological problems than six months with a good psychiatrist." And Jung had a graphologist on his staff.

Paul de Sainte Colombe went beyond reading character from handwriting, and in collaboration with the renowned French psychologist, Dr. Pierre Janet, tested and proved the validity of graphotherapy, a technique that he explains this way: "Character sets the individual pattern of each handwriting and is so inseparable from it that a voluntary handwriting change, once achieved, produces a corresponding change of character."

Dr. Janet continues:

> *Graphotherapy now gives us the quickest and most*
> *effective means yet devised for reaching the subcon-*
> *scious mind and utilizing its tremendous power to*
> *treat our psychological problems and character defi-*
> *ciencies. As informed psychologists know, there is a*
> *connection between mind and graphic gesture through*
> *the nervous system. This connection is a two-way cir-*
> *cuit. Thus, the mind not only influences the hand as*
> *it writes, but the process is reversible, and the hand—*
> *through voluntary writing exercises—can give com-*
> *mands to the subconscious which, sufficiently and*
> *regularly repeated, are obeyed.*

Among the problems which he lists as being successfully treated through graphotherapy are introversion, unsustained will power, lack of self-confidence, excessive drinking or smoking, sexual disturbances, timidity, laziness, depression, and emotional instability. Clinically tested in Paris at the Sorbonne from 1929 to 1931, graphotherapy is now practiced in several European countries and is employed with notable success in the treatment of disturbed children at the Psycho-Pedagogic Center at the University of Paris.

Kathi de Sainte Colombe, who carried on her late husband's work, says that many people become suicidal because they cannot find themselves or handle their problems. Since the intention is reflected very clearly in handwriting, a careful study of the script can prevent the tragedy.

By the same means, many broken romances can be healed, and separations prevented. The greatest contributing factor in marital unhappiness is the general inability of people to communicate freely. This is still another problem that yields to graphotherapy, a practical method, which, if you are of a mind to, can change a great many things; and through these changes, you will be on the way to finding fulfillment in love. For love is an irresistible force that promotes health and happiness. And graphotherapy can help us find our loving nature—if we are willing to turn love on by being loving.

# $\mathcal{T}$HE PALMISTRY

## *chapter seven*

OF LOVE

*Never was there a hand that did not exactly
reflect the brain that directs it... To get to the
secrets of the mind embodies the effort toward
which scientific hand-reading aspires, for
mind is the guiding force in life.*

—William G. Benham

$\mathcal{N}$ow that we've seen what the hand can reveal in the way it produces script, let's look more closely at the hand itself and the secrets held within its own configurations.

No guide need tell us of the meaning behind the touch of a hand—the gentle caress and the warm clasp of a lover's hand are obvious messages of tenderness. Nor do we need a guide to interpret for us the meanings of gestures—that universal language of speaking with the hands which contains its own "I love you" gestures, but understanding the form of the hand and its markings requires a bit of instruction if we are to learn the natural capacities and emotions of our lovers.

Examine your hands and the hands of your loved one. Within them lies still another key to discovering your compatibility and predicting possible pitfalls; within them lies the mirror of your life with your lover.

The philosopher Marius Schneider refers to the hand as the physical manifestation of our inner beings. Throughout human history, the hand has been used as a major symbol for numerous ideas and states. It is no wonder that in time the sixteenth-century art of chiromancy, or palmistry, has become a refined method for gauging a person's potentials in life.

Chiromancy involves more than analyzing the fine lines in the palm of the hand; we first have to take the general view—the view of the whole hand itself. This is called chirognom.

Watch your lover's hands as he or she holds them in repose. The manner in which the fingers are held while at ease tells a complete story about your lover's innermost feelings. Fingers held wide apart indicate generosity; but a thumb tucked under the other fingers shows fear; at worst it may indicate that the person is embarking upon a falsehood. This secret language is an invaluable tool for learning about another person; it is one of the languages of the body that is mastered by top actors and actresses in their portrayal of emotions.

The skin of the hand can tell much, as well. Naturally coarse and rough skin indicates a person who has a less complicated personality. The more finely textured the skin, the more sensitive the individual; many psychics have extremely fine skin.

Wise doctors often look at the nails as a clue to the state of health. But the stigma of the word "palmistry" is so entrenched that when an article appeared in the *Journal of the American Medical Association* correlating the various markings in the palm with certain diseases, the theory was dubbed dermataglyphics! A rose by any other name! The article treated the subject as a new discovery rather than a scientific art discovered thousands of years ago.

Now, take your lover's hands and hold them, palms downward, in your own. Let's look first at the general shape of the hand.

# *Back of the Hand View*

## Basic Hand Shapes

Hands have three basic shapes: the conical, the spatulate, and the square. There is also the mixed type of hand.

*The Conical Hand* is distinguished by long fingers that taper toward the ends, thin rather than thick palms, and, usually, long nails. If your lover's hand has this general shape, chances are good that he or she is an impulsive kind of lover, but one who inclines toward the artistic and creative aspects of life.

*The Spatulate Hand,* distinguished by flat, ladle-tipped fingers (wider at the tips) and a thicker palm and large thumb, is the sign of a hard worker. Here is a person who will make a staying effort at romance, who will not take it lightly.

*The Square Hand* is broad with large fingers which are square at the tips; the palm itself is often square, especially at the wrist. The entire hand is rather large, and the palm is neither thick nor thin, but medium, with a hollowness in the palm. Persons with hands of this general shape are doers; they put their intelligence into their acts. Here is the go-getter, the person who acts on love, instead of sitting around and pining for someone.

*The Mixed Hand* is actually much more common in nature than any of the three pure types; this is the hand which has distinctive traits of each of the other varieties. A square palm with conical fingers must be perused carefully; which is more dominant in the hand—the shape of the palm or the shape of the fingers? It is the dominant character that will reveal to which of the three pure types the individual's personality inclines. When reading the mixed hand, it is wisest to analyze the individual features separately.

## Spacing Between Fingers

So let's now look at the signs of love to be found in the individual features. We'll start with the spacing between the fingers, a feature that can tell volumes of one's character.

Look again at the way your lover's fingers are held in repose—at the differences of spaces between them. Look for the two fingers between which there is the greatest space.

*Fourth and Third Fingers.* When the little finger and the ring finger, held in repose, show more space between them than the other fingers, the individual is driven to act independently. This is someone who, as a lover, will not be influenced by what you—or friends—say about your relationship. He will do what he thinks best; at least, he'll do what he wants to do.

*Third and Second Fingers.* Naturally exaggerated spacing between the ring and middle fingers shows an eccentric nature. This is not very common, but when you see it, be assured that the person is not necessarily conscious of his or her unusual behavior. This would be the kind of lover who, after a nice date and a fine evening, might suggest driving to the beach to catch the sunrise, and stopping on the way to pick up the necessary supplies. Life would indeed be interesting with one whose fingers show this configuration.

*Second and First Fingers.* Greater spacing between these digits suggests a thinker. Here is someone who, though believing in his or her love—thoroughly and with conviction—may not act on it. This is the independent thinker whose capacity to act upon conviction is often hampered by outward situations. If this kind of person indulges in an extramarital affair, he will truly mean it when he tells his lover he wants to marry her. But he most likely won't marry her, since the external circumstance of his marriage will circumscribe any action he may want to take. Or, on the brighter side, this is the type of person who can be convinced of the need to experience different types of love affairs, though he may not at first believe they are "proper."

*First Finger and Thumb.* When the widest natural spacing occurs between these two digits, your lover is the generous type. Extremely wide spacing here indicates one who can tend to extravagance in his or her gifts. Now this may be all well and good during the early stages of romance, but later on, when the relationship takes that turn toward permanency, it may become a problem—when, for example, he begins buying expensive gifts for all your friends and family, and there isn't enough spending power to go around. This configuration can also indicate a liberal, free mind, a generosity of spirit and lack of judgmental attitude—in many ways, a perfect lover.

## Finger Size and Shape

The size and shape of one's fingers are another clue to the heart. We have to be able to interpret the combinations of the configurations, as well as each individual feature; keep this in mind as we analyze the fingers' individual traits.

When we inspect the fingers, we have to look at them both from the palm side up and the palm side down to make a good analysis. This is true especially when we speak of the general shape of fingers. When you look at your *inamorata's* fingers, notice whether they are generally—viewed from both sides—straight, or generally bent, as if out of proportion with the others. Look closely to see if, when the palm is turned upward, the fingers are set evenly over the palm; that is, does the base of each finger align with the others? Or do the bases of the fingers form a downward-turning curve?

Generally straight fingers tell us that the person has sound judgment. He or she is not apt to flights of fantasy about impossible love, and overall is a person capable of realistic ideas and action.

Generally crooked fingers tell us that the person is not the most realistic person in the world. Here is the lover who may try the impossible and whose judgment is not the best. Extremely crooked fingers reveal an unbalanced mind.

## Tips and Joints of the Fingers

The tips of the fingers tell another story. There are three basic shapes to the fingers: pointed, square, and spatulate. When we consider these shapes we'll also consider the joints, whether they are knotted or smooth.

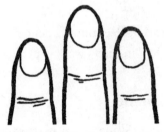

*Pointed Tips.* If your lover's fingers have pointed tips, he or she is a thoughtful person. Look closely—is the pointedness of the fingers extremely exaggerated? Here you may have a daydreamer and a fantasizer, one who indulges in capricious mental activity. "I love her, I love her not," may be a phrase going round and round in his or her head. Now look at the joints of the fingers, viewed palm-down. Are they smooth? This is the sign of the believer. This person will tend to be highly impressionable, and will believe it when you say, "I love you." Knotted joints indicate a more judicious person, both generally and in love.

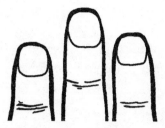

**Square Tips.** Square-tipped fingers are an indication of a rational mind, of an individual wedded to reason. There are very few impulsive love affairs in this person's life, but if the fingers are extremely square at the tips, reason may tend toward the fanatic. Here is the person who believes it may be highly reasonable to continue your affair—if only it didn't interfere with a reasonable, rational life. Smooth joints on square-tipped fingers show an optimistic rationalist, one who sees the bright side of reason in relation to romantic feelings; knotted joints indicate a more meticulous thinker, someone who may take forever weighing the pros and cons, then the cons and pros, of your affair's rationality. Philosophers have these joints.

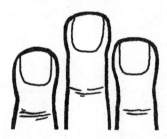

**Spatulate Tips.** Spatulate fingertips indicate a person of action. Here is the lover who won't sit around weighing all sides; this person puts emotions to action. Smooth joints show a tendency to be pragmatic; indecision is this person's pet peeve. This is the "I love you and you love me, so let's get married already" type. Knotted joints indicate an optimistic, enthusiastic doer; this is the person who achieves great results from individual efforts, and the kind of lover who will work hard at developing the good side of your relationship. The wide tips of the fingers on the spatulate type shows they are innovators.

## Thumb

The size and shape of the thumb is as important a key to character as the sizes and shapes of the fingers. When you are reading your loved one's hand, be sure to take into account this digit. The longer the thumb, the more apt your lover is to be faithful, not only to you but faithful to self as well; a very short thumb on the other hand indicates fickleness and inconstancy, both mental and physical. A thick, prominent thumb shows that the person is a strong character; a smaller, less prominent thumb, of course, reveals the opposite.

# Palm-Up View

Now that we've looked over many of the aspects of chiromancy from the back of the hand, let's turn those loving hands palm up and examine them in more detail for the more elusive clues to the emotions such as in the fingers, mounts, and lines. Let's look first at the way in which the fingers are set above the palm.

## Fingers

When all the fingers align at the base in the palm, the individual is quite balanced in the different forces that affect his or her life. This person, when in love, will not be swept away by emotion without balancing it against other factors. However, if one of the fingers seems to be more dominant than the others—that is, set higher in the palm than the others—the characteristics of that finger will dominate the person's character; if one finger is set lower in the palm than the others, the characteristics associated with that finger will be less powerful in the individual's personality.

What are the characteristics of the fingers? Here, we get into the deeper analysis of the palm itself. Each finger is named after the

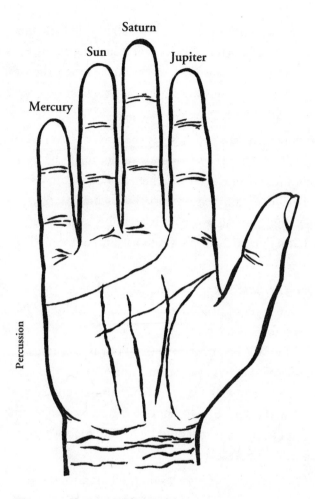

**Figure 1: Fingers and their chiromantic names**

"mount" over which it is placed, and each mount has its characteristics. For convenience's sake, we'll refer to the fingers by their chiromantic names (see Figure 1):

- First or index finger—Jupiter
- Second or middle finger—Saturn
- Third or ring finger—Sun (also referred to as Apollo)
- Fourth or little finger—Mercury

Recall that when one finger is set above the base line of the others, that finger's characteristics will dominate the personality; and that, conversely, if one finger is set lower than the others, those characteristics will be weak in the person. Let's go over the significance of each finger.

*Jupiter (Index Finger).* This is the finger of rule. A long Jupiter finger is found in one who tends to dominate his or her partner. Depending, of course, on whether the finger is pointed, square, or spatulate, that domination may be mental or physical. A short Jupiter finger reveals a person who shuns responsibility and fights back (either mentally or physically) against authority because of low self-esteem.

*Saturn (Middle Finger).* Generally the longest finger of the hand, this is the finger of prudence, or caution. Too long, and the person may tend toward the morbid in this regard. If the finger is pointed, the caution will be primarily mental but it may result in guilt feelings if he or she acts against caution. A long, square, or spatulate finger may very well activate that cautious attitude. Here is the more discreet person. The shorter the Saturn finger, the less caution. Ideally, this finger should be neither too short nor too long—the ideally discreet lover.

*Sun/Apollo (Ring Finger).* Often referred to as the finger of art, the Sun finger provides an invaluable clue if you are looking for someone who is capable of enjoying things of beauty. A long Sun finger reveals a character that appreciates artistic, creative endeavors; but too long, and the person's enthusiasm may spill over into gambling; here's the speculator, in business and in love. Too short, and the person may lack artistic sensibilities.

*Mercury (Little Finger).* This is the finger that tells whether a person is capable of level-headedness and self-management. A long-to-medium little finger indicates that the individual is quite capable of taking care of his or her own affairs. Too short, and the person may be totally disorganized and without social or business tact. Don't look for tact in the emotional realm, either, from the too-short-Mercury lover. Average length reaches to the joint of the Sun finger.

The palm itself is full of hidden secrets about a person's character. Volumes have been written on the art of reading the lines and mounts of the palm. We will touch on those areas that relate to the emotional life—those clues we need to draw a clearer picture of our love and our lover's capacities.

## Mounts

Keeping in mind the different general significance of each hand, let's turn to the mounts. Figure 2, page 225, shows the following mounts:
- Mounts under their respective fingers: Jupiter, Saturn, Sun, and Mercury
- Mount of Venus
- Mount of Mars
- Mount of the Moon

*Mount of Jupiter (below the index finger).* A well-developed Mount of Jupiter—prominent and well placed under the first finger—shows an affable person. This is a social go-getter, a good mixer at parties, gregarious and outgoing. As a lover, this person won't be the stay-at-home-for-some-TV date, but will want to get out and about with others. Too dominant a Mount of Jupiter could indicate vanity and conceit. If this mount is placed more toward the middle finger's base, the individual could be self-conscious. These people are the most beautiful people around at parties, and will take too much pride in their appearance. If the mount is closer to the thumb than the first finger, you may end up with a permanent relationship or marriage, since this indicates a love of family. If your lover has no Mount of Jupiter, he or she may be an extremely humble person, though likeable among his social circles.

*Mount of Saturn (below the middle finger).* It's seldom that you will find a prominent Mount of Saturn. When it is dominant, it indicates a person of caution and prudence to an extreme. Inclination in love is toward the morbid and pessimistic, and at times expressions of devotion may be seasoned by a touch of hypocrisy. The average-sized Mount of Saturn shows someone who is not frivolous about life or emotions, one who takes love seriously. The lack of this mount may indicate that your lover lives with certain fears, which he or she covers up with laughter (usually at the wrong time) or by taking inconsequential events too seriously. A mount leaning toward the first finger indicates a person with a good sense of self-worth, one who won't use a relationship simply to build up ego. A Mount of Saturn that is nearer the ring finger shows an individual who needs solitude and cannot be crowded.

*Mount of the Sun/Apollo (below the ring finger).* This is the mount of the arts. If your lover has a well-developed Mount of the Sun, he or she is either an artistic person or a lover of the arts and things of beauty. Does your lover have a very pronounced Mount of the Sun? This indicates an extremely sentimental type—the champagne, the flowers, the quiet table in a favorite restaurant may be a typical night out. An average position and size of this mount indicates a gentle and tender lover. A shoulder is there for your tears, and a heart to beat with yours. If your lover's hand has no Mount of the Sun, his or her love of art will be weak, and temperament passive and bitter. If this mount tends toward the little finger's base, the person tends to have a just disposition, a calm temperament, and don't be surprised if this person brings along a pet cat on your first date: this is an individual who adores animals. A Mount of the Sun leaning toward the middle finger indicates a person who loves children and family life, so be prepared.

*Mount of Mercury (below the little finger).* A well-developed and centrally placed Mount of Mercury indicates the physical type of person—a good athlete, out of doors and in. He (or she) will be

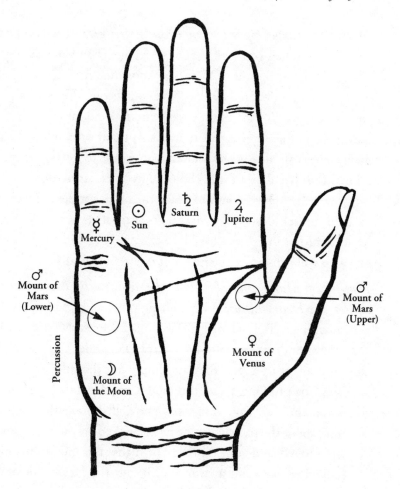

**Figure 2: Major mounts of the palm**

a cheery soul, but too dominant a mount may indicate an excess of this carefree spirit, to the point of heedlessness—your one-night-of-great-fun-and-so-long character. A person with no Mount of Mercury may tend to be without joy—a morosely despondent type. The farther this mount is toward the outer edge of the hand (the percussion), the more daring he or she is, the more possessed of spirit and *joie de vivre.* The closer it is to the ring finger, the more your lover is the comedian of the crowd. This person will find something humorous in just about any situation.

*Mount of Mars–Upper (below Mount of Jupiter and under the Life Line).* When you look at your loved one's hand and see a well-developed upper Mount of Mars, you know that he or she is a brave one. Dashing, unfettered by fears, and courageous, this is another of your go-getters. But too pronounced, and this mount can indicate a downright rashness and a false bravado, a person without good judgment. This can also mean a lover who is apt to get involved (or uninvolved) heedlessly if the choice represents daring-do. The farther down the upper Mount of Mars, the more apt the individual is to commit self-destructive or other-destructive acts. No upper Mount of Mars indicates a total lack of courage and in a lover someone who will run before the first hint of a problem surfaces.

*Mount of Mars–Lower (below the Mount of Mercury and under the Heart Line).* With Taurean qualities of endurance, the person with a well-developed and well-placed lower Mount of Mars is steadfast and emotionally in control. This does not mean that emotions are not present; they are simply not the ruler of this person's life. Too prominent, and this mount can signal the overly secretive lover, the one who won't kiss and tell, but neither tell you anything about the past, which he or she will portray as a mysterious dark spot to which no one is privy. The higher this mount, the more the individual possesses a strong spirit and the greater his or her steadfastness. The lower it is placed, the less fortitude; an extremely low mount can indicate a withdrawn personality, shy beyond reason.

If there is no lower Mount of Mars on the palm, you are faced with someone who is lacking in self-control and may be fickle.

*Mount of the Moon (below the lower Mount of Mars and at the percussion side of the hand).* This is the mount of imagination, the part of the hand that exhibits the degree of the soul's poetry and reverie. Too prominent, and the individual may be given to a life of daydreams and capriciousness; he or she may conduct a love life in the mind only and neglect the facts. Reality and fancy will collide in this person. Here is the lover who may believe he's in love because he has attributed characteristics to you which, in fact, you do not possess; and no amount of proof from you will make any difference. No Mount of the Moon indicates a person without imagination. A date may involve a hamburger at a fast food eatery and a TV show; don't expect a late night out with this person. The farther down the Mount of the Moon (the closer to the wrist), the higher the person's sense of imagination; the higher it is, the more jealous his or her thoughts. A lover with a big Mount of the Moon may well begin conjuring all sorts of sordid situations in which you might be caught if you break a date or don't answer phone calls.

*Mount of Venus (below and at the base of the thumb).* The Mount of Love is an appropriate subtitle for this area of the palm. Passion resides here, in all its manifestations. A well-developed and well-placed mount shows a strong capacity for pure love and romance; the person with this attribute is ignited in love, and you will feel the sparks. An extremely prominent mount indicates a sensuous person, one who expresses passion best in physical terms. The farther toward the Life Line, the greater the sensuality; in this position, the Mount of Venus also indicates a love of the finer things in life and a person who is unhappy without luxuries, including a luxuriously sensual relationship. When this mount leans farther away from the Life Line, toward the thumb side of the palm, it indicates that an individual's passion and love are directed toward pure forms. You'd probably get a poem or two before you'd get to the bedroom, but it would be verse of the most sublime nature, enough to stir the fires of your soul. A palm with a flat Mount of Venus reflects a personality without the capacity for passion, mental or physical, as well as a cold heart, closed to love.

## Lines

Traveling from the hills of love, we go now to the rivers—the lines that life has etched into the palms. Shown on Figure 3, page 229, are the following lines.

- Life Line
- Head Line
- Heart Line
- Fate Line
- Sun (or Fortune) Line
- Health Line

The lines of the hand you use are always forming and changing as your life changes. We'll assume, for convenience, that your lover is right-handed. This means that his or her left hand's lines and mounts depict the natural tendency of the life—inborn capacities; the right hand's markings indicate the accomplished reality of the present, and are apt to change.

***The Life Line*** begins between the thumb and the Jupiter finger and travels around the Mount of Venus toward the wrist (see Figure 3). The direction of this line is downward; that is, the first year of life is recorded at its top, the last year at the point at the wrist where it ends. It reveals a life's longevity and its events. A short Life Line can be mended by good living habits; a long Life Line means just that. The more deeply etched this line, the stronger the individual—the more powerful his or her life force.

***The Head Line*** begins at approximately the same place as the Life Line and extends across the palm, toward the percussion of the palm, ending, usually, just short of it (see Figure 3). A Head Line that tends to slope downward indicates an individual of idealism. A deep line reflects the power of the person's thoughts; a shallow or ill-defined Head Line may mean that the individual has little or no ability to concentrate. A long line indicates varied interests, which may, however, mean a variety of interests in love objects.

If the Life Line and Head Line are joined at their beginning points, the individual will be judicious in the choice of a mate. Separation from the Life Line indicates a bold lover—one who makes a more daring decision in the realm of love.

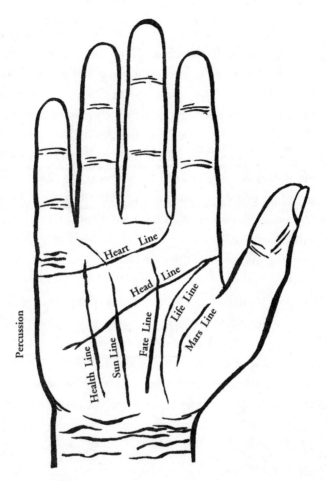

Figure 3: Major lines of the palm

*The Fate Line* can take four major positions in the palm. In Figure 3, the Fate Line is shown as beginning at the wrist and extending through the Mount of Saturn; this is the ideal configuration and indicates the person will have a spectacular career—one to which he or she was fated. A second position is a Fate Line that begins from the lower part of the Life Line and extends upward. The person with this Fate Line will have a good life, especially later—how much later depends upon at which point the Life Line and Fate Line separate.

At that point, the person's life will be more successful. (The mid-palm indicates the ages from 32 to 35.) When the Fate Line begins in mid-palm, the individual will lead a peaceful life until his or her mid-thirties or forties. Then the action begins, as fate takes over and guides this person in new directions, which may include a passion-ate and new love affair. The Fate Line that begins on or near the Mount of the Moon and extends upward and toward the middle of the hand means that the person's life and love may be greatly influ-enced by other people. He or she may marry someone more due to outside pressure than as a result of true feelings (though this is not always the case).

Depending upon where the Fate Line ends, the person's life may end in riches (ending at the Mount of the Sun), in fame (ending at the Mount of Jupiter), in a halted career (ending in mid-palm); or it may end well but not spectacularly (ending on the Mount of Saturn).

The longer the Fate Line, the more one is ruled by the externals of his (or her) life; the shorter, the shorter the career. When this line stops against the Head Line, drastic change in attitude is needed or the individual may make a fatal judgment in life; when it ends against the Heart Line, an unfortunate judgment, based on matters of the heart or sentiment, will be made, unless fate is changed by wisdom.

***The Sun (or Fortune) Line*** is closely associated with the Fate Line. Not everyone possesses this line. Figure 3 shows a Sun Line begin-ning from the Fate Line and ending on the Mount of the Sun; this indicates a person who will become famous through his or her own efforts at developing personal talents. When the Sun Line begins at a point along the Life Line, the person's life will be of an unusual sort, but, again, success will be earned through the individual's own efforts. A Sun Line beginning at the lower Mount of Mars indicates success and fame earned in middle age. When this line originates at the Mount of the Moon, the person's success will not be self-earned, but will be obtained largely through the efforts of others. As with the

Fate Line, the ending points of the Sun Line mean different things. Ending at the Mount of Mercury—business success; ending at the Mount of the Sun—celebrity and financial success; ending at the Mount of Jupiter—success of a personal, social, or political nature.

Take a quick look at the Sun Line on your lover's left hand. Do you see a more deeply etched line in combination with a prominent and highly placed Mount of the Moon? If so, your inamorata loves not only you, but ostentation and display as well. Here is your fancy dresser, your big spender, your big party giver. He or she is the poser—watch this person pass in front of mirrors!

**The Health Line** is the line farthest toward the percussion of the hand (see Figure 3). Ideally this line rises from the Fate Line and ends at the Mount of Mercury. Occasionally, a palm may possess no Health Line, especially if the hand is firm and strong. The absence of this line is not a negative indication, especially if the individual is healthy and strong. The straighter the line, when it exists, the healthier the individual. The longer it is, the longer the person's life will tend to be. If the line is crooked or broken, attention to good health habits is required and nutrition should be studied.

**The Heart Line** is our primary concern. This is the line that appears above the Head Line, begins beneath the Mount of Mercury, and extends to the area below or near the Mount of Jupiter (see Figure 3). A perfect Heart Line is long and deep and runs across the palm along the base of the mounts. This line represents not only the affectionate side of a person's nature, but also the physical blood circulation and the condition of the life's organ, the heart itself. A highly placed Heart Line—one that runs very near the base of the mounts, or intersects them—indicates a jealous, passionate, and possessive person. This is the lover who not only refuses to take no for an answer but may just camp outside your door until you change your mind. If the Heart Line passes low, the individual may possess a cold, recalcitrant nature and be capable of selfishness and deceit, though this may also indicate a person of strong religious beliefs, especially if the mounts are all well developed.

If your loved one enjoys new ideas and displays intellectual curiosity, chances are that his or her Heart and Head Lines are placed widely apart. Placed close together, these two lines denote a closed-minded individual—not your exciting love affair, by any means.

If the Heart Line is shallow and short, there is an indication that the individual cannot love for long, but will flit from affair to affair. In conjunction with a short and small thumb that tends to lean inward in repose, the shallow and short Heart Line indicates a person who has a great problem with fickleness and infidelity. This may also indicate that the person is a poor lover physically because of a lack of good nutrition.

A dark, deep red Heart Line, running stiffly from one side of the palm to the other, indicates a violently jealous nature and strong displays of temper. In Figure 4, this type of Heart Line is shown in conjunction with an exaggerated upper Mount of Mars, a combination suggesting not only violent jealousy, but extreme sensuality as well. The person with this type of configuration in his palm may be without any emotional or sensual control.

Lines under the Sun (ring) finger show very good fortune. Each line brings happiness from different areas of their life.

When the Heart Line begins far up on the Mount of Jupiter, the indication is that there is ideal love but very little sensuality. Figure 5 (page 234) illustrates the extreme of this case. Perhaps a person with this sort of Heart Line would not make the best marriage partner, but he or she would be a stimulating romantic friend.

Such a person must learn to be more practical, or else he or she may be subject to lack of material success because of a difficulty in reconciling romantic ideals with external realities.

When the Heart Line begins with a fork within the Mount of Jupiter, as in Figure 6 (page 235), we see an indication of the highest type of ideal love. Here is a potential marriage partner who would be practical, constant, loving, and sensuous.

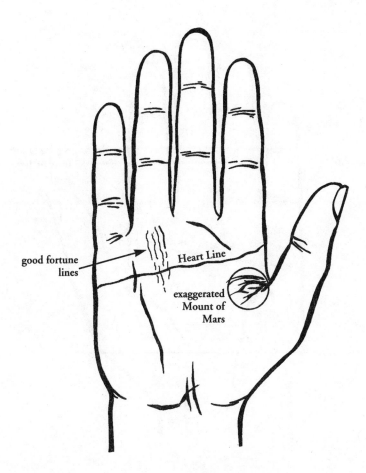

good fortune
lines

Heart Line

exaggerated
Mount of
Mars

**Figure 4: A deep, red Heart Line with exagger-
ated Mars suggests violent jealousy
but extreme sensuality**

When this line begins on the Mount of Saturn, there is an indication of a subdued, uneventful love life, one that lacks passion—in
other words, a partner who will secure for you a humdrum sort of
existence. If the Heart Line is also very deep and uneven, the person will have a long life of hard work, with subdued feelings of love
and passion.

If your lover's Heart Line begins with a double prong, one starting at the Mount of Jupiter, and one at the Mount of Saturn, he or

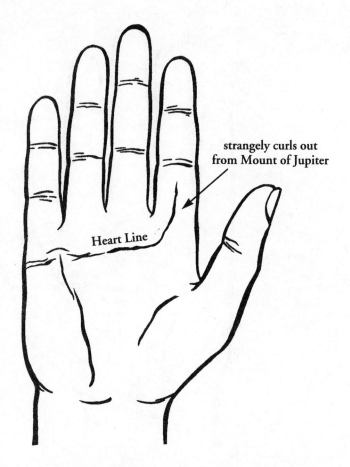

strangely curls out
from Mount of Jupiter

Heart Line

**Figure 5: Heart Line begins far up the Mount of
Jupiter—ideal love but little sensuality**

she is capable of committing errors in judgment in the pursuit of
love. A prong running from the Mount of Jupiter gives magnetic
power to attract the opposite sex, while a prong running from the
Mount of Saturn gives gloomy thoughts and inconstant behavior.

A Heart Line broken under the Mount of Mercury, near the percussion of the hand, indicates a love affair or marriage broken
because of the person's own fickle nature. Figure 7 (page 236) shows
a Heart Line "joined" to a Head Line by numerous lines of influ-

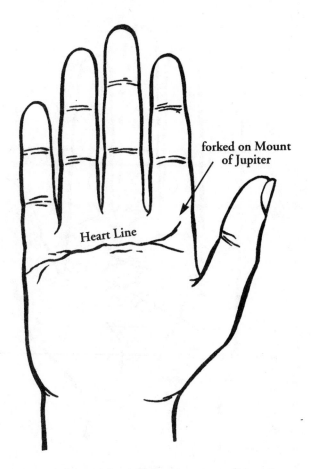

forked on Mount
of Jupiter

Heart Line

**Figure 6: Heart Line forked with Mount of
Jupiter—the highest type of ideal love**

ence. These tiny connecting lines between the two indicate illness
caused by sorrow from temporary loss of love—love sickness.

When there is an unusually high number of these lines of influence between the Heart and Head Lines, the person's life may be
too greatly influenced by the opposite sex.

A group of small lines, or bars, cutting through the Heart Line
bears witness to repeated disappointments in love. Dents or breaks
in the line show grief. When the line is chained so that it appears to

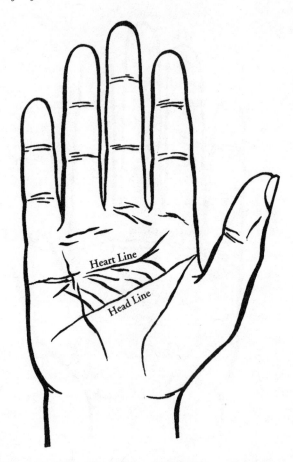

**Figure 7: The Heart Line "joined" to a Head
Line by numerous lines of influ-
ence—love sickness**

have "islands," passing love affairs may be indicated (see Figure 8).
It's generally believed that each of these islands represents an emotional entanglement.

If an island occurs on the Heart Line under the Mount of Saturn,
a brief love affair may interfere with that person's steadier romantic
prospects. If one occurs under the Mount of Jupiter, the love affair
will be a passing fancy, and will not bring about any grave conse-
quences to more serious romantic quests.

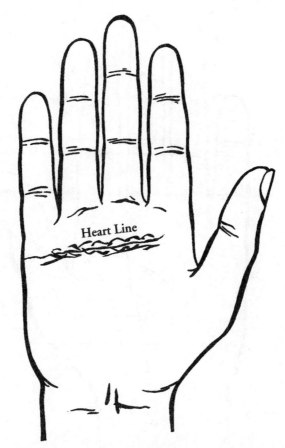

Heart Line

**Figure 8:** Passing love affairs may be indicated
when the Heart Line has "islands"

When a Heart Line and a Fate Line are connected so that the point of connection ends in a chain on the Heart Line, as in Figure 9 (page 238), the person tends to be flirtatious. He or she may become involved in secret intrigues. Generally, this is a sign of inconstancy in affairs of love.

There are two more features of the palm which point to the romantic life: the Girdle of Venus and the Marriage Lines. Figure 10 (page 239) shows the positions of these lines in relationship to the Heart, Head, and Life Lines.

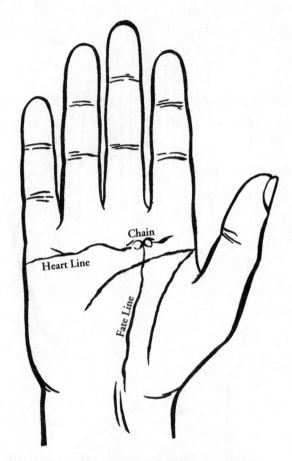

**Figure 9: A chain made by a Fate Line/Heart Line connection—flirtatiousness**

*The Girdle of Venus* is not a feature everyone possesses, or if present, it is often faint or broken. Younger people tend to have this feature, and it fades with the years. Generally, its presence denotes an excess of emotion; if the Girdle deepens and remains in the palm past the twenties, it can indicate a type of sexual hysteria or an individual who is unduly preoccupied with sexual matters. While a person with a pronounced Girdle of Venus may make an unpredictable marriage partner, he or she may compensate with a very active artistic or

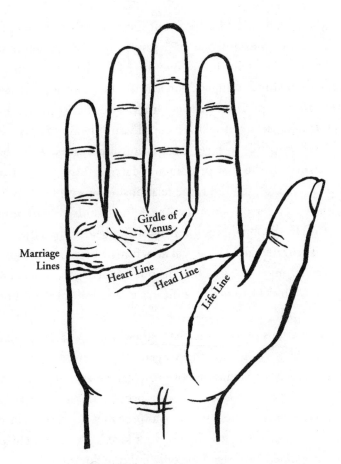

**Figure 10: Girdle of Venus and the Marriage
Lines in relation to the Heart,
Head, and Life Lines**

poetic nature; in the case of great artists, who usually have the Girdle
of Venus, the drive toward art acts to tone down an overly active sexual nature.

*Marriage Lines* can mean important emotional ties which may or
may not be legal marriages. As shown in Figure 10, these lines are
located at the upper palm's percussion, near (or extending onto)
the Mount of Mercury. There is one line for each serious emotional attachment.

Look for these lines on both of your lover's hands. The ones on the left hand indicate someone else's love for your lover; the lines on the right indicate your lover's own love for others. In both the left and right palms, though, Marriage Lines mean real, lasting relationships. The position of these lines varies between left and right hands because a real relationship doesn't always happen the moment someone fails in love; the relationship begins when that love is returned. If the first prominent Marriage Line is lower on the left palm than on the right, the relationship was probably initiated by the other person—not the one whose hands you are reading—and it also probably took a little while before the object of the love reciprocated and the actual attachment began. The longer the line, the stronger the attachment, but a Marriage Line passing beyond the Mount of Mercury indicates a fanatical, perhaps one-sided attachment.

Watch for various signs connected to these lines. A Marriage Line composed of little islands, or chains, generally means a person has had, or is capable of having, emotional attachments that are too dependent upon or too close to other people. If the chains also appear in the left hand, the intimacy was probably a consequence of the other's emotional state, not that of your lover's. Generally, chains on the right-handed Marriage Line only indicate flirtatiousness.

Breaks in a Marriage Line can mean separation or divorce. A broken Marriage Line with the two fragments overlapping each other can mean a separation followed by a reconciliation; at least the emotional attachment remains, whether the actual relationship does or not.

When a Marriage Line is crossed by a line of influence that leads from the Mount of Venus and cuts through the Life, Head, and Heart Lines, it indicates a troubled marriage, caused perhaps by the interference of parents or other relatives.

## Special Configurations

The finer points of your lover's romantic nature become clearer when you consider some of the special configurations attached to the major aspects of his or her palm. We've already seen how chains or islands on a line can add new dimensions to the meaning of that line, or how lines of influence can alter an interpretation. Forks, stars, crosses, and triangles (see below) are indications of finer points in your loved one's romantic life. Let's consider these.

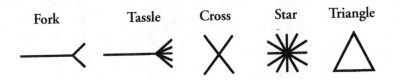

A cross at the end of the Marriage Line indicates the passing of a loved one. A triangle in this position means an extremely happy love life. If the Marriage Line ends in a star, chances are very good that marriage with this person will be lasting and happy. A very distorted fork at the end of the Marriage Line, with one prong going deeply into the Mount of the Moon, shows a disposition toward violence and passion.

Figure 11 (page 242) shows a combination of stars on the Life Line and the Mount of Venus, in conjunction with a sloping Head Line. Note also the deep black spot on the Mount of Venus. Here is an indication of a glib, seductive lover, who cares only for the release a brief emotional attachment may give. This type of selfishness appears in a person with a deep black spot on the mount; a star resting near the spot could mean that there has been some love tragedy. Three stars near the Life Line without the deep dot is a sign that your lover is passionate, perhaps a person with a "conqueror complex," but one who is sincere and capable of having a truly honest relationship. With the dot, he or she is a passionate conqueror, but lacks sincerity—a relationship probably won't work out well.

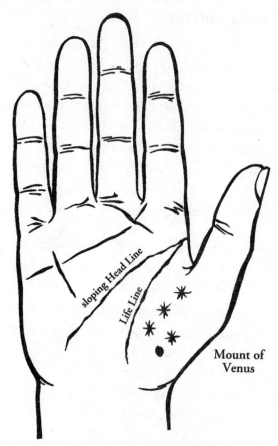

**Figure 11: Stars and a sloping Head Line—
active erotic imagination**

A star right on the Life Line indicates someone who may meet with calamity because of persons of the opposite sex; one or more stars directly on this line may also mean that this person possesses something in his or her psychological makeup that attracts misfortune (unless this tendency is thwarted by reading Chapter Ten on love and sex).

When a star on the Mount of Venus near the Life Line is accompanied by a sloping Head Line, as in Figure 11, you may be dealing with a highly sexed individual who possesses an active erotic

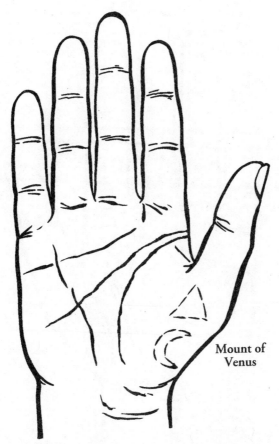

**Figure 12: An experienced seducer will most
likely have one of these signs on
the Mount of Venus**

imagination. So, depending upon your desires, be warned or
encouraged by this sign.

Figure 12 shows a Mount of Venus with a triangle and a crescent,
or half-moon. In actuality, the clarity of the signs won't be this clear.

A triangle in this spot means that the person does not rule out
extramarital affairs; indeed, the person with a triangle on this
mount may go outside his or her marriage to find a permanent lover
while continuing to live with a spouse.

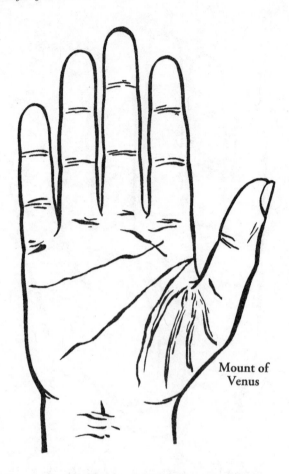

Figure 13: Concentric lines following the Life
Line—a person easily influenced
by the opposite sex

The half-moon on this mount signifies a neurotic imagination.
An experienced seducer will most likely have one of these signs.

The simple lines of influence from the Mount of Venus must also
be studied to recognize the refinements of your lover's romantic
nature. In Figure 13, we see an example of many concentric lines
following the Life Line inside the Mount of Venus. Here is a person
easily influenced by the opposite sex. If the lines are very strong and
long and located very near the Life Line, these influences are more

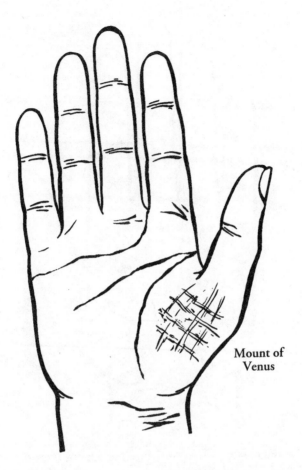

**Figure 14: The entirely crisscrossed Mount of Venus is a good indication of a neurotic personality**

powerful. Such a person may have weak willpower and easily be the dupe of an expert seducer.

Be ready to tackle a complicated but interesting person if you see a configuration on the Mount of Venus as shown in Figure 14. The entirely crisscrossed Mount of Venus is a good indication of a neurotic personality—not sinister, but complex, especially when it comes to the emotions.

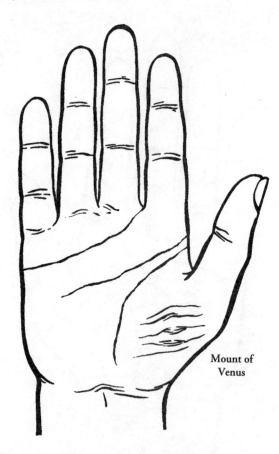

Mount of
Venus

**Figure 15: Deep horizontal influence lines in-
dicates an overpowering influence
on the opposite sex**

When the Mount of Venus shows strong, deep horizontal influence lines from the second joint of the thumb to the Life Line, as
in Figure 15, watch out! Here is someone with an overpowering
influence on the opposite sex; you stand a chance of becoming an
innocent victim of a Mephistophelean power. If these horizontal
lines of influence have islands, as two of the lines in Figure 15
have, your lover may have previously had many affairs. These
islands indicate a Casanova component in the personality.

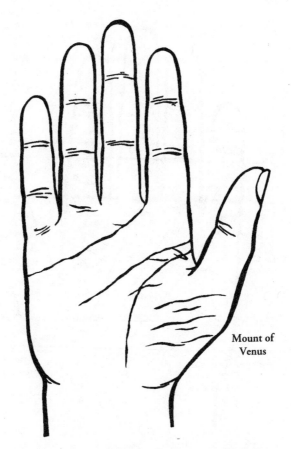

**Figure 16: These Mount of Venus lines indicate
a lover greatly influenced by family**

If it's in-laws you want to avoid at any cost, then it's best you don't push toward marriage with someone who possesses Mount of Venus influence lines as illustrated in Figure 16.

Here is a lover greatly influenced by family. "Mom never cooked it that way" would not be an unusual statement around this person's home.

Different lines of influence running from the Mount of Venus to other mounts signify different refinements of character. In Figure 17 (page 248), four more common influence line configurations are shown.

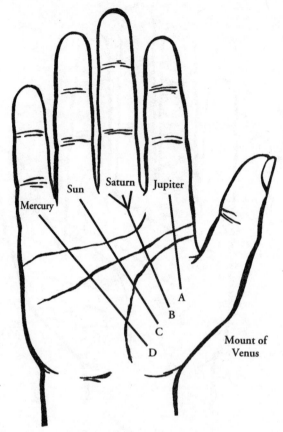

**Figure 17: Different lines of influence signify
different refinements of character**

First, there's the influence line that runs from Venus to the
Mount of Jupiter (A). Here's the schemer, imbued with ambition
and egoism, consumed by the drive for success. As a lover, he or she
isn't the most romantic person around, as career will be placed
before emotional love.

The influence line running from Venus to the Mount of Saturn
indicates a depressed, moody, and uncommunicative lover. As this
person grows older, he or she may end up living in an ivory tower,
detached from outer life. If the influence line ends in a fork, as it

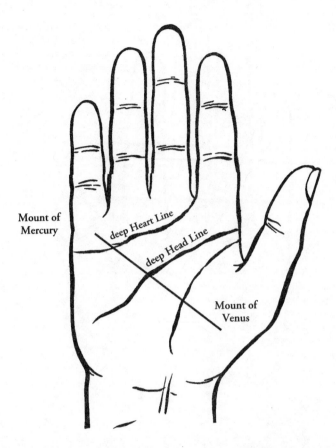

**Figure 18:** This influence line shows what may
be a stormy love life; a strong-feeling
person for a short term romance.

does in the diagram, marriage with this person would be unhappy
for both people (line B).

The line marked C, ending at the Mount of the Sun, is the most
favorable indication for romance and a permanent relationship. A
person with this line of influence has a good chance to become
famous, to gain wealth as well as celebrity; he or she will be aided
through life by close friends. Love and romantic attachments will
receive due attention in this person's life, even though career accomplishments will be significant. Read Chapter 10.

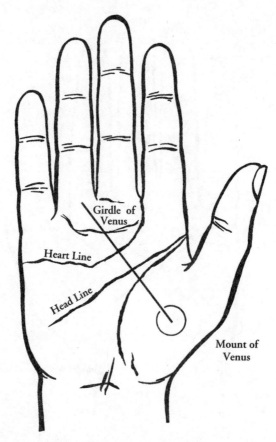

Figure 19: Sudden passion and perhaps infidelity are indicated by this line of influence from the Mount of Venus

The influence line marked D, ending at the Mount of Mercury, indicates a personality with lofty ideas and a great aptitude for science. His or her "other world" attitude is conducive to a warm, lasting relationship.

Figure 18 (page 249) shows an interesting combination: the line of influence begins toward the center of the Mount of Venus and intersects a long, deep Heart line as well as a long, deep Head Line, ending at a high point on the Mount of Mercury. This individual's love life may sometimes be stormy; he or she probably already has a history of repeated difficulty in romantic ventures. Not your best bet for the long term, but a strong-feeling person for the short.

Another interesting possibility for a line of influence originating in the Mount of Venus is shown in Figure 19. The line begins in an island on the mount and runs directly to the Girdle of Venus, intersecting both Heart and Head Lines. Sudden passion and perhaps infidelity are indicated here.

I had a case of a woman who possessed just such a configuration. She was quite attractive and passionate, and she was about to enter into a love affair destined for misfortune. She realized that her good name, her fortune, perhaps even her reasoning were threatened by such a romantic adventure, but she left her husband and her reputation for the young man—who happened to be her cousin.

Figure 20 (page 252) is another example of a special case of influence line beginning on Venus. Here, it starts with a star on the mount and ends with a fork on the Mount of Saturn. When someone possesses this sign, chances are his or her marriage may end in death or serious illness.

Broken marriage is also indicated by the configuration shown in Figure 21 (page 253). Here the line of influence begins in a star and ends in an island at the Mount of Mercury. A guilty intrigue involving the person's career is indicated—an intrigue that will be connected with or result in divorce, lawsuits, and general marriage troubles; but wisdom can change this.

If the line does not begin with a star, there is no indication of career intrigue but romantic separation and lawsuits are still possible.

One last example of the way influence lines can affect the basic meanings of a palm's secrets. Figure 22 (page 254) shows a long and deep Heart Line, in conjunction with a marked Girdle of Venus and many horizontal lines of influence across the Mount of the Moon and sloping Head Line.

If your lover has such markings, he or she possesses an active imagination. Common sense will go to the winds; a vivid mental

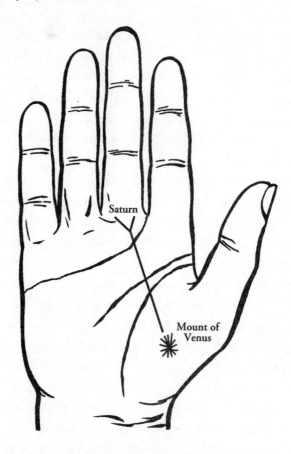

**Figure 20: A star ending with a fork on the Mount of Saturn—marriage ends in death or illness**

imagery will rule this person's love life. The many-lined Mount of the Moon indicates jealousy, generally, sexual jealousy. In combination with a vivid imagination, this individual must learn to overcome jealousy in general.

The palm contains untold volumes about a person's life. Here, we've gone far to demonstrate the emotional side which the hand can reveal—no one aspect, we must remember, should be considered without looking at it in combination with the others. Though everyone possesses signs of emotional imperfection, these signs can

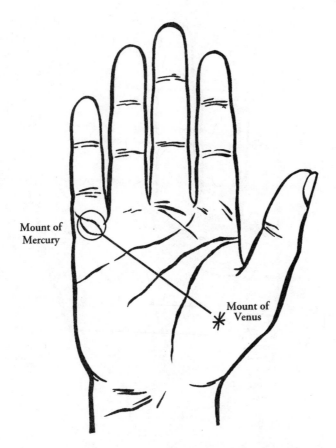

**Figure 21: A star ending in an island at the Mount of Mercury indicates intrigue involving a career**

be changed as the person changes through life's experiences. Again, see Chapter Eight.

We are all our own guides. The signs in our hands alter to speak of these internal changes as we change our attitudes toward life—through living—and on love—through loving. Destiny is not beyond our control; attitudes control our lives enough to change the way destiny writes in our palms! Giving love to another is one of the most dramatic ways of altering destiny—for ourselves and for our loved ones. When you improve your character, you improve

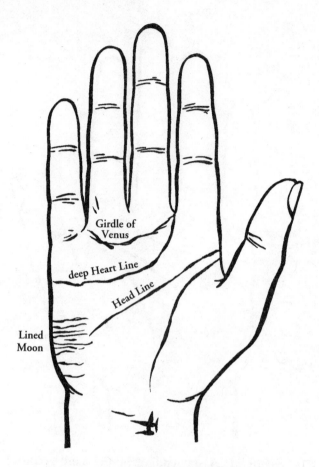

Figure 22: **Many lines of influence on Mount of the Moon—an active imagination combined with jealousy; if low they are travel lines, usually by sea**

your destiny. We can alter and achieve and create the course of our lives. Remember the old saying, "As a man thinketh in his heart, so is he." What we think (we do have control of what we say to ourselves) controls what we attract to us. So feed ourselves constructive, loving thoughts and be in control of our destiny, for the lines of the palm change as we change our thinking and learn how to take healthy care of our bodies. We are in control of our destiny!

# *T*HE COLORS OF LOVE

## *chapter eight*

*The aura of love is a rainbow of colors
that splash us with the warm rain
and sunshine of creativity.*

—A. Andrews

*I* don't know what it was, but from the second we saw each other we knew we were meant for each other."

"We both knew right away we were on the same wavelength."

"We just felt close, right from the beginning."

These are certainly not uncommon declarations. Surely, we all have memories of having met someone we were immediately attracted to. That irresistible pull which can unite two lovers from the first moment seems so natural. Or we can recall feeling a dynamic vibration from a person who enters a room, or when we first shook hands with that special someone. "Love at first sight," though it may be a cliché, is another expression of this instantaneous feeling of romantic recognition. Recognizing each other from a past life could be one of the answers, but these feelings are based on more than mere romantic fancy; they are the result of two people possessing similar auras. Although the feeling is usually interpreted as intuitive and immediate like or dislike, the cause actually comes from two people's auras mixing as they meet.

# Auras

What are these auras? They are not just some sort of fanciful invention by science fiction writers. They do exist. Kirlian photography, a special process in film technique, makes it possible "to photograph the apparent energy emanating from the body," as the Kirlian scientists describe it.

The resulting photographs are very striking, capturing exactly the shifting colors, tones, and hues of this field of energy—the aura—as it curls flamelike from the body.

The process of Kirlian photography has provided technical science with proof that the ancient occult science of the human aura is not imagination. The subtle magnetic emanation that is generated by each of us has been studied by occultists for centuries, and has gone under different names in different languages. But the idea behind it is always the same: there is a peculiar body energy or life force derived from the atmosphere around us. The first experimenters with this force learned that it had characteristics analogous to the force field around the common magnet.

We each possess a "magnetic" field that radiates from us in the same way that the Sun's rays emanate from its center. This is the aura, and it partakes of and reflects our mental, spiritual, and emotional states. We all create the characteristics of our own auras by our mental, spiritual, and emotional habits. The temperamental pattern which you have made your habitual response to certain situations is reflected by a specific color in our aura; good or poor health (mentally or physically) is also reflected by characteristic auric colors.

So the aura is an extension of a person's character; it is the aura we are "feeling"—with our own aura—when we feel instantaneously conscious of the strength of another's personality and charisma.

Yet, very few people are capable of actually seeing the human aura in any degree or intensity without the aid of Kirlian devices. Highly evolved people—known as "sensitives"—are capable of discerning these energy radiations. Until technical science caught up with occult science in this area, it was only through the reports of sensitives that we knew the colors and shapes that auras could take.

The well-known auric instructor Barbara Martin says that if a person is healthy, rays of shimmering silver are visible in strong, straight lines emanating at a 90-degree angle from the body. Rays that seem to droop or hang close to the body denote ill health or fatigue in a person. Likewise, if a sensitive herself is indisposed or fatigued, her own aura will be weakened, as well as her capacity for auric sight.

Ordinarily, the human aura extends up to eighteen inches, sometimes two feet, away from the body and has various shapes, depending upon an individual's natural mental and emotional states. Barbara Martin's interpretation of the shapes of auras is one of the most dependable. In her work *The Fascinating Aura* she writes that the less mentally developed person will have an aura that closely follows the outline of the body, one which is usually square across the bottom and top. (Does this ring a bell for the epithet "He's a square"?)

The higher the mental development of an individual, the more egg-shaped the aura. (Here we have some evidence for the truth in the expression "egghead.") A person who is highly evolved, both mentally and spiritually, will radiate an aura that is slightly pointed at the top and at the bottom. The level of a person's development will determine the width and depth of a person's aura.

Auric colors are another indication of one's emotional and mental state. To discern the predominant colors of an aura, in addition to the size and shape, is to discern a person's sum total character on all levels—including, of course, how capable a person is of giving and receiving love. Ancient occult science, as well as modern technical science, has shown that each color reflects something different about one's emotions and habitual temperament. At UCLA, where some of the most intensive research is being done on auras via Kirlian photography, studies that Masters and Johnson never thought of were conducted on couples during the act of making love. Using the Kirlian film process, researchers photographed different couples during sexual intercourse. They saw that the auras of those who were involved merely in a sexual encounter were quite ordinary. But when Kirlian photographs were taken of a couple who were deeply and sincerely in love during sexual intercourse, the auras of both showed up with magnificent power, light, and color.

## Color Symbolism

The power of love has color, and that has now been proven for all, from the faithful to those who find proof only through cold, mechanical means. It was not the Kirlians who first studied the meanings of colors in our temperaments, however; the ancient Egyptians first formulated the idea of correspondence between the levels of human consciousness and the color spectrum. So before we go further with how to use these colors for our own benefit in love and life, let's go over them and see what each indicates.

***Red.*** One of the primary colors, red is the symbol of life. It is the color of pure energy and power. Man's life energy is shown by a beam of vivid red light radiation, the vital energy flow. Pure red means enthusiasm and righteous direction. People with a great deal of red in their auras possess strong minds and wills and show a warm, affectionate nature. This is the color of the most profound of humankind's passions: passionate love, passionate courage, and passionate hatred. The purer the color, the healthier these passions. When the color is darker or muddied, the physical self has taken over, and passion has become self-centered.

*Yellow.* Reflecting humankind's intellect and brainpower, this is a stimulating mental color. Its presence indicates that the mind is receptive and always working, even when the individual who possesses it is in repose. The golden shades of yellow reflect a highly evolved person, one who has developed innate capacities and attained a great amount of wisdom. When pure yellow shades into gold in an aura, the individual is probably in the process of developing higher capacities. Generally, pure yellow is the predominant auric color of optimistic, capable, and intelligent people who use their intellect in their dealings with love and life. These are not worriers, but are high-spirited and thoughtful people. Muddy yellow hues, however, are a negative sign; they indicate jealousy and suspicion, as well as idleness and a tendency to daydream and fantasize.

*Blue.* A spiritual color, blue denotes a preoccupation with religious beliefs and a devotion to altruistic causes. A person with a predominance of blue in his or her aura will overcome all obstacles in search of knowledge. This is an inspirational character, artistic, and in harmony with nature. The truth is this person's concern, especially in matters of love. The love is the pure kind of love, based in mutual trust and loyalty. The brighter the shade of blue, the more self-confident the individual and the more optimistic the character. Paler shades of blue indicate less self-confidence and positivism. Indigo blue in the aura denotes a high spiritual nature; one whose aura is dominated by this color is fortunate, for its dominant presence reflects attunement to the spiritual self. The greatest integrity and sincerity attainable by humankind is possessed by such a person.

*Green.* A color that is actually the mix of the primary colors blue and yellow, bright, shining green in the aura reflects a peaceful and pure person who is a lover of the earth and nature and who finds fulfillment in beauty. This is also the color of individualism and renewal; it represents a person growing in knowledge and balance. A pure blue green is a sign of the Ego, of a person who has an inborn sense of charity and love of the human race in general. It represents a wide variety of ideas on the mental level and an animated, versatile, adaptable nature. A gray-shaded green is the color of diplomats and those people in power who act for the good of people whom they govern, rather than for the good of themselves. A muddied, speckled green aura shows self-centeredness and a reign of Ego. A person with a predominance of muddy green is involved in personal affairs to such an extent that outside matters become irrelevant.

*Violet.* A rare color to dominate auras, this is the hue of spiritual serenity, of a person willing to put his or her talents into service for humanity's higher capacities. It contains both the blue color—spirituality—and the red color—vitality and power. It is no wonder that throughout human history, kings and queens have adapted this color as theirs, in the same way they adapted the (often false) idea that they were divine beings. This color hardly belongs on the physical plane; indeed, only prophets and saints have been known to possess this as their predominant auric color. However, certain highly evolved individuals (intellectually or emotionally) will show some shades of this color, mixed with others, in their auras.

*Orange.* A mixture of the primary colors yellow and red, pure orange shows enthusiasm of an intellectual nature toward life. The life-of-the-party type of individual possesses a powerful orange ray and is the soul of energy, an active, energetic person who tends to dominate others. People with any shade of orange are those to whom responsibility and authority are second nature. The determined, ambitious individual with the pure orange ray can become the selfish, egotistic person in pursuit of personal fame and reputation, in which case the aura will be dominated not by pure orange, but by a grayer, muddier hue. Overall, the pure orange ray denotes someone whose determination will bring success; the danger lies in the possible misuse of that success. A well-balanced individual will retain an orange hue throughout life.

***Brown.*** A mixture of all the primary colors, brown denotes the color of the manager, the businessman. It is connected with material acquisitions, and the power to make money. A person with this as a dominant auric color is conventional and industrious; emotions remain at bay in pursuit of objectives and accumulation of worldly goods through ordinary but well-managed means. The more personal wealth this person accumulates, the darker the brown auric shade. Brown denotes a stick-to-it-iveness that is necessary in commerce and business success, though not perseverance in emotional affairs—indeed, such willfulness will take its toll on his capacity for true love. When the hue tends toward greenish brown, the individual will be selfish, grabbing at anything within material reach.

***Gray.*** People with gray as the predominant auric color are not very common, although hints of gray will appear in many people's auras. In predominance, this is the color of the narrow-minded person. Surely not the world's greatest love prospect, this person is without imagination and approaches everything with extreme conventionality. People with at least some gray in their auras are formalists in all they do, be it in business or love. Marriage first and then the bedroom. The more gray in an aura, the more likely the person is to be a loner—a persistent individual who will give up love and friendship to complete his or her worldly task of turning each stone along a slow and careful way: everything according to the rules.

**Black.** Black is actually the absence of color—not really a hue at all, but color's negation. It is associated with evil in its pure form, or of negativity. In an overpowering negative mood of resentment, a person's aura can expand to a huge black cloud that fills the room and has its effect on everyone around. A jealous tantrum against your lover will fill the house with blackness. True colors mixed with black produce a toning effect. Very often, a person on the brink of death will have an aura speckled with black. A person who possesses an evil, harmful nature will have an aura of deep crimson laced with black—viciousness personified.

**White.** Also not a pure color in and of itself, white is the blending of all colors' light rays, and as such it is present in everyone's aura to some degree. When white combines with other hues, it produces pastels, and each pastel of a pure color will denote a higher quality of that pure color. For example, red and white in the aura, or pink (as it appears), is usually associated with youthful vibrancy and innocence. This is the color of love and health, of those who lead a quietly modest life of love and art. There is no jealousy or negativity in the person who has pink as a dominant auric color. Others will be attracted to a predominantly pink aura because of the feelings of devotion and loyalty, vitality, and love it exudes. Yellow-white, or very pale yellow, as the dominant color of an aura denotes an "ivory tower" kind of life. This person has given up—temporarily, perhaps—the struggle for wealth and position in favor of intellectual pursuit. Here is a person who can be ultimately altruistic and capable of the purest form of love. When pastel yellow is combined with or muddied by greenish brown, the individual uses mental powers to develop offbeat ideas and can become fanatical.

When white mixes with blue to produce pastel blue, or blue white, high idealism is indicated. The predominance of this auric color represents a person capable of transmitting a wonderful sense of tranquility to others.

*Opalescent hues* in auric colors are other variations which show a high development in the individual. These mother-of-pearl emanations are rarely constant in an aura, but come when someone has just reached one of the finest moments of life, when utmost unselfishness and love is achieved.

To see the shape, size, and color of human auras requires years of training and patience. However, when two people are close and love is building between them, it is possible to catch a glimpse now and then, even if you have no training whatsoever. The best time to catch this "glimpse" is just before your loved one is waking up, usually in the dawn or predawn hours. You may see the aura emanating from your loved one's head on the white pillow. During sleeping hours one's aura weakens as the body's activity ebbs. Just before waking the body has strengthened, however, and as the mind throws off sleep, without yet being fully awake, the aura is at its most intense.

There is still another way to experiment for yourself to see whether you have some capacity for auric sight. Place your fingertips together for at least one minute. Then, against a black background, slowly draw them apart. Auric radiations can often be seen emanating from the fingertips. It may take some practice to get this effect; but when you do see it, it will be quite apparent. Your fingers will appear as though united by rays the width of each finger, and these rays will become narrower as you draw your fingers apart. Try it with your lover, and after both of you have pulled your own fingers apart, lay your hands palm downward on the black cloth you use for a background. Watch as each of your auric rays seems to reach for your lover's.

For most of us, auric vision takes time and formal instruction, but what we stand to gain from auras does not only involve our ability to see them. We know that auric colors are of nature, that knowing what they mean is knowing nature's message to us. Knowing this, we can "use" auric colors as a point of meditation, not only to strengthen our own capacities for love, but to "send" love to others.

## Color Meditations

Let's say that you want to heighten your feelings of devotion to your loved one, that you want to rid your self of your jealousy about this person and increase the pure love you have. Red, white, or pink are the auric colors you will meditate on to achieve this. You are going to think pink, quite literally, and you are going to do so in a meditative state of relaxed awareness.

The best method for beginning meditators is to place a slip of pink paper on a white background before them. Look at this color, concentrating only on the pink slip of paper. When intrusive thoughts enter your mind, make an effort to push them aside. "Get into" the color before you. Close your eyes and try to visualize only that color.

Once you feel the color pink firmly in your mind, sit in a comfortable chair, your head upright, your arms relaxed and at your sides. Close your eyes and begin by breathing deeply and evenly through your mouth several times. Do it slowly; if you begin to feel dizzy, slow down your rate of breathing—don't just sit there and blow big gusts of air. Rather, breathe in and out until you begin to relax with the exercise.

Now, with your eyes still closed, visualize the color pink. (You may need to have the pink slip of paper within sight at first, to glance at, if you have a problem visualizing it.) Still in your relaxed breathing state, concentrate only on the color pink. You'll find it easier to do now than at first, before you had done the breathing exercises. Your next step is literally to bring the color into your body centers. The illustration on the next page shows these centers called chakras by the Hindus. Visualize the color pink descending down, through the chakra at the top of your head from above, swirling in a clockwise pattern around and into the other chakras. Concentrate and feel it descending (clockwise) around the "third eye" energy center, then farther down, to swirl around and into the throat center. Once you feel the color penetrating this center, visualize it swirling even farther into your body, circling your heart center (clockwise, again), then penetrating this chakra. Feel it there for a moment, and when you are satisfied and can visualize your heart center possessing pink, concentrate on the swirling pink color, and send it down to your spleen area. From your spleen center, send it in a clockwise motion down, around, and into your solar plexus center. From there go to your spinal center, at the base of your spine.

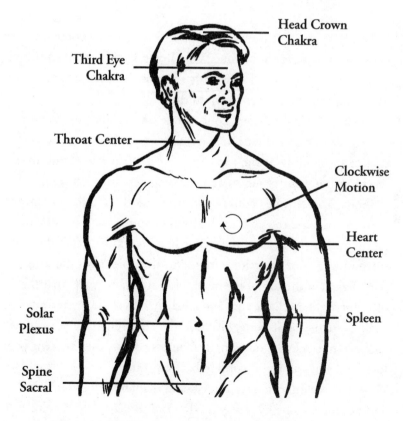

**Bring the colors into your chakras (body centers)**

This will take time, and don't be discouraged if at first it takes many sessions to feel the color descending through just the first chakra at the top of your head. Each time you meditate on pink, you will be able to "send" it farther into yourself more easily and in less time. Once you are able to visualize the color in each chakra, picture the strand of color being locked into the solar plexus center in a kind of bow. Once you can do this, your aura will possess much more of the color pink (in this case), and your character will be witness to this change, even if you or your loved one do not possess auric vision. Remember, the aura is a sort of color translation of our inner selves and of those things that are important to us. Just know what each color means in your character.

What if you want the person you love to get over some jealousy he or she may have about you? What if you want to send your love, to surround your loved one with the pure essence of your love? With color meditation you can do this.

In your meditative state, concentrate on the color pink and pull it into your chakras first. Now, visualize your lover and his or her chakras, beginning at the top of the head. Visualize a pink thread reaching out from your solar plexus center, through your other chakras, to a point just above your lover's head. (You do not have to know or visualize the physical location of your lover—just the mental picture of the person and his or her chakras.) Picture the color surrounding your lover for a moment, then picture it entering the first chakra, at the top of the head. Now mentally "pull" that thread of color right back to you and push it down through your first chakra. At the same time, visualize the color entering your lover's chakras (in clockwise motion) as it enters yours. You have sent your love, and you will feel it coming back to you.

It's terribly important to understand that any color you "send" to another must come back to you. To send someone else a color is to send it to yourself, as well. So be warned—do not play around with color meditation; do not try to harm someone by sending black, for instance. It will only come back to you.

When you are meditating to bring down the light (color) into your aura, you are changing it in a way that vibrantly affects not only yourself, but others, especially those whom you love. If you want to make a truly smashing impression on your first meeting with a new potential love, make an impression on yourself first by spending twenty minutes meditating on the color whose characteristics you wish to possess. Heads will turn when you enter a room if you are possessed of a good color. No, people probably won't actually see your aura, but they will sense the character of that color in you. They may not know why they find you so magnetic or attractive, but they will be attracted.

So, to review the important characteristics of each auric color, and to make matters a little more convenient for color meditation, here are the basic principles of each color.

## Basic Color Principles

| | |
|---|---|
| Red | Life. Pure energy. Warm affection. Enthusiasm. Also passion. Anger. Danger. |
| Yellow | Intellect. Openness. Optimism. Ability. |
| Gold | Wisdom. Higher consciousness. |
| Blue | Altruism. Inspiration. Calm. Harmony. Artistic nature. Truth and love. |
| Indigo | Spiritual nature. High integrity and sincerity. Intuition. |
| Green | Energy. Earthly peace. Balance. Individualism. Renewal. |
| Blue-green | Ego. Human charity. Human love. |
| Violet | Spiritual serenity. Spiritual power. |

| | |
|---|---|
| Orange | Activity. Intellectual enthusiasm toward life. Ambition. Responsibility. |
| Brown | Perseverance. Materialism. Managerial talent. |
| Gray | Formalism. Conventionality. |
| Black | Negativity. Evil. |
| White | The highest magnitude of spirituality. |
| Pink | Vibrancy. Love. Lack of jealousy. Modesty and art. Devotion. |
| Yellow-white | Intellectual pursuit. Developing conscious- ness. Pure love. |
| Blue-white | High idealism. Tranquility. |

There is another type of color exercise that both you and your lover can do and makes for a pleasantly intimate evening, without a blaring television. For this exercise, you'll need slips of colored paper, one slip for each of the colors. This is something that each of you should do separately, without watching the other. Afterward, you can compare notes to see how your colors correspond.

First, on the back of each colored slip of paper, write a number or a letter. Then lay out all the colored slips, color side up, against a white background. Without thinking about the colors, select the color that immediately strikes you as your favorite of the bunch. Pick it up and turn it over, placing it above the row of colored slips. Now, look again at the row of colors. Again select the first one of those remaining colored slips that immediately strikes you as your favorite. Place this one to the right of the first selection you made, above the colored slips. Keep repeating this, each time selecting the color that immediately strikes you as the "best" of the remaining colored slips. Remember not to pause and think about what a color means or to render any other judgments about associations you may have with a particular color; just pick the one to which you automatically and instantly are drawn. When all the slips have been chosen, jot down the numbers (or letters) of your selections, going from left to right—that is, in the order you chose them.

Next, ask your lover to do the same, but don't prompt and don't hover while your lover is making selections. When your lover is finished and has jotted down the numbers of his or her selection of colors, compare them with yours.

Basically, your first two color selections will represent those qualities that you are working to attain. The next two color selections will reflect qualities that you now possess—the colors that a sensitive would be able to see as your dominant auric hues. The third two or three selections reflect traits and qualities you possess but aren't using in your love and life right now, for whatever reason, but mainly because these qualities do not fit your aspirations.

By these first three sets of choices, you should be able to tell, in a general way, if you and your lover have similar auric colors—that is, similar characters and similar traits. In other words, you should be able to see if you are basically compatible. If among these three sets of choices both of you have at least three colors in common, you are on the way to a fine romance. This doesn't mean that the colors have to correspond directly in the exact order you chose them. All it means is that if among each of your first six or seven choices of colors, there are three mutually chosen colors, you are pretty compatible. Upwards of those three, great! For each direct similarity (if you both chose red as the second color, for instance), the greater your chances at true, lasting romance.

But what about the last several colors? Well, these are colors that reflect characteristics you are in the process of rejecting. The last two or three choices of colors are probably reflections of traits you have already rejected altogether, so pay attention to your lover's choices in the final colors as well. There may be some rough times ahead, for instance, if all the colors you chose first turn out to be the ones he or she chose last! But then, if that's the case, it's probably already apparent to both of you that things aren't as close to paradise as you'd wish!

The aura, or that energy field around each of us, must be "recharged" from time to time by contact with other people. We improve each other's auras with a balancing of polarity between the "negative" energy of woman and the "positive" energy of man. The terms "negative" and "positive" in this context do not mean "bad" and "good," but are used to denote opposites. This is the Yin and Yang of nature, and when these two polarities come into physical contact, the auras are enhanced and heightened. An exchange of energy takes place where each polarity meets and is energized by its opposite. It's a soothing effect, even when sexual intercourse is not involved.

It's interesting that the American eagle, our national symbol, has a beautiful instinct for going through the ritual of love every twenty-four-hour period—but not necessarily for sexual culmination. American eagles will come together and roost, touching each other. The mere physical closeness is instinctively important at day's end. They are drawn to each other by nature, for the balancing and strengthening of their auras, to feel whole again.

Touch is important for us, too. Each time we pat another on the back in a gesture of fondness, we exchange auric energy and reinvigorate ourselves and our capacity for love. Especially in these times of depersonalized urban life, when it is actually possible to go for days at a time without touching another human being, it is important for our emotional and mental survival to become close to someone, to reach out a hand and touch. No matter how mechanical society becomes, we will always need contact with other's auras in order to energize our own. Nature is truly beautiful to give us this need for each other's aura.

Can you think of any moment as close to paradise as when you and your lover are in each other's embrace? Savor this feeling, for it is not only pleasurable, but healing to the body and soul.

# THE NUMEROLOGY OF LOVE

*chapter nine*

*Nature geometrizes.*
—Pythagoras

We've seen that the signs of love are within the stars, the face, handwriting, the hand itself, and in auric colors. Now, using that same key of love, we'll unlock some of the mysteries of numbers and search for the finer details of the character and soul of romance in ourselves and our loved ones.

In the scientific art of numerology, numbers are more than tools for expressing how much or how many; they are expressions of ideas. Each number is a garment for a concept, and within each concept are ideas about love. The greatest philosophers of ancient Greece thought of numbers as the essence of universal harmony. Plato said that numbers have a harmony, the same harmony of movement as our souls and our cosmos. Pythagoras stated that the universe is arranged according to numbers.

Numerology is the science of interpreting the laws of nature and the human spirit through numbers. It is the pure study of the meaning of numbers that comes down to us from the ancient scholars. Modern technical science uses a mere portion of this ancient knowledge about numbers in its linear equations to interpret only linear ideas. Numerology uses all the ancient knowledge about the working and harmony of the cosmos, and the way numbers can be used to interpret the universal laws, linear and nonlinear. And love is nonlinear; it comes from emotion more than from logic.

One of the basic ideas behind numerology is the cyclical nature of our lives. We are constantly moving in and out of cycles. We feel this in our romantic lives where love is concerned; we have upswings and downturns. Nothing is constant except change. We begin life on a path, but that is a path of change, no matter who we are. It is a path that takes us only into cycles, ever changing, always altering the way we are, the way we shape our destinies, the people whom we love and who love us.

Numerology can help us interpret both our original path and our current cycle. By comparing what we learn about ourselves and our lovers in this way, we can come to a deeper understanding of each other and avoid unnecessary pitfalls in our romantic lives.

Each of us possesses three basic numbers at all times. There is the number of the birth path, which is constant; second is the birth name number, also constant; third is the number of the day you were born, another constant.

But the current cycle changes each year. We have numbers to determine the paths we will take through all our cycles; then, the number that is always and purely the individual who is on this path; and, third, the number of our day of birth. On top of that we also have our ever-changing social cycle.

It's quite a simple matter to find out what each of these numbers is via numerological addition and reduction. In numerology we use only the nine digits: 1, 2, 3, 4, 5, 6, 7, 8, 9. The numbers 11 and 22 have a special significance in numerology, which we will discuss later.

First, let's determine the three numbers for a person named Gail Maureen Philips, born on December 6, 1943.

# *Y*our Birth Path Number

This number is based on your complete birth date. To compute it, add the year you were born to the number of the month you were born, to the day you were born. Gail was born on December 6, 1943. You will find her birth path by adding:

$$
\begin{aligned}
+ \quad & 12 \text{ (December)} \\
+ \quad & 6 \text{ (day)} \\
+ \quad & 1943 \\
\hline
= \quad & 1961
\end{aligned}
$$

Next, using numerological reduction, we reduce the number 1961 to one digit by adding all the digits across:

$$1 + 9 + 6 + 1 = 17$$

But 17 still is not a one-digit number, so we add its digits:

$$1 + 7 = \mathbf{8}$$

So, the birth path for Gail Maureen Philips is the number 8.

# Your Birth Name Number

This number is based on your name, meaning the name you were given at birth, the name on your birth certificate. To compute this number, we assign numerological values to the letters of the alphabet in a simple order:

| A | B | C | D | E | F | G | H | I | J | K | L | M |
|---|---|---|---|---|---|---|---|---|---|---|---|---|
| 1 | 2 | 3 | 4 | 5 | 6 | 7 | 8 | 9 | 1 | 2 | 3 | 4 |

| N | O | P | Q | R | S | T | U | V | W | X | Y | Z |
|---|---|---|---|---|---|---|---|---|---|---|---|---|
| 5 | 6 | 7 | 8 | 9 | 1 | 2 | 3 | 4 | 5 | 6 | 7 | 8 |

Let's take the name Gail Maureen Philips and find out what her birth name number is by adding and reducing the numerological values of the letters in her name.

Her first name is 20:

G (7) + A (1) + I (9) + L (3) = 20.

By numerological reduction this becomes 2 + 0 = **2.**

Her second name is 32:

M (4) + A (1) + U (3) + R (9) + E (5) + E (5) + N (5) = 32.

Reduced, 32 is 3 + 2, or **5.**

Her last name is 44:

P (7) + H (8) + I (9) + L (3) + I (9) + P (7) + S (1) = 44.

Reduced, 44 is 4 + 4, or **8.**

The next step is to add these three reduced numbers:

2 (First name) + 5 (Second name) + 8 (Last name) = 15

Reducing this number, we get 1 + 5 = **6.**

And so, Gail Maureen Philips' birth name number is 6.

# Your Birth Day Number

The number of the day a person was born is the third personal number, and it does have some significance in interpreting character. It often happens that we become romantically interested in someone, but aren't yet familiar enough to feel comfortable asking his or her year of birth. "When's your birthday?" usually nets an answer like "September 10th"—*sans* year. Computing that person's three life numbers is then impossible. Even if you know the person's real full name and can compute the birth name and the current cycle number, the exact birth path number will be unknown. In such a case, it's possible to use just the number of the birth day as a *sketchy* substitute—in this case, the 10th, which reduces to 1 (1 + 0).

Your three basic numbers—birth path, birth name, and birth day—never change; they are your permanent lucky numbers. There is another number that changes every January. It is called the current cycle number or personal year number.

# Your Current Cycle Number

This is the number of your present social cycle or year. To find it, you simply add your birth month number and birth day to the present year. Let's see what the cycle number is for Gail Maureen Philips in 1998:

$$
\begin{array}{r}
+\quad 12 \text{ (December)} \\
+\quad 6 \text{ (day)} \\
\underline{+\ 1998} \text{ (any current year)} \\
2016
\end{array}
$$

Again, we reduce this figure by adding its digits together:

$$2 + 0 + 1 + 6 = 9$$

So, Gail's cycle number in 1998 is the number 9—Nine Year.

Two numbers are interpreted both prior to and after they are subject to reduction—the number 11 and the number 22. If, for example, after adding and reducing the digits in your lover's birth name, you reduce to the number 11, the birth name is the number 2 and the number 11 (1+1=2); with 22, it is both 4 and 22. In cases such as these, you will have to read both the significance of the number 4 and the significance of 22 (or 2 and 11) for a complete understanding of the vibratory influences of the birth name. These two special numbers, 11 and 22, are *master numbers*. If an individual is living on the positive side of the number 2, he or she can become an 11. The number 4 person can also become a 22.

Each of your numbers will have some bearing on understanding the whole person, since each number we are connected with is another thread in our entire harmonious connection to the universe of life and love. So as we go on to reveal the significance of each number, keep in mind that all of us have vibrations from more than one number—the number of our birth path, the number of our birth name, the number of the day of our birth, and the number of our current cycle.

# *Your* Number Meanings

Let us proceed with the explanations of the vibrations each number gives us, through the combinations and influences of our birth path number, the number of our birth day, and also our birth name number. (Remember: Use only the name on your birth certificate.)

We have influences from all three of these basic numbers. Two or more identical numbers intensifies the qualities and vibrations of that number. So be aware of each of these three number influences while reading the following pages. (For the explanation of your current cycle number, see page 291.)

# Number One

This is the number of the naturally aggressive and showy lover, the person who takes the lead. Love is more important than shelter or food to Ones; it is a necessity, not a luxury. For One to live without love would be as meaningless as a lumberjack living without a forest.

Creativity, originality, and a certain unorthodoxy are keynotes for people with this as one of their numbers. There are possible pitfalls having a One lover; for example, he or she may become selfish in love. Number Ones have a tendency to live as though the Sun itself revolves around them.

They are great lovers, but if a tendency to egocentricity has developed within them, they will make love simply for the pleasure it gives them, paying far less attention to giving pleasure in return. Ones who have allowed their self-centeredness to take over are smug and self-satisfied. Giving-oriented One lovers, on the other hand, are independent and exciting; they are willing to experiment.

Independence in both thought and action is of utmost importance to One; they are people who may easily be reformers in society and reformers of their lovers' romantic and sexual habits. They can be arrogant in a way that is supremely attractive to members of the opposite sex. A poet would say that Ones have heart. They cannot be cowed, bullied, or bluffed. They possess initiative and are not afraid of new starts; they dance to their own tune.

Ones may be restless due to an awareness of their own creative force. If one of your lover's numbers is One, encourage change as he or she feels inclined to change. These people need change, and if circumstances in their lives—or lovers in their lives—fight against this change, it can be disastrous for their character; they need change like flowers need the Sun. These are not people who write on the air; they must possess the air and its many winds of change.

People with the astrological signs of Leo or Aquarius respond well to Ones. Libra, Gemini, Aries, and Sagittarius also harmonize with them. But Scorpio and Taurus should be cautious in dealing with Ones; their needs are for constancy and faithfulness, whereas Ones will always need change.

## Number Two

(Read also Number Eleven.) An individual of gentleness and grace and a lover of fine things, a Two is a person of emotion and organization. These are people whose greatest contribution to a lover is the ability to provide a sense of emotional security. They can create a loving home out of a few sticks of furniture, and they have the capacity to feel at home—and make you feel at home—no matter where.

But this very capacity to make any place home may lead to possessiveness. People who have Two as one of their numbers must be on the alert not to be possessed by their possessions. Possessions, to a Two, can be furniture, paintings, and books—or, on the more negative side, purely the human object's affection.

On the positive side, Twos provide the roof over your head, the food on your table; they impart a security that allows their lovers freedom to be creative. Love with a Two can indeed become one of nature's miracles.

Two, like the astrological sign Cancer, is associated with the Moon. Because of this lunar connection, Twos tend to be moody. They are changeable beings, shifting from mood to mood as the sea shifts its tides. These people make mountains from the molehills in their minds. During "down" periods, Twos can take the slightest criticism as a sign of utter rejection, so it's important that Two's lover understand mood swings and be careful with words and actions during those moody times.

People with the astrological signs of Cancer, Taurus, Pisces, Scorpio, and Virgo are naturally attracted to Twos. Capricorns, Libras, and Aries are rarely attracted.

# Number Three

This is the number of presence. Threes are unhappy when confined; their love cannot be expressed or grow unless they are in contact with other people. These are people who must be able to experiment, to give full play to their intellectual curiosity, to see and be seen. They are energetic both in thought and action, and expect their lovers to appreciate their energy.

These people are artists by nature; without circumstances that allow them society with others, their art dies, as do their inner selves. Some people can be alone on a mountaintop and still develop their capacities for love; not so with a Three, who has to be among people to develop these capacities. These are people whose love grows within their relationships.

Because they need to be around other people in order to find and express their love, Threes are exciting people who tend to be the life of the party; they're usually attractive to others, and because they are people who are always looking to expand their horizons, they may begin thinking of the next love—the next experience—rather than accept the present love and experience. At the same time, this tendency allows them to become philosophical and to develop ideas into full-blown concepts, instead of wrestling them down by shotgun, scattering half-blown schemes here and there.

Proper diet is important for a Three individual; his or her mental and physical energies require a sensible diet. Threes in restrictive situations, where they don't have freedom to express their energetic drives, may turn to abusing their diets by overeating. If your lover is a Three and gorging him- or herself, chances are something in your relationship is hampering them. Are you or your lifestyle interfering with your lover's freedom of mental and physical expression?

The more excitement and intellectual confrontation you provide in your relationship with a Three, the better your love life will become; a clash of ideas stimulates this person. Without excitement, without experimentation, without the chance to expand his or her horizons, a Three becomes a robot. So curb your Three lover only in vain; trying to keep all his or her excitement and charm for yourself will literally destroy that excitement; your lover may become fat, boring, mean, and frustrated, and you may end up wondering, "Where is the person I married?"

The astrological signs of Sagittarius and Gemini are attracted to Threes. People born under the signs of Leo, Aries, Aquarius, and Libra also have an affinity with this number. Threes have to be a bit careful in dealing with Geminis, even though Geminis are attracted to them; it's a case of opposites attracting. Virgo and Pisces individuals are not the best matches for the active, energetic Three.

## Number Four

(Read also Number Twenty-two.) An unusual person by conventional standards, Four is willing to tear down, when life's circumstances make this necessary, in order to rebuild. Fours can be alone in a crowd and are people most others find difficult to understand. Like astrological Geminis, Fours seem to be drawn in two directions at once. They can see the need for taking care of the mundane details that are part of making a relationship work, but at the same time they're able to hurl logic to the winds and give their all to pure emotion and affairs of the heart.

Emotionally, Fours often are like volcanos, ready to explode. Relationships are not easy with them. When everything seems to be going well, an emotional storm may be just around the corner. In love, these people have to take things as they come, one step at a time. If they get locked into an emotional corner by hurrying things, explosions are bound to occur. "Don't Fence Me In" could easily be their theme song when it comes to forming romantic attachments.

They permit logic to have equal time with their emotions, but once emotion knocks on their door, they really can't allow love to stick one foot in; the whole door gets thrown wide open, and all the good resolutions made on the altar of logic are tossed out the window. So, in many ways, love is a dare for the Four individual.

Dilemmas are good for these people. They need to be working out problems, coming to individual solutions. This is probably why they are so difficult to read, and why they are capable of tearing down the structure of their lives and starting all over again (once they've reached their personal solutions).

They are always challenged by life and love; but it's from this challenge that movement comes. If your lover is a Four and has fallen into a routine groove without obstacles to hurdle or challenges to meet, he or she may become lethargic, and love for you may begin to disintegrate. It's better for a Four to have problems to overcome than to sit in absolute pleasure and vegetate. When everything on the surface of your relationship is going smoothly, Four will indeed begin to vegetate—until the moment when the volcano underneath erupts.

Scorpios, Taureans, and Leos are drawn to Fours. Fours will also find affinity with people born under the signs of Cancer, Pisces, Virgo, and Capricorn. Taurus can be a case of opposites attracting, so some caution is advised here. Though Fours tend to attract opposites, they don't always attract what is good for them. Leo is another case in point. Aquarians may be attracted to Fours, but again, this may be good for the Aquarian, but not so good for the Four.

## Number Five

Some of the most active people around, Fives are both intellectual and emotional when it comes to love; they can fall either way. If your lover is a Five and has fallen intellectually, he or she will still give physically, but you may detect the strain this dichotomy causes.

These people are natural analysts—of everything. For example, once they've attained a goal, they'll begin to analyze its worth and to worry about it. "Well, she can't be so great or she wouldn't love me" would not be an unusual statement from the lips of a Five. Self-esteem is one of their major problems. They're constantly preserving it, and this becomes a major obstacle to their happiness. In most cases, they have to resolve this for themselves; there is little their lovers can do or say to prove that they're just fine as lovers and people.

Fives are able to naturally exude an inner sexuality—and to go out and lure what they want to get. The question to pose to them is: "Do you always need what you want? Is what you want actually the constructive thing for you?" Nature provided Fives with analytical minds; the answers to these questions are available within them. Fives can benefit from giving their intellectual curiosity full play. As a lover of a Five, it is not good for you to be restrictive in this sense. These are people who also tend to be very romantic and avoid looking into details or paying attention to their analytical nature. You may notice a tension in your Five lover; this is the creative tension between the need for romanticism and the need to analyze the practical side of a relationship.

Do not dominate Fives. In a relationship their mercurial minds should be given full play. They should not be held back, goaded into pulling punches, or forced into being just like everyone else. They must be allowed to build their own self-esteem and to exercise their own freedom of choice. If they're allowed to make their own mistakes, free of the restrictions of others' values or rules, they can be the best of lovers in a lasting, personal way. These are not people of the majority; they are a special minority whose needs must be fulfilled on their own terms.

Gemini, Sagittarius, Virgo, and Pisces are most attracted to Five individuals. Leo and Aries people are also drawn to them. Sagittarius and Five are opposites; they are attracted because they have much to learn from each other. Five may feel an attraction to Virgo and Pisces if he or she senses weakness, but as a rule, these are not the best matches.

# Number Six

Like Threes, Sixes are artists. But here the similarity ends. For Sixes are supremely affectionate individuals—sometimes, alas, to the point of distraction. The clinging-vine type is the negative side of the affectionate nature.

Like Taurus, a Six has a good voice for singing and speaking; this quality is matched in Six with an ability to express things well and dramatically. Their need for expression is extraordinary, and if no outlet is available, they begin to deteriorate inside. Like Threes, they will die inside without an outlet for their artistic nature. They also need love, and a lover with whom to be affectionate.

Six is associated with the planet Venus, the symbol of love. This means that Sixes are receptive individuals. They are open to emotion and relationships. But, as I've said, their affection can smother a lover. It's as if this tendency to be sweet permeates every level of their lives, for Sixes tend to have blood sugar related maladies: hypoglycemia or diabetes. The image of a sugary person, then, is pointedly accurate on every level in the portrait of a Six individual. Sixes should avoid refined sugar.

It's not at all difficult to feel at ease with a Six. He or she is a natural diplomat. Sixes can bring together people who have opposing views; they are natural mediators. So, if you are in a relationship with a Six, don't be surprised if he or she is always trying to get people together.

People born under the signs of Taurus, Libra, and Aries are drawn to Six individuals. The Aries attraction is matched by Six on the physical level; though good sexual relationships can grow here, a lasting relationship with Aries and Six can pose real problems. It's never lukewarm, but either very hot or very cold. It's the very aggressive Aries type whom Six attracts. Leo, Sagittarius, Gemini, and Aquarius are other astrological signs, which have an affinity with Six. Sixes should be cautious in relationships with Cancers and Capricorns.

## Number Seven

People with seven as one of their numbers hold their heads high, seemingly above it all. But inside, they may well be going through tortuous self-doubt. Outwardly assured, Sevens are inward perfectionists, always striving, constantly trying to achieve the impossible. These are people who heed their inner voices; because of this we have come to call them "spiritual" types. Indeed, the attainment of the impossible is a spiritual endeavor, and Sevens, to this extent, are truly spiritual.

We may wonder why Sevens sometimes are susceptible to drugs or alcohol. These people are often striving within themselves, but their striving is pitted against incredible external odds. Imagine Walter Mitty without comedy.

Some Sevens appear painfully shy; others appear supercilious, eternally censuring and correcting others. But no matter how brash and harsh they may seem on the outside, they are brooding and worrying inside, trying to measure themselves against their high, spiritual standards.

Love with a Seven, then, is no lighthearted matter. Sevens will strive to make their love with another glow—almost literally. Their criticism and censure of lovers is not done out of inner maliciousness or vanity; on the contrary, it is done out of love, and out of that striving to make the almost-perfect into a perfect creation. A love affair with a Seven can be a gift to you, for it affords you the most intimate, private contact with someone who knows and practices constant self-criticism and improvement. Reach for the stars with your lover if he or she is a Seven, and you just may get there, though the going will not always be easy.

Often, Sevens tend to be secretive about their love affairs. They may find it delicious to have clandestine meetings and subtle flirtations. This side of a Seven makes a love affair spicily exciting, but for a lasting relationship, you must gain the Seven's confidence; you must expose your own inner secrets, and in return you'll receive more love and affection than you ever imagined possible.

Sevens, like anyone, show their sides in numerous ways. An aggressive, humorous person may be a Seven; a sultry, suspicious person may have this number; or a shy, retiring individual may possess this number. The key to a Seven is the integrity of his or her inner self, the search for perfection. As a lover of this type of individual, it's up to you to draw that perfect nature out; you stand only to profit from it.

The astrological signs Pisces, Cancer, and Scorpio are naturally attracted to Sevens. If you are one of these signs, and your lover is a Seven, both of you must exercise extra caution to keep from drifting out of contact with day-to-day necessities. If you can do this, all levels of your love will be of the most sublime nature imaginable.

## Number Eight

Since ancient times, eight has been the symbol of the snake about to strike. It is also the number of the organizer, the number of responsibility, of ambition, and of goals. Eights are people who mean business. They are the kind of people who accept responsibility and receive great rewards for taking it.

Don't be put off by the demeanor of an Eight person. He or she may be forbidding; it's part of being down-to-earth. Eights often appear to be the taskmasters, and in many ways, they are. They allow you to get away with nothing; no game-playing is allowed in the arena of Eight. They are disciplined and they expect discipline from their lovers, so don't become romantically involved with an Eight unless you, too, mean business. The stakes are high, and Eight plays for keeps.

Nothing is halfway where Eights' love is concerned. They accept the responsibility of a relationship, and they offer security, both emotionally and materially. Involvements with Eight individuals are therefore real commitments—commitments you must do your utmost to represent. You cannot be flirtatious around Eights the way you can around Threes or Fives. Involvements have to be based on the promise "I am yours."

With all their receptivity to commitment, though, Eights need some demands made upon them for the sake of curbing their immaturity. In sexual relationships, this side may come out in statements such as "Ask of me and I shall produce." A bit of humility is needed for the Eight person to develop into a mature individual who is capable of true love. As an Eight's lover, you'll have to tone down his or her pride in sexual prowess, so that the "see what I can do" becomes "we each have something to offer; what I have is this umbrella of love and protection."

If it's a full commitment to an Eight you are interested in, ask for something—but don't make demands if you are only flirting; Eights are serious about love.

Capricorns and Cancers, because of their romantic intensity, make good matches for Eights.

## Number Nine

Nine represents the circle of completion; the symbology of this number, like the symbology of all numbers, is based in fact. In this case the circle of completion—the symbology—is obvious, for a circle is composed of 360 degrees and reducing 360 numerologically results in $3 + 6 + 0 = 9$.

Nine is also the symbol of human love. The English word "love" numerologically reduces to 9.

Nine is universal appeal; it is the institutional number; it is distribution, getting your message across to others. Nine is the universal language, just as music or mathematics is. It is the number of Right, the number of the crusaders.

Humanitarianism is associated with this number; and although we tend to think of humanitarians as meek do-gooders, true humanitarians—those who possess nine as one of their numbers—are more the Carry Nation type, wielding a hatchet for the cause of Right. They are aggressive. But then aggressiveness gets things done. Toward what better purpose to put aggressiveness than humanitarian efforts?

Principles and laws are important to Nines, whether they are using those ideas to make a romantic relationship better, or to correct a social injustice.

On the more negative side, Nines tend to attract lovers that take more than they can give. Nines may have pasts filled with affairs in which people used them as crying towels. They tend to be involved with people who have burdens to be lifted—burdens Nines will gladly assume. But this accepting others' burdens is destructive, and ultimately for Nine will lead to the end of a love affair. A developed and mature Nine knows that accepting others' burdens as his or her own is a mistake and does something to correct the inclination, but a Nine who is not mature will want to feel needed; taking on his lover's burdens as his or her own will be simply a *convenient* way to get over insecurities. Nines will buy your love by tending to your problems (at the expense of his or her own self-development).

On the positive side, the mature Nine is a natural counselor—sans that brand of emotional blackmail inherent to the immature, insecure Nine.

As a lover, a Nine may seem cool, detached, wanting only to do the appropriate thing, but he or she is a virtual volcano once those emotions are triggered by the right person. Nines can be aggressive in affairs of the heart. He or she is the lover who at first seems to have your personal welfare at heart, but who may become a devouring, insatiable partner once the relationship gets going. This is so because Nines hold back until the very last moment; their love is as powerful as their aggressive capacity for humanitarianism.

Nines are also artists like Threes and Sixes; they won't let their independence of thought be curbed for the sake of a romantic relationship. If your love is real, you can help your Nine grow and develop artistically by allowing that freedom to create; denying it will only make an ogre out of a lover. Accepting it will allow love to bloom to its fullest flower.

Don't seek a gentle lamb when you pursue a Nine, for they are aggressive in everything, and if he or she is holding back today, it is only for the purpose of storing that energy for use in humanitarian or love efforts tomorrow. Once you've earned a Nine's trust and love, prepare for a person that will completely let go; the volcano of love will erupt, emotionally, sexually, and intellectually.

Aries and Libra are naturally attracted to the fiery Nine. Cancer and Capricorn may find life quite difficult with these people, unless they make extra efforts to adapt to Nine's artistic need for freedom.

## Number Eleven

(Read also Number Two.) One of the master numbers, Eleven is able to start from nothing and build a world with his or her hands from available resources. Elevens are innovative, progressive, and they have a natural humanitarian quality.

Elevens are natural romantics; they see only the best and as a consequence attract people in a mutually advantageous manner.

This is the person who won't press love upon you until you are comfortable. "Are you warm enough? Do you want anything to eat or drink? Would you like some music?" These are all questions an Eleven will ask before the bedroom question arises—certainly before the subject of lasting love arises. This is what I mean when I say Eleven is a humanitarian. Far from a selfish lover, an Eleven is naturally considerate and loyal. Elevens hold fast to friends, lovers, wishes, hopes, and dreams. Being in a relationship with an Eleven is like having an eternal love affair, one that doesn't get turned off when you're out of bed. It's pleasurable in bed and out.

It is not unusual for Eleven's lover to compare his or her own shortcomings against Eleven's finesse. If you find yourself as a lover of an Eleven chiding and blowing up because of your own insecurities, remember that Eleven will most likely overlook these emotional storms; remember that Elevens hold a master number.

Don't be afraid to experiment sexually with an Eleven, for this is a person incapable of being shocked or scandalized by unorthodoxy, whether it occurs in the bedroom or the sitting room. These are experimental people, and the ability to experiment is often the one thing that keeps sexual love alive.

Cultivating an adventurous spirit is the key to keeping life in your relationship with an Eleven. Elevens are apt to change quickly, so avoid falling into ruts with them. One sure way to lose an Eleven is to insist on sameness in everything, or to sermonize about orthodoxy and issue complaints.

If you want an exciting, different lover, one who is not wed to tradition and contemporary mores, look for an Eleven.

Both Aquarius and Leo are highly compatible mates for a master number Eleven. Both of these signs possess power and love without dependency or orthodoxy.

## Number Twenty-two

(Read also Number Four, when derived from 2 + 2.) The other of the master numbers, twenty-two is a number marked by destiny. Twenty-twos seems to be apart from the crowd and society. Like Fours, but on a higher level, these are people who are willing to tear down in order to reconstruct. Also like Fours, Twenty-twos have a negative side: tearing down merely for the sake of destruction—the nihilist at work to no end except the end itself.

On the positive side, the more mature Twenty-twos are master builders. They'll replace the gingerbread cornices with something more substantial and lasting. These are the people who, by analogy, are the pure refrain under a symphony's orchestral arrangement; they are the melody, the architects of life.

In love, nothing is halfway with this number. Don't get involved with a Twenty-two on a mere flirtation level. No lukewarm exists in Twenty-two's emotional repertoire. All or nothing is the name of the game—except it's no game. Intensity is the keyword here. Romantic game-playing is a trap only for those who play it with a Twenty-two.

Style is a Twenty-two trademark, but it's a personal style made up of individual methods. And so it's possible to learn a great deal from Twenty-two lovers. They're on their own, emotionally, intellectually, and psychologically. We call such people "old souls." Translation: they are wise. A parent may have vanished from home, for whatever reason, when Twenty-two was very young.

People with this number are never likely to be simply uninvolved; they tend never to find anything easy. Some of the world's greatest revolutionaries had Twenty-two as one of their numbers. Perhaps many would write it off to coincidence, but the planet Pluto, which rules this number, was discovered in the same year as the very first and famous Detroit sit-down strikes—revolutionary action which led to better working conditions for everyone.

Intensity, total commitment, and dramatic change for ultimate good are all elements of Twenty-two, so be prepared for these things in a romantic attachment to Twenty-twos. Be prepared also for a generous life, a home that is comfortable and supplied with the best of everything. Be ready to play hard, to work hard, and to love to the fullest.

The most compatible astrological signs for this number are Scorpio and Taurus, but Scorpios and Taureans must work hard to meet the Twenty-two lover on his (or her) own level.

Having studied numbers—the Pythagorean, the Hebrew, the Egyptian, and so on ad infinitum—I have found through personal experience that the simple date of an individual's birth does reveal a great deal about his or her life and, more importantly where we are concerned, about love tendencies and romantic potential. So we are going to approach this subject more comprehensively now, by examining birth month, day, and current year.

# *Your Current Cycle Meaning*

Life is cyclical—the cycles of the planets and the stars. We never remain long in the same cycle. Love surges up and swings down. Only change is constant.

Here we are discussing the nine numerical cycles. Each of the nine cycles is repeated every nine years. Do you know which one you are in this year?

As described earlier, you can determine your current cycle or personal year number very simply by adding your birth month and day to the current year (see page 275 for an example). The result is your current cycle or year number.

Every number cycle does have its love vibration and potential. The most obvious cycles are numbers five and eight, which usually dominate love and/or marriage cycles; next is one. Sometimes when your social cycle corresponds with a surge of creative energy, you find an outlet in special or unique relationships. Two gives a tremendous drive and desire for security; it's associated with the Moon and the zodiacal sign of Cancer, so many persons have a liaison or even a marriage while under the dominant Two Year—for reasons of security or for practical business purposes, to form a joint enterprise or partnership, to enhance the value of a product. It's not a very exciting kind of romantic number, but it is a necessary one for some people; it gives a feeling of security that is not always easy to obtain (until the secrets are learned).

The most intriguing number to be under for the year is seven because you must be wary of fooling yourself. It's not necessarily easy for others to deceive you, but there is a great tendency for self-deception. While in a Seven Year you seem to look through rose-colored glasses, to be Neptunian; in some cases you perceive the world as if through drugged senses. You think, "This cannot really be happening to me." You feel as if it's another world. This cycle has to do with motion pictures, television, the world of illusion, so naturally, on the positive side, it can be beneficial when you find yourself behind or in front of the cameras. This is a good cycle to study and prepare for.

When nine is the dominant digit for the year, it usually indicates a time when a relationship is put to a test, a time when events and situations are finishing rather than starting. The real challenge to an individual under the dominant Nine Year is not to look back to the past or hang on to it, but to have the courage to raise his or her sights to new horizons. It's always difficult to let go of something you've become used to. Habit patterns are very difficult to break and these patterns rear their ugly heads in strong ways in the Nine Year. But also remember "love" itself, when numericized by its letters, equates with nine. It's the completion, but completion need not be the end of or cut off of a relationship. It could be the completion of all the rough edges around a sphere, so that you begin to roll with the punches; you find better ways of distribution, you are able to reach more persons with your product, with your thoughts and your ideas. You become the Universal, the Renaissance, rather than being limited to any one category.

I will now give you the keywords that apply to the nine cycle years. Which one are you in at present?

## Current Cycle Keywords

One Year   Don't be lazy! This is the opportunity that you've been waiting for the last nine years. Plant the kind of seed you want to come up. Whatever you sow now, you will reap later. Start things. A year for action.

Two Year   Wait. Time not so much for action as attraction. Things come to you if you are quiet and receptive. Things are germinating. Collect. You are ready for accumulation.

Three Year   Enjoy. This is the year to cultivate the old and make new friends. Entertain. Accept invitations. Cheerful year—optimistic. You may try to undertake too many things. Be careful not to scatter your energies. The flowers planted two years ago are now ready to bloom. Enjoy them. You are in a halo light. Share your enthusiasm with others. Time to express.

Four Year   Get down to brass tacks. Keep busy. A work year, not a year to loaf. Build and dig in, and prepare for the vacation next year. Put all affairs in perfect order. Follow a healthful diet. Be practical. Work—be dutiful.

Five Year   Get out of the rut. This year feel free. Go! Opportunity will be found outside of the ordinary routine. Let go of old things. If in business, advertise and promote. Be ready for happy surprises.

Six Year   What is yours will come to you. You will be needed in many directions. Be adjustable—narrow down a bit. Enjoy home life. You may move. Ease things into place. Don't hustle or bustle. A good influence for expanding friendliness, contentment, and love in the home. Cook—work—clean. Comfort those you love.

**Seven Year**    Prepare. Time for reflection and perfection. Good financial vibration if you don't strain. Await developments. Spend lots of time alone to get acquainted with your powers, future desires. Analyze everything. Take up new studies. Listen to the voice within.

**Eight Year**    Power year! Now is the time to compel things to come to you. Expand—take a chance. Great forward strides and great rewards! You gather all the fruit of your past seven years' activity. Plan—think—act. Power is in the air for you!

**Nine Year**    Completion. Prepare for a new beginning next year. Weed out all dead wood. Finish up and throw out all that has delayed or hampered you. A burden is taken off your shoulders. Clear out—relinquish. Humanitarian year.

Every birth path, birth name, birth day, and cycle has its love vibration and potential. When you have looked through the meanings of numbers and reflected on the vibration of each that you and your lover possess, try to combine them to form a whole picture. Within the romance of these numbers is the equation of your love. Find your work, work for love, and cherish it when it comes to you.

Through these numbers find what you have in common in character and in practical mental and emotional stamina. One or two numbers in common indicates happy companionship and the joy of being together.

To love and be loved completes the plan of divine creation and breathes the music of the spheres upon us all. Love is eternal; it is ever present. It never seeks to possess or hold; love just loves. Through the illumination of numbers we can learn to love more— life, children, ourselves—and cease to criticize and judge others. True love will walk in, for the way to love is written in our numbers. Be true to your numbers and your numbers will be true to you.

# $\mathcal{A}$ QUESTION OF LOVE AND SEX

## *chapter ten*

*The deepest need of man is the need to over-come his separateness, to leave the prison of his aloneness. The full answer to the problem of existence lies in true and mature love.*

—Erich Fromm

*And I would like to add...Separateness is only an illusion, a false sense of isolation existing in your imagination, for we are all one. We are all part of the Universal Intelligence.*

—Jeraldine Saunders

$\mathcal{O}$ur lives should be filled with love, be noble, creative, and joyous. This can be accomplished through knowledge of the subjects we have covered so far in this book but first we must remember that *thoughts are things*. Our lives are influenced by our thinking. Successful, happy people have knowingly or unknowingly drawn upon this additional factor to achieve their success in matters of the heart and in prosperity in general. We are all given this faculty by the Universal Intelligence. We all develop it to a different degree. People who have attained satisfaction in their lives, whether in love or career, thereby achieving growth and development, have dared to picture in their minds (I call it image) their desires and wishes so that this force within them is stimulated. Thus the Universal Intelligence within you works on these images until these images become your life.

We know now that if the heavens were photographed from the very spot where we wore born, at the moment of birth, we would have a picture of our unique planetary setup—our very own horoscope. In other words, we would have the hand of cards we were dealt at birth. This may sound a bit frightening to some who would conclude from this that everything in life would then be fated. Of course we know that, yes, our horoscope is the hand we were dealt at birth—but it is up to us to play that hand. Knowing the significance of each card we hold, we can better play the game of life. This is where free will comes into play.

"The truth shall set ye free" is certainly a very powerful saying, in all aspects of life, especially our love life.

We should utilize the signs in our palms, face, and horoscope because they were all given to us as light to help us find the safest and most enjoyable paths to take in life, particularly in romance.

With this knowledge we can learn to appreciate our individual uniqueness and realize we are the design of the Universal Intelligence. We must learn to love and appreciate ourselves. Until we do love ourselves, it is impossible to love others.

If you are one of the many people who find self-love difficult, it is helpful to try the following:

> *Pretend for a while you are your own parents, or the loving parents you would like to have had. Sense what love they would feel for you—precious you. No one in the world is just*

*like you; you are lovable. Keep practicing this routine. Once you train your thoughts to say loving things to yourself, you will automatically hold your head higher, walk more gracefully and with more authority; your voice will give out the sound of assurance and confidence. Your love life will be enhanced.*

We all have a powerful arsenal for improving our love lives and our lives in general. This vast arsenal is books! Read them. Every person who knows how to read has the power to improve life, to make it full, interesting, and joyous.

Keep an open mind when reading. You will learn the difference between knowledge and information. Accept what you will. Educating yourself on all subjects is possible—just by reading.

"How do I deal with my sexual feelings? How do I cope with them?" We've all asked—and been asked—this troublesome question, but the answer we most often hear or read concerns how sex works—the "birds and bees" part of it. We don't get the answers we need most. This most important part of our life is not taught anywhere in our public educational system, despite innovations in clinical sex education. I doubt that you can find a course in any school in the country dealing with preparations for coping with our *love* problems—how to relate successfully to another human being.

Let's start with a basic, simple, natural need—the need to touch another person. Touching is so important in all friendships, from a simple shaking of hands to embracing one another. The inclination to touch is natural, and it isn't reserved solely for the opposite sex. Most Europeans still greet each other with hugs and kisses on the cheek, regardless of the gender mix. If you've been to Europe and experienced the uninhibited expression of friendship, you will understand its naturalness in human relationships.

This touching means that there is something needed or desired between two bodies for purposes of balance. Touching is the first and most basic physical sign of the capacity for releasing your true and loving nature.

When we overcome certain barriers and reach out and touch, many of our inhibiting emotional conflicts can be healed.

Sometimes you reach out a hand to a lost soul who feels all alone, and that person will have to fight to hold back tears as a result of your gesture. This happens because for the first time in years, perhaps, this person witnesses the translation of a spiritual love into physical expression. It is such a contrast to the protective shell that most of us wear; upon the first physical expression of the spiritual connection between all people, one is easily overwhelmed.

We carry this further with the act of sexual intercourse—when you allow your aura to merge with another's. During this ultimate physical extension of a truly spiritual union, there can be no doubt about the goodness of the sex act for both people. When we are into a spiritual feeling, there is an automatic desire to translate that into physical terms—the act of making love. Of course, considering the epidemic of AIDS, the dangers of promiscuity should be uppermost in the minds of the  sexually active.

To know what is right for you in sex, you must know who you are. There is no right or wrong where sex itself is concerned, but it is the social conditioning in each of us—the rules of our culture—that makes us feel this or that is correct or incorrect. We have to learn to deal with this conditioning. This doesn't mean that we have to conform to our manmade cultures.

We may have an inner conflict when our minds are divided between what we have been taught was right (according to the rules) and that which we *feel* is right. The trick is to strive to understand the *real* truth. Your purpose should be to conquer your brainwashed subconsciousness and fill it with thoughts that are based on decisions communicated by your *true* inner voice. The inner voice is the voice of truth, and in each of us it is the reflection of Universal Truth. Each person must learn to make his or her own inner voice powerful, to outshout that conditioned, brainwashed, subconscious—that is only a reflection of "manmade rules." The real you inside is a diamond that needs polishing; the conditioned you is merely a rhinestone. Which do you want to possess?

Ah, but you must listen to your *own* inner voice, for the inner voice of one person does not necessarily point the right way to Truth for another. As an example, the Samoans had had no trouble with their sex lives until the Western missionaries forced their reserved training and sex hang-ups on this beautiful and natural civilization. But just because the early, premissionary Samoans had come upon a way to approach the truth where love and sex were concerned, their way may not work so well everywhere. Once, for instance, when my daughter returned from a date with a very charming young man, she came to wake me up, all upset. "Mother," she said, "there must be something wrong with me! You know how long I've waited for Bill to ask me out. Well, tonight I found out that he's just as perfect as I thought he'd be—but I met his best friend tonight, and now I think I'm just as crazy about him, too."

"Don't worry," I said, still half asleep, "in Samoa this would seem perfectly natural."

"But, Mother!" she screamed, more anxious than before. "This is not Samoa!"

And she was right. We have to deal with life as it is lived where we live it.

To help us decide what is best at this time and in this place, we each have an inner guide; and if we are living in tune with nature, it is easier to hear it, easier to trust it. If we can get in touch with our inner guide, thereby expelling that brainwashed subconscious, we could listen and know when a relationship has a true, honest basis, and we could feel fulfilled within ourselves. Then we would never have a sex problem, wondering what's right and what's wrong.

"How do I know when my subconscious has led me astray?" you may ask. When we have worry, guilt, anxiety, and frustration as a

result of our sexual life, we had better peek into our subconsciousness and see if what we are feeling is coming from that true inner
voice—or from that brainwashed voice. The latter is the inventor of
old wives' tales and ego trips. The former has nothing to invent,
because it is the truth, and the truth simply exists in each of us with
no need of its own for guilt trips.

Passions! Ah, feelings. The turbulence of the emotional area—
this is what makes the world go round.

When we allow our emotions to work for us, in harness, so to
speak, with our intellect, we can move our ideas into action. So we
must not repress emotion, but try to understand and use it to our
own benefit.

The beauty we see in our loved one, the beauty we see in
nature—what would these be without emotion? Our emotions can
give us this feeling of oneness with all life, and they can give us
complete awareness of the Presence within. This awareness is a sen-
sation of love. Perhaps the word "God" means love.

Think of "God" and "love" as verbs, not nouns. God is a name, a
symbol, but while a name it is not a person and not a place. It is an
activity, an action that originates from within us. That action can
be "self-givingness." A glimpse of self-givingness is available to us
when we make love. Love isn't abstract when we make love; it's a
demonstration of the nature of God in action, nature's wisdom in
the tune of life.

The New Age recognizes that shared sex involves shared auras,
mutual orgasms and "tying the knot" of chakras that flower
together. Never fear, however, as long as your love and togetherness
is enjoyable, that your sex life might not match someone else's standards. The importance of sex is wide-ranging—everything from letting sex be a mad and furious master, to hugging, to holding hands,
to celibacy. Bliss can be achieved anywhere along the scale. The
choice and practice is yours. This latitude, this wide range of expression, permits you to approach sex however it feels most comfortable.

The trick is to utilize the information in this book to find a lover whose desires are compatible with yours.

No one can give you love. You can love others, but you cannot get it from others. It is already there. Other people can merely awaken it in you.

Let's take a look at the subconscious mind. The subconscious has no reasoning power, but when we grasp subconscious knowledge we have taken the first step toward being able to make that part of the mind work for us and not against us. The subconscious mind, because it has no reasoning power, believes and records everything our conscious mind tells it, just as a computer accepts, without criticism, all the data we feed to it. We all talk to ourselves, whether we realize it or not, and our subconscious mind records all these conscious or semiconscious conversations. In addition, it records all we have done, seen, and learned throughout our lives. So you can just imagine what a collection of misinformation most of us have been stashing. The subconscious is the recording center of our social and cultural conditioning; this is where the files are.

Now, the moment we behave in a manner that is out of accord with the data stored in that recording center—in a way that is contrary to our conditioning—we run into difficulty. The conscious mind may be at one level, while the subconscious mind is at another. Think of the last time you went through some changes. Perhaps you felt lost, adrift at sea without a lifeboat; surely you felt nervous and upset, as though you were passing from one place to another without a map. Of course! You had no map—all you had was a glow of light that you wanted to reach—but that glow was *you*. It was strong enough to reach your subconscious mind, so you set about making some changes. But nothing you'd done before in your life was like this, so the old recording center bucked and rebelled and made you feel uncomfortable. "This does not compute," is what that conditioned voice inside was telling you.

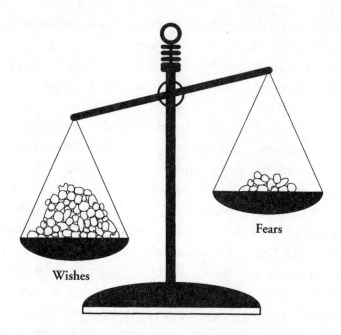

Figure 22: Simple visual analogy of your subconscious: Each pebble in the pans
of the scale is a thought. You determine which way the scale tilts.
Make your wish-thoughts outweigh
your fear-thoughts!

Nervousness and fear have nothing to do with right or wrong—
only with whether or not what you are doing and feeling violates
your previous conditioning.

When you've made it through a change—and haven't run away
to the conditioning rules—you know that there is hope.

We can start improving our inner selves immediately by feeding
our subconscious constructive data. We can compose our personal
inner conversations—our thoughts—from the kind of information
we want stored in that recording center. Since the subconscious
mind believes whatever we tell it, and because it has no reasoning
power, we must be careful with the kind of thoughts we dwell upon.

We can release guilt, tension, and all sorts of negative feelings by feeding constructive, positive data to the gullible subconscious mind. (See Figure 22.) We can reprogram that brainwashed subconscious by heeding the feelings of personal needs. We can shout down that wrong voice by doing the right thing and thinking thoughts we want stored. What a powerhouse this is! Make your subconscious work for you, rather than you for it. Gaining control of the subconscious is probably the most vital of all human achievements.

Tell yourself that your love needs must be met—and sure enough, those needs will be met. Believe they will be. Tell yourself that any of your needs must be met, and the way to meet them will come to you. *We tend to move toward that upon which we dwell!*

Sometimes we cannot control our surroundings as much as we would wish. There is one thing, however, we all have the power to do, and that is to consciously control our attitude toward our environment. Two people can be experiencing the same situation, yet each can react differently. One might feel delight, the other boredom. It depends upon what attitude was chosen. I say "chosen" because we have the power to choose our attitudes. We can consciously change our thoughts to ones that bring happiness. So it's not what happens to us, but *our attitude* toward what happens to us that determines whether we will be happy. Remember, we do have control of our attitudes.

Don't worry about past mistakes. We've all made them. Put in the proper focus, mistakes can create a strength within us that gives added insight and helps us continue to grow. When we forgive ourselves for past mistakes, we have reached the first prerequisite for realizing love, for at that point we are ready to accept ourselves, and so are able to love ourselves. Universal Intelligence loves us regardless of what mistakes we've made, big or small.

Misuse of physical relationships most often is born out of a lack of love for ourselves. Learning about our own uniqueness from the Mantic Arts, such as those we've explored in this book, can help us accept ourselves simply as we are. Just as no two snowflakes are alike, no two humans are meant to be exactly alike. When we learn to accept ourselves as unique, we have arrived at the beginning of learning to love ourselves and begun to gain higher self-esteem. Once we love ourselves, we are able to love others. When we've learned to love others, the love we give out will just naturally bounce back to us.

We are all filled with love. Allow the protective walls to be let down so love can flow out; with this release, it comes rushing back.

Possessiveness and jealousy stem from warped data that we have fed our minds.

The more we allow our loved ones freedom to demonstrate their own individuality, the less reason they have to fear losing a part of themselves in our presence—and the less reason they have for wanting to leave us. In fact, knowing someone cares enough to allow us to be ourselves breeds "that loving feeling." The Indian poet Gibran phrased it so beautifully: "Let there be spaces in your togetherness."

Our feelings of happiness come in part from knowing that we are acceptable in the eyes of our loved ones. Of course, true maturity is not so much doing what others consider right or wrong, but being able to maintain and sustain and handle what we believe in principle and still relate to our fellow human beings without being rejected. This is the challenge: to keep one's own views and standards even when they may not be popular, and to do something effective about getting those views to others subliminally.

One of the rarest accomplishments is to keep pure truth and cunning in oneself, side by side and in balance; when in balance, your cunning will enable you to express your pure truth—your innocence.

Keeping one's own values and beliefs in focus, though the onslaught of authority and orthodoxy tries to make us follow the herd, is a powerful way to hang on to your integrity and sanity. If you "know your own worth," the Persian poet Hakim Sanai wrote, "what need you care about the acceptance or rejection of others?"

When we have love problems, remember there is a power within us free to move through us as perfect wisdom in all relationships.

When you can feel happiness, joy, and fulfillment, you are on the right path for *you*. When you feel disappointment, frustration, fear, possessiveness, and guilt, you are on the wrong path. Keep in mind that it is not what we do but how *we feel* about doing it that creates either conflict or happiness.

Those of us who are lucky enough to have found our soul mates may feel as Lara did in *Dr. Zhivago* when she said to her lover, "It is as though we are taught in Heaven to kiss, and then brought to Earth to see if we learned our lesson well."

The many dimensions of love that grow and expand between people can be truly beautiful.

We have to realize that we are dealing with an inborn need to love at intellectual, emotional, spiritual, and physical levels. All these feelings must be taken into consideration when choosing a mate, but when sex begins too soon in a relationship, the wonderful feeling that the sex act gives can sometimes make the physical level of the relationship obsessive and block the feelings that come from other levels. We might even allow this single feeling to determine whom we shall marry.

We must develop on all fronts to keep Eros (the Greek God of sexual love) from becoming our mad and furious master. As strong and as powerful as Eros is, you cannot trust it, because of the conditioning in our society. Perhaps, years ago, Eros could be trusted in Samoa, but not here or now, with all our misconceptions of what is basic to happiness.

If, as I have said, all the brainwashing was removed to allow the Divine Intelligence within us to take over, then we could hear it tell us what our true needs are.

The brilliant Dr. Leo Fishbeck, author of *Dare to Dream*, feels the reason we should but can't always trust our inner voice is what he terms "our sociological arrested development." He explains that in our society there are certain areas and certain dimensions of love that have not been brought out in us and have not been encouraged. Most of the mistakes we make sexually are due to being out of touch with ourselves.

So, the only answer is to start forgiving yourself of all past mistakes and begin with self-love, and develop the awareness of who this person is that is called *you.*

We are all born into a state of the highest good.

We are all a part of the Universal Intelligence.

*We are all a channel for love!*

Remember: You tend to move toward that upon which you dwell...*so dwell well!*

# *index*